Fringe Voices

Fringe Voices

An Anthology of Minority Writing in the Federal Republic of Germany

Edited and translated by
Antje Harnisch,
Anne Marie Stokes
and
Friedemann Weidauer

Oxford • New York

First published in 1998 by
Berg
Editorial offices:
150 Cowley Road, Oxford OX4 1JJ, UK
70 Washington Square South, New York, NY 10012, USA

Berg is the imprint of Oxford International Publishers Ltd.

Library of Congress Cataloging-in-Publication Data

A catalogue record for this book is available from the Library of Congress

British Library Cataloguing-in-Publication Date

A catalogue record for this book is available from the British Library

ISBN 1 85973 127 9 (Cloth)
1 85973 132 5 (Paper)

Typeset by JS Typesetting, Wellingborough, Northants.
Printed in the United Kingdom by WBC Book Manufacturers, Mid Glamorgan.

Contents

Contents

Contents

Acknowledgment

The editors would like to thank Louise Speed of Wayne State University in Detroit, Michigan, Prof. Craig Decker of Bates College in Lewiston, Maine, and Jennifer Hayward, The College of Wooster, for their input on the style of our texts and translations.

Part I
Introduction

Germany, not a Country of Immigration?

'The Federal Republic of Germany is not a country of immigration'. This is the official political line the Federal government has pursued so far. But the social and political realities belie this assertion: the six million foreigners currently living there should be proof enough that Germany has in fact become a land of immigration.

The presence of millions of foreigners in Germany – people who are not German citizens but have been living in the country for generations – calls forth a number of paradoxes which complicate the relationship between German citizens and non-citizens as well as the debate on what should be done. While most politicians would insist that they are in favour of good relations between citizens and foreigners, nothing has been done to alter the perception of many Germans that these people will always be in some sense 'foreign': the absence of laws regulating immigration into Germany, together with the unchanged practice of basing citizenship on ethnic origin, forms the legal foundation of a mind-set regarding people who have immigrated into Germany as a group which will always be markedly different from ethnic Germans. This of course makes the most well-intentioned attempts at integration even more difficult.

From the very beginning of its existence, there has been migration into the Federal Republic:[1] about nine million Germans who were expelled from Polish territories in the aftermath of the Second World War and another three million from East Germany (the so-called *Übersiedler*) entered the Federal Republic in the 1940s. There has also been a continuous flow of ethnic Germans from Eastern Europe (the so-called *Aussiedler*): about 1.5 million since 1948/9. And in the wake of the collapse of the communist states of Eastern Europe, the flow of ethnic

1. For brief accounts of the post-war history of migration into Germany in English, see Nora Räthzel, 'Germany: One Race, One Nation?' *Race and Class* 23.3 (1990): 31–48 and Eva Kolinsky, 'Non-German Minorities in Contemporary German Society', *Turkish Culture in German Society Today*, eds David Horricks and Eva Kolinsky (Oxford: Berghahn, 1996), 71–111.

Germans has increased once again, with migration from East Germany assuming enormous proportions. Officially, however, this does not constitute immigration since both *Übersiedler* and *Aussiedler* are technically Germans. In the 1950s, and even more in the 1960s after the construction of the Berlin Wall (1961), migration from the East diminished. At this point, West Germany began to recruit workers from southern Europe to fuel its economic miracle. But, officially at least, this work migration did not constitute immigration either, since it was supposed to be of a temporary nature only, as reflected in the term *Gastarbeiter*, 'guest worker' – even if the reality soon looked different.

As already indicated, not all immigrants entering Germany have similar status. For, in contrast to most Western nations, the Federal Republic defines citizenship biologically. While one is an American if one is born on American soil (*ius soli*), one is a German if one is born to German parents (*ius sanguinis*). This principle leads to the following absurdity: the ethnic German from Russia, who lived in Russia for most of his/her life and doesn't know any German, typically has little problem acquiring German citizenship, but the second- or third-generation child of Turkish parents, who has never been to Turkey and speaks German like a native (for s/he is a native), would have a much more difficult time if s/he wanted to become a German citizen. It is not impossible for a foreigner living and working in Germany to acquire German citizenship, but it is difficult and costly and usually requires that one give up any other citizenship. The fact that dual citizenship is usually not an option forces people to make tough decisions, for property and inheritance laws in their countries of origin often only apply to citizens.[2]

However, Germany's major parties have started to engage in a debate on how to change the country's immigration laws and the momentum is growing for a change in some of the more outdated laws and policies. Among the reforms (in most cases proposed by either the Green Party or the Social Democrats) that look likely to meet some success in the German legislature are ways to allow for dual citizenship, to make it easier for second-generation 'guest workers' to receive citizenship, and to give long-term foreign residents of Germany some of the privileges that so far have been linked to citizenship, for example limited voting rights. It

---

2. For an extended discussion of the legal issues involved, see Günter Frankenberg, 'Zur Alchemie von Recht und Fremdheit. Die Fremden als juridische Konstruktion', in *Schwierige Fremdheit. Über Integration und Ausgrenzung in Einwanderungsländern*, eds Friedrich Balke, Rebekka Habermas, Patrizia Nanz and Peter Sillem (Frankfurt: Fischer, 1993), 41–67.

should also be emphasized at this point that, apart from the peculiarities of German immigration law, long-term legal residents have always enjoyed the same social welfare benefits as German citizens, and, in this sense at least, Germany has assumed more responsibility for its non-naturalized inhabitants than some of the other industrialized Western democracies.

But the hitherto unchanged legal status of foreigners in Germany makes it easy for Germans with citizenship to remain caught in the illusion that Germany does not have to face immigration problems like other countries. *Article 16* Instead, the issue has been sidestepped via the intense debate over Article *asylum* 16a in Germany's constitution (the *Grundgesetz* or Basic Law), which up until recently guaranteed unconditional asylum to people persecuted for political reasons. Instead of debating the number of people allowed to immigrate and the criteria for such a regulated immigration into Germany, or debating changes in the ways in which one can become a German citizen and the concomitant possibility of granting dual citizenship, the political discourse on immigration focused on such issues as what constitutes persecution for political reasons and who might be taking advantage of this article in the Basic Law. It is not difficult to imagine how such a debate can divide people trying to immigrate into Germany into 'legitimate' cases and those 'abusing' Germany's seemingly liberal constitution, while failing to confront the fact that Germany has to find ways of dealing with its share of massive worldwide migrations that are occurring for economic as well as other reasons.[3]

The current migrations are a result of the growing number of people affected by legal, political and economic uncertainties in their home *push factors* countries, which in turn are the consequence of a number of factors. Two of the most important ones are the power vacuum left behind by the collapse of the Warsaw Pact and the failed attempts to bring about changes in the economic and political structures of Third World countries. One could interpret this partially as belated effects of nineteenth- and early twentieth-century colonialism. The patterns of dependencies established then have not completely disappeared.

However, while the debate on the asylum law can be seen as an attempt to sidestep the real issues, it nevertheless could not help addressing them

---

3. For a history of the asylum law and current discussions of it, see Klaus J. Bade, *Ausländer, Aussiedler, Asyl. Eine Bestandsaufnahme* (Munich: Beck, 1994), 91–146 and Günter Frankenberg, "Zur Alchemie von Recht und Fremdheit," in *Schwierige Fremdheit*, 41–67, particularly 55–60.

indirectly.[4] Paragraph (1) of the current legislation, which specifies that 'anybody persecuted on political grounds has the right of asylum', was part of the original document which went into effect on 23 May 1949. On 28 June 1993, paragraphs (2) to (5) were added as amendments, since the growing number of people entering Germany and demanding asylum under Article 16a was perceived as a threat to social stability. The wording of these paragraphs reflects the immediate concerns the politicians in charge had in mind when they drafted them.

Paragraph (2) specifies that persons entering Germany not directly from their homeland but after a stopover in a third country shouldn't have waited until they arrived in Germany. The paragraph specifies that they could already have applied for asylum anywhere their plane had landed on its way, provided the respective countries honour international agreements protecting refugees. One could argue that the politicians used one of the contingencies of international traffic, the fact that most flights into Germany make a stopover in one of those countries, to 'stem the flood of refugees', a phrase often used in this context.

The intention behind this paragraph is twofold. First, refugees from the Third World will no longer be given the chance to stay in Germany for as long as it takes to process their request for political asylum, something which at the height of this 'flood' often took years. The assumption behind the amendment, thus, is that most of the asylum seekers have come for economic reasons, an assumption which disregards the fact that in the 'trouble spots' of today's world, economic, social, religious and political problems can scarcely be isolated from each other.

The second intention behind the amendment is that those countries in which the refugees make a stopover will be forced to 'take on their fair share' of them. One could, of course, claim that the legislators were aware of Germany's geographic location when they made the law: it is surrounded on all sides by one or more layers of countries with democratic constitutions. This means that almost no political refugees will be allowed into Germany, certainly none who have travelled by land. Less than ten years ago, a political dissenter from East Germany would have been welcomed in Germany, even if he or she first crossed the Baltic Sea to reach Sweden

---

4. See Lutz Hoffmann, who reads the asylum debate as an 'alternative to debating the constitution' ('Globale Stabilisierung. Neue Aspekte der Wanderungspolitik nach dem Ende des bolschewistischen Imperiums', in *Einwanderungsland Deutschland* (Göttingen: Lamuv, 1993), 10–17). For a discussion of the economic side of the issue see Bert Rürup and Werner Sesselmeier, 'Einwanderung: Die wirtschaftliche Perspektive', in *Schwierige Fremdheit*, 285-304.

or Denmark. The amendment seems to indicate that the times for this kind of political refugee are over, that most of those claiming this status for themselves have other motives.

Paragraph (3), meanwhile, talks about enabling the German legislature to 'specify countries where the legal situation, the application of the law and the general political circumstances justify the assumption that neither political persecution nor inhumane or degrading punishment or treatment takes place', i.e. to make blanket statements on where political persecution is taking place. In reality, however, almost any such statement would be problematic: are Turkish Kurds never political refugees just because Turkey has a democratic constitution and has special member status in the EU? Can conscientious objectors from the former Yugoslavia never apply for political asylum because the territory of which they are citizens now seems, in the eyes of German legislators, to be ruled by law?

Again, as these two examples show, generally a combination of a number of different factors motivates people to leave their home country and look for a more peaceful and prosperous life elsewhere. The 'classic' political refugee, as defined by German law, no longer exists, and the new legislation indirectly admits this: it is seeking to protect its affluence by preventing the growing number of people from the trouble spots of today's world from using its erstwhile liberal law as entry ticket. The 'asylum debate' could therefore be termed an intentional misnomer because everyone involved in it knew that Germany was trying to tackle much greater problems than its alleged concern to be able to discern the 'real' political refugees from those 'abusing' the asylum article. In particular, the paragraph pertaining to the responsibilities of all other similar countries reveals that the legislators were well aware of the fact that Germany is being confronted with its share of global migration movements – in the face of which, the paragraph seems to imply, the rich countries should join forces to protect their privileges. Put less polemically, Germany is trying to force the countries surrounding it to share the economic and political burden of large numbers of immigrants. One has to keep in mind that many of these countries already had in place much more restrictive immigration laws that made Germany the logical choice for migrants aware of these differences. It is therefore not entirely justified to accuse Germany of repeating the grave mistakes it made in its past and of reneging on its historic responsibility. Such accusations of course hit Germany in one of its sorest spots and lead to overreactions on the part of German politicians and other public figures, who either arrogantly defend Germany's position or promise too much in the way of reforms. A historically informed response to such allegations

global
migration
movements

is to point out that, on the one hand, Germany's special responsibility is that towards groups persecuted for ethnic reasons (as the main culprit in this regard in the first half of this century), and, on the other, beyond this Germany is simply responsible for its share of the economic problems brought about by mass migrations, just like any other industrialized country.

Article 16 was written into the German constitution with the best intentions, but the situation to which it responded has changed. It was meant to protect people from political persecution of the kind many had to suffer at the hands of the Nazis, and it was also intended as a signal at the onset of the Cold War that the West would offer political dissidents from the East a safe haven. Nowadays few people would fit these fairly narrowly defined criteria for recognition as political refugees. Historically speaking, Article 16 also presented an alibi for the postwar West German government to atone for just one of the sins of the Nazi regime, political persecution, when in fact the largest number of people persecuted by the Nazis were members of ethnic groups and not political dissidents. If German immigration laws were to reflect Germany's special responsibility resulting from the era of totalitarianism, they would above all have to protect people displaced by ethnic strife in their home countries.

What remains problematic about the recent reform of Article 16 of the Basic Law, however, is that it leaves untouched Germany's definition of itself as a community based on ethnic origin, and hence also preserves, implicitly, the resulting negative attitudes towards foreigners, which find their worst expression in open racism based on ethnic difference. If immigrants could attain citizenship and thus the same legal status as ethnic Germans, the general perception of immigrants as outsiders or indeed intruders might be changed. If immigrants were to gain equal legal status through clearly defined regulations, ethnicity as a means of differentiating between 'Germans' and 'foreigners' would cease to constitute the defining criterion. Furthermore, if all ethnic groups had the same legal status, ethnic differences could then be discussed as the basis of a positive definition of one group in comparison with others, not as something which merely determines whether one 'belongs' in Germany or not. Difference could be brought into play as a contribution to the whole of society instead of a means of discrimination. As it stands, however, the law reinforces the divisive perspective. One can hope that, as an outcome of some of the more recent debates, the relatively fast reform of Article 16 will be followed by another constitutional reform that will abolish or at least modify the outdated German *ius sanguinis*.

wow.

Germany as a Multicultural Society: Legal Challenges, Ideological Shifts and Socioeconomic Realities

Different models for a multicultural society cannot be discussed until foreigners have attained the same legal status as all other citizens. In the absence of such a policy, ethnic differences as the ground for differences in legal status will continue to undermine any multicultural model. But the situation is somewhat paradoxical. While equal legal status might motivate one or the other ethnic group to assimilate to the majority culture, it is at the same time the only guarantee for any group to be able to express its ethnic differences without fear of reprisals by the majority culture.

This is very different from what is going on at present. While there seems to be an almost exaggerated hope in some parts of the political spectrum that the influx of foreigners and their cultural contributions will help Germans out of what is generally perceived as cultural stagnation and provincialism, it seems it would be hard to motivate the various ethnic groups to live up to these overdrawn expectations. While attempts have been made by almost all of the political parties and by other groups to offer foreigners ways to participate in the political and cultural life of the Federal Republic, these same groups are becoming increasingly ↑ eco. marginalized economically. And economic marginalization tends to margin- reinforce ethnic differences and exacerbate social marginalization. Ethnic alization difference therefore might be resorted to as the strongest source for forming a positive definition of self if all other means are being withheld by society dignity. value. worth.

And Germany needs the contribution of its foreign citizens for a variety of reasons, not least of which are economic ones. It has been estimated that Germany needs about 300,000 immigrants per year in order to compensate for the shrinking 'ethnic' German population and for the concomitant deficit in the budget of, among other things, the mandatory state pension fund.[1] It is economic criteria such as these which are driving the reform of immigration laws in other countries. It seems that Germany has been somewhat slow to face up to these realities. For it is only logical that, if the Federal Republic is not a 'country of immigration', then laws regulating immigration would not be necessary or even appropriate. The current manner of handling immigration represents a combination of three different procedures which are not coordinated with each other.

There is first of all the processing of asylum seekers according to the newly formulated Article 16 of the Basic Law. Whatever arrangements are being made for them, their stay in Germany is assumed to last only until the political circumstances leading to their persecution have changed, thereby making political asylum for them unnecessary.

Then there are the rules pertaining to those working in Germany legally (the so-called guest workers or *Gastarbeiter*). Acquiring a permanent work permit and permanent residence in Germany as well as becoming eligible for German citizenship is a time-consuming and complicated procedure. It takes fifteen or eight years of residence in Germany (depending on the age of the applicant) to become eligible for citizenship. The applicant has to demonstrate 'assimilation to the German ways of life', have a sufficient and secure source of income, and represent a 'valuable addition to the population'.

Work permits are not granted based on criteria of the job market such as demand for certain types of qualifications (as is the case in the USA, for example) but more or less on the ability of the person in question to demonstrate that he or she is currently employed. People who become unemployed for a longer period of time can consequently have their work permit revoked, which means they have to leave Germany. For those eligible, applying for German citizenship is not always a very attractive option either; it requires that one gives up the citizenship of one's country of origin. Together, these aspects of German immigration law combine to keep foreigners working legally in Germany exactly what they are called: guest workers. However, as mentioned earlier, this is fortunately the area within debates over German immigration law where currently new models are being discussed that have reasonable chances of becoming law.

Finally, there are the special immigration laws which apply to people of ethnic German origin from Eastern European countries. They become German citizens based on their ability to show that they have kept their

---

1. For a discussion of the economic side of the issue, see Bert Rürup and Werner Sesselmeier, 'Einwanderung: Die wirtschaftliche Perspektive', in *Schwierige Fremdheit*, 285–304.

special for ethnic Germans

Germany as a Multicultural Society

ties with German culture. As one can imagine, this is very much open to subjective interpretation and susceptible to changes in the political climate. As it is now, different rules apply to almost every different ethnic group present in Germany. The only way out of a debate which continues to bring up the question of the ethnic origin of the different groups in question would be immigration laws and procedures which disregard the ethnic origin of the applicant. Therefore, quotas for the different ethnic groups like those used in the USA would not present a solution either, because quotas also focus on the ethnic origin of the applicant. While the attacks on certain ethnic groups in recent years seem to suggest that the concept of a multicultural society has completely failed in Germany, to be sure of this one would first have to try to change the legal situation of immigrants so that it does not reinforce ethnic divisions. *ethnic-blind...*

It is absolutely essential to redefine German citizenship so as to modify its current basis, i.e. ethnic origin (*ius sanguinis*); this would change matters not just for those seeking to immigrate into Germany but also for the ethnic Germans who already live there. The *ius sanguinis* is not based on a clearly defined historic event such as the founding of a new state. It has no historic point of reference, but is based on the myth that at one time there was a clearly defined territory inhabited solely by 'Germans' and that this community in some sense still exists today despite the massive migrations and territorial changes which have occurred in the meantime. Ethnic Germans today are defined as the descendants of this mythical community. Individual identity is therefore not based on a conscious allegiance to the state into which one was born or has immigrated, but on *inertia* a feeling of belonging to a group whose origins are shrouded by the mists of prehistoric times. As a consequence, the individual may well believe that fairly recent historic developments should not alter this situation.

Basing German citizenship on something other than ethnic origin, however, would involve a redefinition of the German people as a *new basis of cit. ship* collective. It would also mean that once and for all the definition of what now constitutes Germany would be tied to its present geographical shape, which is the result of recent history, and not on the dreams of an imagined space which was once inhabited by 'Germans' alone. Lastly, it would render the majority of Germans conscious of the existence and contribution of non-ethnic Germans in their midst. Between 1960 and the mid-1990s the number of 'foreigners' living in Germany grew from about 700,000 to about seven million (from 1.2% to 8% of the total population). More than half of these seven million, moreover, have been living in Germany for more than fifteen years. And one-third of the present population immigrated into Germany at one point or another. The legal

– 11 –

situation which continues to privilege ethnicity helps to prevent these facts from forming part of the consciousness of the ethnic Germans and from changing the ways in which one defines what is 'German'. For it supports the belief that those who can claim that they belong to this imagined community have stronger bonds with each other and are hence justified to fend off those 'who do not belong'.

That the debate about how many 'foreigners' Germany can absorb has intensified has to do not only with the sudden increase in the number of asylum seekers (caused by, among other developments, the collapse of the Soviet Union and other Eastern European countries, the continued crises in some of the Middle Eastern countries, and the breakup of Yugoslavia), but also with internal developments in Germany's social and economic system. Perhaps the most important change is taking place in the economy and affects all industrialized countries, including the Federal Republic. This change could be characterized as large portions of the workforce shifting away from work in industry and manufacture to other types of work, particularly to the service sector. For the immigrant workers this means two things: while on the one hand they are still exposed to familiar forms of xenophobia and prejudice in the new jobs, the integrational forces of the labour movements represented by the industrial unions and the large workers' parties (such as the Labour Party in England and the SPD in Germany) have largely disappeared as an ever-decreasing number of workers is actually represented by them. While these organizations themselves have never been completely free of ethnic prejudice, they nevertheless helped fight the discrimination by employers as well as the racism of state institutions such as the public welfare offices. Whether in Germany or other European countries, the labour movement had been at the forefront of the battle against ethnic prejudice.

The structural change in the economy is accompanied by a similarly pervasive change in society as a whole. The shift away from industrial labour is paralleled by the weakening of what could be called the republican model of society. Before, the role of the state and its institutions was perceived (to create equal conditions for all members of society) (schools, for instance, were supposed to provide the basis of equal opportunity for everybody to participate in society), something which in turn meant that an equal share of responsibilities was expected to be shouldered by each citizen. This attitude was still prevalent in the reform movements of the 1960s and early 1970s, most visibly in the plans to reform the educational system. Since that time, the approach has changed fundamentally. The emphasis now is on the specific needs of individual groups and their specific contributions to society, which do not add up to one coherent whole any more. A symptom of this shift can be seen in activists of the 1960s and 1970s turning away from mass organizations to what might be called 'special interest' groups. One of the negative symptoms of this change is the increased visibility of right-wing neo-Nazi groups, which are not held together by shared values but by a shared hatred of everything that is 'different'. A youth movement gathered around positive, perhaps utopian, ideas does not exist any more; the new 'youth movements' gather around negative ideas such as racism and xenophobia. And the leaders of the neo-Nazi groups seem to have perfected a way to fill the vacuum created by the absence of a different kind of youth movement. These changes certainly have contributed to intensifying discussions about the possibilities and limits of a multicultural society.

[margin: ← hate]

Nevertheless, there still exists a broad public sphere within which the problems of minorities and migrants are being discussed, a public sphere which reacts to right-wing activities in imaginative and effective ways. If it comes to shows of strength, this spectrum of German society can count on numbers which dwarf the small but highly visible neo-Nazi groups. No right-wing attack on foreigners has been left unanswered by these progressive groups, which can count on support in all strata of German society.

Clearly the lack of viable political solutions to immigration or the so-called 'foreigner problem' is related to feelings of xenophobia and racism, as are the physical attacks, which are extreme expressions of these feelings. Right-wing groups are on the rise all over Europe, but nowhere is violence as prevalent as in Germany. And nowhere does it seem to be as tacitly condoned by a large proportion of the population. Nowhere, however, is public outrage over these attacks so strong as in Germany.

[margin: foreign prob]

It is not altogether surprising that racist violence has been more prevalent in the East.[2] Germans in the new states view themselves as the losers of unification: unemployment is skyrocketing, housing is scarce and, like food and other necessities, it has become more expensive, if not unaffordable. Sharing in the wealth of the West was a major impetus for the people in the East to push for unification. This dream has not come true. And the foreigner is an easy scapegoat for all that has gone wrong. In addition it must be remembered that Germans in the GDR were even

[margin: losses]

2. It is true that racist attacks came under the spotlight after unification, and it is also true that they occurred mainly in the East. But this should not fool us into thinking that racism and xenophobia are problems only in the so-called new states and that resentment did not exist prior to unification. The most fatal attacks occurred in Solingen and Mölln, i.e. former West German cities.

less used to living with 'foreigners' than those in the FRG: the workers and students from other socialist countries who lived in the GDR were housed in buildings which were segregated from the native population and had little contact with them. In addition, officially at least, anti-Semitism and racism, as well as xenophobia, did not exist in the GDR; but, as recent events prove, those sentiments were merely repressed, not eradicated. Finally, what was said about the demise of the republican model perhaps applies to the former East Germany as well. This particular republic laid out very clearly for each citizen what it could provide and what it expected. In addition, young people in particular were kept busy around the clock and year round by the various activities of the mass youth organizations. The new order could certainly not provide a new feeling of belonging and thus left a vacuum in the reunited Germany, which again could be used by demagogues of the worst kind.

Sociologists, psychologists and political scientists – among others – have tried to explain xenophobia and the recent outburst of violence against foreigners through reference to social causes such as lack of work and housing, individual psychological factors and anthropological notions of the fear of anything different or strange, as well as to the peculiarities of German history.[3] Whatever the reasons for the violence, and there are probably a number of factors at work, it is puzzling that the German authorities have reacted with relative nonchalance to such atrocious crimes. The left-wing extremism of the 1970s called forth much more aggressive reactions from German politicians: terrorists were hunted down, and a whole new set of laws was created to protect the state from any kind of extremism. Consequently, the authorities now have plenty of legal means at their disposal to prosecute extremists, means which, initially at least, were not employed.[4] When arsonists were excused by extenuating circumstances, politicians seemed to be indicating to the perpetrators that they understood their hatred. Only because of immense international pressure and massive demonstrations organized by antiracist alliances within Germany itself have authorities become tougher on this kind of

---

3. See for instance Maya Nadig, who explains xenophobia and violence by referring to a number of different social and psychological factors playing into each other ('Die Ritualisierung von Haß und Gewalt im Rassismus', in *Schwierige Fremdheit*, 264–284).

4. See Freimut Duve, 'Terror in Deutschland', *Angst vor den Deutschen. Terror gegen Ausländer und der Zerfall des Rechtsstaates*, ed. Bahman Nirumand (Reinbek: Rowohlt, 1992), 19–27. Hans Magnus Enzensberger argues similarly in his essay printed in the same volume, comparing how the police dealt with 1970s and 1980s ecological and peace movement demonstrators with how it reacts to right-wing violence today ('Über einige Besonderheiten bei der Menschenjagd', 14–18).

crime. It now seems that the executive branch of government had been holding back to a degree that the majority of Germans could not understand any more. The call for changes in the political make-up of the present government might in part reflect annoyance with its *laissez-faire* attitude and the wish of a majority for a government that takes a more active role in these events. Tougher legal penalties for racist crime have done much to reduce attacks on foreigners. But more still needs to be done. As outlined above, reform of the legal foundation of citizenship and immigration would be a further prerequisite for tolerance and acceptance. Mind-sets and attitudes, however, need to change as well. Changes in how people think do not occur automatically with legal changes, but the latter can facilitate them. Furthermore, literature and other cultural endeavours could contribute significantly to altering the attitudes and mind-sets of Germans towards the minorities who live in their midst.[5] If one considers the (in comparison strong) interest of Germans in cultural matters and events, this does not seem like a utopian notion.

5. Claus Leggewie among others suggests a comprehensive concept for immigration and integration as a prerequisite for change, which includes legislation concerning immigration and citizenship as well as anti-discrimination policies ('Vom deutschen Reich zur Bundesrepublik – und nicht zurück. Zur politischen Gestalt einer multikulturellen Gesellschaft', in *Schwierige Fremdheit*, 3–20, particularly 6–8, and 'Der rechte Aufmarsch', in *Angst vor den Deutschen*, 52–74, particularly 63–65). See also Hans-Jürgen Heinrichs, who insists that a change in legislation alone does not get rid of xenophobia ('Von Fluten, Wellen und Strömen', in *Angst vor den Deutschen*, 28–51).

3

Minority Literature and its Role in a Multicultural Society

Although the situation in the Federal Republic does not seem to promote thriving cultures of 'foreigners', in the last two decades minorities have become increasingly visible in the cultural arena. This volume attests to a diversity of voices which not only enrich the German cultural scene, but also force us to question concepts of a unified identity and a homogeneous national culture. While selecting texts for our anthology we were guided by the principle of diversity. We include the voices of various ethnic groups, which came to Germany from different places at different times for different reasons. In addition, we have aimed to present diverse voices from each group, diverse in terms of generation, gender, ethnicity and religion.

Common to all texts collected in this anthology is that they were originally written in German by authors who live in Germany or lived there for a period of time in the past. They deal with questions of identity and homeland, culture and language as well as gender, race and class. They address issues of family and community, as well as religion and history, particularly in its German variant. They describe what it means to be black and German, or Jewish and German, or Turkish and German, or Rumanian and German, etc. in contemporary German society. At the same time, however, they are unique voices: engaging, provocative and stimulating. We do not claim that they are completely representative of any or all minority groups. This anthology should serve as a starting-point for further discovery of the rich and diverse voices of contemporary German culture. This book is part of a search for a new multicultural definition of German society, an attempt to promote understanding and respect, to counter fears and prejudices, and to awaken curiosity and interest.

The anthology consists of different types of texts – essays and short stories, poems and excerpts from novels – written over a period of about twenty-five years. Foreign residents in Germany first found a voice in

guestworker literature

the late 1970s with the so-called *Gastarbeiterliteratur*.[1] This was the term given to a body of texts which concentrates on the everyday life of the foreigner or, more specifically, the foreign worker in Germany, on his struggles with work and housing as well as problems with the natives and their prejudices. The overarching goals of this literature were twofold: to protest against inhumane living and working conditions as well as prejudice and intolerance and to foster understanding between Germans and foreigners. The publication and circulation of these texts was made possible through a network of groups, small publishing houses, journals, and series such as *Südwind Gastarbeiterdeutsch*, which was edited by Franco Biondi, Rafik Schami and Jusuf Naoum among others.

The texts anthologized in volumes such as *Zwischen Fabrik und Bahnhof* (Between the Factory and Train Station) or *Im neuen Land* (In the New Country) relate subjective experiences and are by and large of a didactic nature. In good enlightenment tradition, they seek to educate their readers, thus envisioning a better world. Biondi's story in this volume and Schami's fairy-tale-like fables remind us of this belief in the betterment of humanity through education and enlightenment. Similarly, although not sharing the belief in the possibility of a better Germany, Lea Fleischmann sets out to enlighten her non-Jewish German fellow-citizens about the nature of contemporary Germany by telling them why it is impossible for a Jew to live among them.

It is more difficult to find a common denominator for the literature of the late 1980s and the early 1990s. Instead of instructing readers on how to create a better world, the texts deal with deterritorialization and the concomitant loss of identity. Rather than having integration – and assimilation – into German society as their overarching goal, the authors of these texts investigate their own cultural origin(s) and mixed identities. In literary terms, they go back to their non-German heritages and mix them with German cultural traditions: they combine words, images and motifs as well as myths and ways of storytelling from different cultures and traditions, which thus illuminate and challenge each other. Authors

---

1. For descriptions and analyses of this literature, see for instance Horst Hamm, *Fremdgegangen freigeschrieben. Einführung in die deutschsprachige Gastarbeiterliteratur* (Würzburg: Königshausen und Neumann, 1988), Gino Chiellino, *Am Ufer der Fremde: Literatur und Arbeitsmigration, 1870–1991* (Stuttgart: Metzler, 1995) and Hartmut Heinze, *Migrantenliteratur in der Bundesrepublik Deutschland* (Berlin: EXpress Edition, 1986). For an overview in English, see Heidrun Suhr, 'Ausländerliteratur: Minority Literature in the Federal Republic of Germany', *New German Critique* 46 (Winter 1989): 71–103 and, more specifically focusing on Turkish-German writers, the recent *Turkish Culture in German Society Today*.

such as Emine Özdamar and Rafael Seligmann, for instance, self-consciously situate themselves in the German tradition; however, they just as self-consciously reread and rewrite its conventions. And they not only rewrite German traditions, but in turn situate themselves in other traditions, Turkish or Jewish for example. Such mixing allows them to question ideologies of unity and purity still prominent in contemporary Germany.

Migrants' literature in Germany is written within contemporary German cultural paradigms, but it is also written against them, rewriting them in the process. With its political message on the one hand and emphasis on subjective experience on the other, minority literature of the 1970s and early 1980s reflects prevalent literary trends of the time, such as Literature of the Affected (*Literatur der Betroffenheit*) and New Subjectivity; like the evolving workers' and women's literatures, migrants' literature of this period insists on the intimate relationship between the personal and the political. The mixing of cultural traditions and questioning of unified identities common in migrants' literature of the late 1980s and 1990s, on the other hand, evokes post-modernism, the most prevalent feature of contemporary German culture: not the playful relativism of a post-structural post-modernism or the aestheticizing of the political, but a post-modernism that has a political agenda. This is particularly true in the German context where notions of a pure national identity and a homogeneous literary/cultural tradition are still very prevalent.

The following anecdote illustrates how Germans often perceive literature by minorities. When looking for a work by Emine Özdamar in a bookstore run by a student collective in one of Germany's old university towns, we were unable to locate the author among the (German) authors displayed in alphabetical order on the shelves. When we then approached one of the salespeople for information, we were told that we would find the book under Turkish literature at the other end of the bookstore. And indeed, there it was, among works by Turkish authors which had been translated into German. The spatial organization of this bookstore conveys an intellectual attitude: minority authors, in this case Turkish-German authors, are not German writers. And, by extension, writing in German and writing literature does not add up to 'German literature', except in some exceptional instances as, for example, in the case of Franz Kafka.

One of the reasons for compiling an anthology of this kind is to make these elements of German literature more visible and to lend substance to the claim that these texts should be counted as German literature as well. However, one should be careful to avoid the pitfalls inherent in the notion of one homogeneous 'German literature'.[2] We would like to suggest that it is futile to compare the texts written by minorities with the texts by established German authors with regard to both quality and quantity. Whenever there have been challenges to a national literary canon, the defenders and apologists of such a canon have pointed out that there simply isn't much good writing by the groups perceived to pose the challenge. *[margin note: measuring stick]* This was the case when German students demanded that workers' literature be included in the curriculum, and to some degree it is still the case with regard to women authors. Again, upholders of the notion of one homogeneous German national literature would most probably claim that the texts in this collection do not live up to what they perceive to be the standard of literary quality, and that the textual basis is not large enough to furnish sufficient textual material for a representative cross-section of this type of literature. They would also perhaps invoke the term contained in the title of this collection: these texts are marginal *vis-à-vis* what is more properly termed German literature.

To avoid the pitfalls in this case means to avoid getting involved in a debate over the quantity and quality of the texts we think should be considered part of German literature. With regard to the number of texts available, a debate on why, at least for some groups within German society, there aren't more texts available would be more fruitful. Such a *[margin note: social inequity]* debate would highlight the inequalities in social status among the different groups, inequalities also reflected in differences of access to educational institutions, a necessary precondition for expressing oneself in writing in a way acceptable to the majority culture.

This argument also provides at least a partial explanation as to why we would consider a debate over the quality of the texts to a large extent irrelevant: texts are considered to be of high quality when they reflect the qualities of writing taught in educational institutions. These qualities in turn then serve as the measuring stick (which is the literal translation of the word 'canon') for the critics who decide which texts 'make it' into the national literature or canon of texts considered representative. For the critics themselves are, of course, products of these same educational institutions. It is therefore easy to see how the process of constructing a literary canon or national literature is both somewhat incestuous, marginalizing those authors who do not belong to the narrowly defined

---

2. See Leslie Adelson, 'Migrants' Literature or German Literature? TORKAN's *Tufan: Brief an einen islamischen Bruder*', *German Quarterly* 63.3/4 (1990): 382–389 and Arlene Teraoka, '*Gastarbeiterliteratur*: The Other Speaks Back', *Cultural Critique* 7 (Fall 1987): 77–101.

circle of the well-educated, and at the same time a way of ensuring that the same socially constructed aspects of literary quality are reproduced over time.

Instead we would like to suggest that these texts should not be approached with the question of 'how close do they get' to the literary standards of established German authors but with consideration of what they might contribute to German literature in ways not easily recognized by the critic trained in traditional ways of reading literature. Where this critic might detect linguistic or rhetorical irregularities, we would like the reader to entertain the question of what these irregularities might say about the language of the majority, how they might help readers to put their received and intuitive ways of 'living in their language' at a critical distance, an act which, in turn, will help them to understand how language functions to construct a culturally specific and at times exclusionary cultural and national identity.

If the texts are considered in this way, the reader will also avoid constructing a hierarchy among the different groups presented here based on some imaginary standard of appropriate modes of literary expression. The texts collected in this volume do certainly differ in tone according to the educational, social or ethnic background of their authors. But again, while acknowledging these differences among the texts, it might be best to reflect upon their specific contribution to German literature and culture and not view them as indicators of their 'rank' within socially and culturally constructed categories.

An analogy to our discussion of the legal status of foreigners in Germany might best convey the approach we have in mind for these texts. We have argued that immigration laws which are not based on the ethnic background of the applicant might perhaps be a prerequisite for allowing the diverse ethnic groups to make their specific contribution to German culture. These laws would replace the current practice whereby ethnicity serves to uphold differences in the legal status of the various groups. Equal legal status would then provide the basis for expressing cultural difference. Similarly, it might be best to consider all the texts gathered here as having equal status within our perception of German literature and culture. Once we have established intellectually this kind of equality among them, we can then go on to point out the specific contribution of each text to German literature and culture. This should ensure that quantity or quality (however it might be defined) will not serve as criteria for the exclusion of some texts, but that each text will be viewed with the intention of establishing its contribution to our understanding of contemporary Germany.

But at the same time we should always bear in mind that the diversity and equality among the different groups represented in this volume do not reflect a similar diversity and equality among the various ethnic groups living in Germany. One graphic proof that not even a book of this nature can approach a semblance of equality among the diverse ethnic groups in German society is the absence of texts by Sinti and Roma, the two groups of 'gypsies' living in Germany. The way in which our society privileges the printed word presented us with no other choice than to exclude them since the only texts we could have used were ones not written by Sinti or Roma themselves but texts based on oral accounts and recorded by other people.

This book should not, then, be seen as a reflection of Germany as a multicultural society, but rather as an attempt to delineate what such a society might look like: a chorus of different voices, each with its own place and the right to voice its opinion without fear of reprisals which in real life might keep these voices quiet. *[handwritten: mission statement]*

But we should also bear in mind that these texts, whether they are autobiographical or purely fictional, whether they are diary entries or poems, are also to a certain degree literary texts; therefore they should not be read as the authentic and unequivocal expression of the opinion, sentiments and thoughts of their authors. All these texts must be scanned and examined for the different levels of meaning they contain. And in so doing we should perhaps leave behind our preconceptions regarding differences in complexity between the various genres. We are, for example, used to viewing poems as probably the most complex form of 'encoding' real-life experiences, while autobiographies are often read as the attempt to record one's life as truthfully as possible. In order to do these texts justice, we would like to invite the readers to engage in an experiment: to read each text in two ways, as the direct and authentic expression of real-life experiences and as a complex literary work of art in which real-life experiences are condensed, encoded and subjected to a variety of rhetorical devices. To give just one example: a short story by a Turkish female intellectual might be about her life as a Turkish intellectual in Germany, but it might also be about something entirely different. What this might be we leave to the reader to discover.

This approach will also prevent the reader from viewing the authors we have selected as representatives of their ethnic group. Ethnicity in each case is only one of several positions which the individual author inhabits in his or her society, and often it might not be the most defining one. Similarities in educational and social background might present a much stronger bond between two individuals than a shared ethnic background. We should therefore read these texts as authors' careful negotiations with all the different groups with which they have something in common in some respects and from which they differ in others. Nevertheless, all these authors have one thing in common: <u>one aspect of their identity is and will always be 'hyphenated'</u>: they are always both Turkish and German, both Jewish and German, etc. <u>And as a result of this, these authors are likely to be more sensitive to the rifts and contradictions which characterize our daily lives than those who have never had to question or were never questioned about their cultural or ethnic background.</u>

Finally, if we limit any generalizations to this one point – that the authors share a heightened awareness for the contradictions underlying each individual identity – we might be able to avoid making one gross generalization: that there is a common denominator to the experience of minorities in Germany. Of course it is natural that the reader will make comparisons. And in the process of comparing, s/he will discover not only similarities but also differences.

Part II
German Jews: Living in a
Double Diaspora

Outside Israel, the Jewish community is growing faster in Germany than anywhere else in the world. This is largely due to the immigration of Jews from the former Soviet republics, who under a special agreement between the two governments are exempt from some of the strict German immigration laws. Still, their total number is very small compared with what it had been before the Nazis took power in 1933.[1]

Being Jewish in Germany today is naturally problematic, and the relationship between Jewish and non-Jewish Germans is still strained by recent history. The Holocaust and the treatment of the Jews under Hitler dominate the dialogue between Germans and German Jews. Much of this has to do with the unresolved problems which both Germans and German Jews of the generations who lived under German National Socialism have bequeathed to the postwar generations. These unresolved problems complicate every aspect of what it means to be Jewish in today's Germany.

Non-Jewish Germans have never been able to formulate an answer to the collective guilt thesis which claims that every German, regardless of his or her position in society, shares responsibility and guilt for the crimes committed by the Nazis. If everybody in German society is guilty, Jews necessarily are constant reminders of this guilt. Thus, the collective guilt thesis keeps reproducing the dividing line between German Jews and non-Jewish Germans as the dividing line between victims and perpetrators.

As a result of this, Jewish culture is not perceived from the perspective of its millennia of existence and of two thousand years of German–Jewish contact. Rather, Jews in Germany are viewed as living reminders of twelve of the darkest years in German history, and knowledge of this other culture on the part of non-Jewish Germans is often reduced to knowledge of its almost complete destruction under the Nazis. Well-intentioned attempts

---

1. There were around 500,000 Jews living in Germany in 1933. While only 25,000 Jews were living in Germany right after the war, today there are around 60,000 Jews in the reunited Germany, but their number is growing due to the influx of immigrants. In the early 1990s 15,000 Jews came from the former USSR. All these numbers vary according to whether one only counts the members of the Jewish *Gemeinden*, the official members of the Jewish congregations (see Cornelia Schmalz-Jacobsen and Georg Hansen, eds, *Kleines Lexikon der ethnischen Minderheiten in Deutschland* (Munich: Beck, 1997), 82–84.

by German teachers to imbue their students with historical awareness by visiting former concentration camps or the initiatives of local politicians for the establishment of Holocaust memorials only serve to reinforce this limited perspective if they fail to promote any knowledge of other aspects of German-Jewish life and culture. Similarly, the representation of anti-Semitic incidents in the media, in the absence of any other images or knowledge of Jewish culture in Germany, creates the sole impression of members of the Jewish community as victims.

In this sense, their cultural history is being taken away from the German-Jewish minority as a source of comfort. The same can be said of its ethnic heritage, which, if at all, received attention only from the perspective of anti-Semitic racism, particularly in the shape of a catalogue of stereotypical 'Jewish' physical features. The memory of how a pseudo-scientific theory of racial differences was put in the service of the attempt to eradicate an entire segment of the German population still haunts the mention of particular features of any ethnic group, something which would be problematic even without this catastrophic period in history.

Religious tradition as the third root of a Jewish identity has also become problematic for Jews currently living in Germany. Often their parents didn't have very strong ties to their religious heritage, and many chose to neglect it in the false hope that assimilation in this regard, too, might pre-empt anti-Semitic sentiments. Today, moreover, the strong influx of Russian Jews, who for decades had to live under a state-enforced secularization of all aspects of life, also brings with it the perplexing prospect of a Jewish community without cultural ties to its religious traditions. Many young Jews view this, if not exactly as an act of betrayal, then certainly as something lacking in their background and are making a conscious effort to return to those religious traditions. This effort is often met by a complete lack of understanding on the part of their gentile contemporaries. For the latter are continuing on the path towards secularization as evidenced by the increasingly small number of people who still belong to one of the Christian churches in Germany.

The state of Israel, which could serve as the focal point for a positive definition of a Jewish identity, is also called into question by non-Jewish Germans. For a number of reasons, Germans on both the political Right and Left tend to sympathize not so much with Israel but with the Palestinians and the Arab countries in the ongoing conflicts in this region. Israel is seen as the aggressor and as an imperialist country which is supposedly denying other peoples their right to an existence. When the Jewish songwriter Wolf Biermann voiced his support for America's war against Iraq because the latter was posing a threat to Israel, he was confronted with indignant rejection on the part of non-Jewish Germans. German Jews, moreover, are just as critical of the policies of the state of Israel as anyone else. However, they are collectively considered as representatives of these policies by other Germans, and any resentment against Israel is vented against them. While most Germans would be careful to establish that they don't have much to do with their own government, German Jews are seen as a collective in full agreement with 'their' government in Israel even though they are in fact German citizens. A German politician in a meeting with the head of the Central Council of Jews in Germany in fact once referred to the Israeli government as 'his', i.e. the Jewish functionary's, government.

This latter aspect is linked to another source of conflict between Germans and German Jews. After a period in which anything connected to the idea of a 'fatherland' had become suspect and had been radically questioned by, among other groups, the student movement of the 1960s, younger Germans now seem to have reconnected to Germany as a place where they belong. The term *Heimat* has experienced a renaissance in Germany. However, while non-Jewish Germans can take the country in which they live for granted, German Jews cannot perceive of Germany as such a place. For they question it themselves, and others, in particular Jews in other countries, also force them to question it. In the essay below, Henryk Broder offers a Jewish-German perspective on the concept of *Heimat*.

In relation to the Jewish communities in other parts of the world, German Jews live in a double Diaspora. As part of the Diaspora they are also constantly reminded by other Jews that they chose to live 'in the land of the murderers', something which American Jews in particular find difficult to understand. Thus, German Jews not only have to face criticism for not living in Israel, they also have to defend their choice *vis-à-vis* the rest of the Jewish community. This aspect is discussed in Seligmann's text 'Zionism' below.

Despite these areas of conflict there are also areas in which non-Jewish and Jewish Germans have had similar experiences. However, this does not make German–Jewish relations any less complicated. While many younger Germans rejected their parents for what they had done under Hitler and in this sense grew up 'without fathers', the same can be said of German Jews: while it is clear that their parents had been the victims, some younger Jews nevertheless reject them because by returning to Germany they have forced them to live in this 'land of the murderers', something which sets them apart from the rest of the world's Jewish community.

An additional commonality is the fact that both non-Jewish and Jewish Germans who lived through the war find it extremely difficult to relate to their children their individual fates. On the one hand, non-Jewish Germans are reluctant to reveal to their children any role they may have played in support of Hitler's regime. On the other hand, the fate of Jewish Germans and their relatives under Hitler is so terrible and incomprehensible that it often seems easier for them to treat that whole period on the level of historical abstraction rather than individual involvement. The encounter between non-Jewish and Jewish Germans therefore leads to a matrix of complex and contradictory emotions: when non-Jewish Germans talk about their parents on the basis of family ties and solidarity, the Jewish Germans serve to remind them of their at least potential role as perpetrators. Jewish Germans' unambiguous solidarity with the generation of their parents as victims, however, is thrown into question when doubts arise as to whether their parents actually built their current existence 'in tandem with the murderers'.[2]

Finally, there is, of course, outright anti-Semitism, which, in spite of what has happened in Germany, is still widespread. About one-third of all Germans would not want to have Jews as their neighbours, would not like to see a Jew as president and believe the Jewish minority has too much influence.[3] Moreover, beyond this widespread anti-Semitism among the German population there are also forms of institutionalized anti-Semitism; in the former GDR, for example, acts of racial hatred against Jews did not make it into the official statistics – a form of denial which had as its basis the claim that a socialist society would outgrow such barbaric forms of human behaviour.

Taking all this into account, it is no wonder that German Jews still adhere to the concept of a 'portable fatherland', a term coined by the nineteenth-century German Jewish poet Heinrich Heine. Jews living in Germany keep the thought of leaving this country alive in their consciousness, fantasize about what to put into their suitcases, and, if they have dual citizenship, make sure they keep it. The irony is, of course, that this behaviour might cause even more prejudice against those who are perceived as 'hearing the grass grow'.

This chapter brings together three writers who have confronted the problems outlined above, and who thematize aspects of being Jewish in Germany in their texts. They have, however, all come to different

---

2. An expression used by Maxim Biller in 'Auschwitz sehen und sterben', in *Die Tempojahre* (Munich: DTV, 1991), 116f.

3. See Rafael Seligmann, 'Wie in der Judenschul', *Der Spiegel* 10 (1995): 62.

conclusions. Henryk M. Broder, an essayist who contributes to many German newspapers and weeklies, was born in Poland in 1946. He lived in Germany from 1958 to 1980 and since then has lived between Jerusalem and Berlin. Lea Fleischmann was born in Ulm, West Germany, in 1947. She worked as a teacher in Wiesbaden and Offenbach until 1979, when she decided to emigrate to Israel. Dr Rafael Seligmann, a journalist and the editor-in-chief of the *Jüdische Zeitung* (1985–7), as well as a lecturer (*Akademischer Rat*) at the *Geschwister-Scholl-Insitute* at the University of Munich, was born in Israel in 1947. He moved to Germany in 1957 and has lived there ever since. Most recently, he has published a series of articles in *Der Spiegel* that focus on Jews of German descent living in Israel.

While some scholars have claimed that there is a renewed and intensified interest in Jewish issues in Germany,[4] the difficulties Seligmann encountered when attempting to publish his novel *Rubinstein's Auction*, from which the passages in this chapter are taken, tell a different story. The manuscript was sent back by several publishers before Seligmann decided to fund its publication on his own. Afterwards, furthermore, it received little attention from critics. Perhaps it is Seligmann's aggressive tone and ironic depictions of Jewish life in West Germany that put publishers off. But it would be a mistake to read Seligmann's irony and sarcasm as yet another example of 'Jewish self-hatred'. Rather, it is more fitting to read them as appropriate means for depicting the idiosyncrasies of a community living in a twofold Diaspora as Jews outside Israel and as outsiders within this Diaspora, the ones 'living in the land of the murderers'.

The texts of the authors in this chapter represent reflections on three fairly distinct periods in West Germany's postwar history. Rafael Seligmann's novel *Rubinstein's Auction*, from which the excerpts in this chapter are taken, is an account of an adolescent German Jew coming of age in the late 1960s and on one level can be read as an autobiographical account of Seligmann's own youth. While there are definite references to contemporary events in this novel (as, for example, the reference to the

4. Sander L. Gilman and Karen Remmler have published a volume of essays with the misleading title *Reemerging Jewish Culture in Germany: Life and Literature Since 1989* (New York and London: New York UP, 1994). Jewish authors have produced at the same rate before and after 1989; what has changed, however, is the amount of attention their writings have received after this historic divide. Jack Zipes, for example, argues that the German Jews have become the focus of attention as 'the most defining Other' since East Germany has ceased to play this role (see 'The Contemporary German Fascination for Things Jewish: Toward a Jewish Minor Culture' in Gilman and Remmler, 15–45).

formation of the 'Grand Coalition' of Christian and Social Democrats in 1966), it can be read as a reflection on the inner workings of the Jewish community at a time when it had not yet received much attention from outside. Some of Seligmann's observations can in fact be seen as his coming to terms with the very exoticism of being a Jewish boy in the Federal Republic of the 1960s. Fleischmann's polemic, on the other hand, is already clearly marked by the politicized language of the 1970s, and as a polemic represents an accurate account of her own position at this point while it might not be doing justice to developments that were in fact put into motion by the political uproar of the 1970s. The picture of an 'authoritarian' German national character she paints was precisely one of the targets of the student movement and the ensuing attempts at social reform of the late 1960s and early 1970s. A character portrait of today's generation of parents would be markedly different, reflecting the anti-authoritarian and liberating impulses that have permeated most of Germany's institutions ever since the turmoil of these decades. Broder's essay, then, can be seen as a warning that despite these reforms the Germans of the 1980s and 1990s have no reason to be complacent about what they and previous generations have achieved in coming to terms with the past. The essay is a brilliant example of why every society needs people who have a different vantage point so that complacency will not lead to a repetition of mistakes made in the past.

−4−

Playing Ass*
Rafael Seligmann

'Shalom Ass.'[1]

'Why are you only just coming home now?'

'That's none of your business.'

'This is how you talk to your mother?'

'Exactly like that! How often do I have to tell you that it is entirely up to me whether and when I come home?'

'But I have to know when I am supposed to heat up the food.'

'As soon as I tell you to do so!'

'Tell me, have you gone completely mad today? How dare you?' She has left her spot behind the kitchen table and is planting herself in front of me in her full height of five feet. 'Do you have no respect at all for your parents? Don't you feel a glimmer of gratitude for Friedrich and me? Since your birth we have done everything for you.'

'Am I supposed to thank you for having brought me from Israel to this Nazi-country?'

'There are other people here, too. Besides, in a couple of years all the Nazis will be dead.'

'And you, too!'

For a moment her light brown eyes widen. But Ass immediately regains control of herself. 'You have completely forgotten how we were doing in Israel, Jonathan. I was sick, Friedrich had no work. How were we supposed to feed you?'

---

* 'Eselei', from *Rubinsteins Versteigerung* (Frankfurt-on-Main: Eichborn Verlag, 1989), 16–20.

1. Though the tone of the following conversation suggests otherwise, this is a word of endearment. In fact, the novel is dedicated 'To Ass', hinting at the obviously autobiographic character of this book. The aggressive tone of the conversation is also an indirect commentary on the often much more polite tone in gentile German families, which might often gloss over problems. Compare Fleischmann's comments on the tone used in gentile German families.

'I see! Now I am the one responsible! In order to save me from starvation you had to come to Germany. The only thing strange about this is that up until today not one person has died of hunger in Israel – something you can't say about the Jews in the German concentration camps.'

'That's long past,' she screams.

'Nothing is past. The old Nazis are still alive and are bringing up children to be new Nazi-pigs.'

'You had trouble in school again!'

'The fuck I had,' I yell.

'I don't understand you. Why do you always have problems with this? Aaron Blau and Herrschi Bierstamm live here, too, and they are content.'

'You must be talking about Arthur and Heinz? Those cowardly sons of bitches don't even dare to be called by their Jewish names. Just wait, soon they will call themselves Adolf and Horst so that no one will get the idea that they are not Aryans. But none of this will be of any use! Don't think that they get teased any less than me. Later on, of course, they'll have surgery on their crooked noses. Maybe that'll help.'

'You talk like scum.'[2]

'That's what I am. As a Jew I do not belong to this society.'

'And what's more you talk like a Nazi. As if all Jews had crooked noses. Look at your father. He is blond and blue-eyed.'

'And he also has a good measure of German stupidity inside him.'

'Righteous Lord, the way you talk about your father!'

'He deserves it! Most Yids make lots of money here at least. The Blaus and the Bierstamms, too. But our Friedrich breaks his back for a few lousy marks in Silberfaden & Ehrlichmann's warehouse ten hours every day. He could have got a great job like that in Israel, too. But of course there he wouldn't have made it all the way up to owning a car, not even one of the VWs loved so dearly by the *Führer* himself. But he doesn't even get anything out of that. Because Friedrich can't even drive. He always has a bright red face when he sits behind the wheel, the midget.'

'God in Heaven, what are you saying about your own father? Have you ever thought about the fact that this "midget" has been feeding you for over twenty years? That he slaves away every day so that you have something to eat and a roof over your head?'

---

2. The German word 'Asozialer', a term from social psychology referring to those who cannot be reintegrated into society. It has become a swear-word now.

'I know this record by heart. I owe you eternal gratitude. The fuck I owe you if you really want to know. Parents feed their kids as a matter of course. Your parents fed you, too.'

'But we were grateful.'

'That's enough! If you don't shut up right this minute I am going to get mean.'

'I'd like to see that.' Her eyes are sparkling.

'You will any moment! I warn you, Ass. If I hear one more word from you I will explode.'

'Well then, explode! Do you think I'm afraid of you?'

'I don't care, I am going to take a bath.' I push her out of the way and go to the bathroom.

'But the food is going to get cold.'

I lock the door, run water into the tub while I am getting undressed. This shouting match has made me feel better. And now a hot bath. I have to wash off all that dirt, the dirt from the classroom and the brothel.[3]

I climb into the tub. The hot water calms me down. I run more water in through the shower-head.

'Why are you taking a shower in the tub? You will flood the entire bathroom.'

'If you don't shut up right now I'm going to come out and throw you into the tub fully dressed.' With some effort I climb out of the water.

'Don't splash water all over the place!'

'I'll splash as much as I like.' And with whatever I like.

'But then you will kindly have to clean the bathroom.'

'I will make a clean sweep of you if you don't shut up soon.'

'What kind of language are you using with your mother?'

'Just wait!' I throw open the bathroom door and dripping with water I rush towards Ass.

'Are you *meschugge*, you'll catch a cold. Dry yourself off right away.'

'Quite the opposite. I am going to get you wet, too.'

'Help! Help! My son has *nebbich* gone completely *meschugge*.'

At least she is retreating to the kitchen. I saunter to my room, throw myself on to my bed and pull the cover over my ears. After a while I feel a pleasant warmth in my arms and legs.

Why did I let Bauriedl get to me like this?

---

3. In the previous chapter, Jonathan auctioned off the seat next to the new teacher on whom everybody, and especially Jonathan, has a crush, probably in an attempt to show his supposed indifference. Embarrassed he had stormed out of the classroom and gone to a brothel where he managed to spend the money but did not accomplish much else.

Why is this always happening to me?

Because I am a cry-baby and a mimosa. But that's going to stop right now. Instead of tears and hurt feelings there is only going to be cold hatred – of the Germans!

OK, I've been lying around long enough now. I get dressed and storm out of my room.

'Where are you going? You can't go outside with wet hair. You are going to catch a cold.'

'If that happens, I will let you take care of me.' I slam the apartment door shut.

5

Zionism*

Rafael Seligmann

'Jonny, you are early. The executive committee is still in its meeting. The best thing for you to do would be to go for a little walk.' Arale Blau seems to be annoyed.

'I am slowly getting fed up, Arthur. I am a member of the Jewish Group Sinai just like you. What gives you the right to kick me out?'

'But Jonathan, no one wants to kick you out. You are simply much too early, more than a quarter of an hour. And we're still in the middle of the executive committee meeting, that's all.' Arale smiles slyly, superciliously.

Just try to provoke me, you pig. 'You have your executive committee meeting, so what? I would like to know what you are discussing, too.'

His smile broadens. 'I do believe you do, Jonny. But, you know, executive committee meetings are not public – unfortunately.'

'Why not?'

'Because we have to make decisions, and you could never do that with twenty people.'

If you don't stop grinning, I'll smash your face in. 'So that's how it works. You make the decisions and let the ordinary people rubber-stamp them.'

'Not exactly. Rather, let's say we get issues ready for the decision.'

'Rather, let's say you can kiss my arse,' I scream.

'But now you're getting obscene, Rubinstein.'

'Obscene is what you are. You are arrogant enough to believe that it is going to go on like this for ever. You decide and we act. You spend our money and we cough it up. And what, exactly, do you do with our money? We pay, and you make off with it.'

His smile has disappeared. 'That's enough now, Jonny! If you don't take that back right now, I'll stick it in your face.'

* 'Zionismus', from *Rubinsteins Versteigerung* (Frankfurt-on-Main: Eichborn Verlag, 1989), 24–35.

Behind Arale's back at the end of the hall way Itzchak Polzig's cylindrical physiognomy comes into sight. In the dance-like walk of the former *Jeschiwa* students our forty-year-old mentor approaches. 'What's going on here? Why are you shouting like this?'

'Nothing, really, Mr Polzig.' Arale's expression fluctuates between devotion and righteous fury. 'Jonny tried to force his way into the executive committee meeting. And when I told him that he wasn't allowed because he is not on the executive committee he became abusive and offensive.'

Polzig pauses for a moment. His inward-turned eyes behind the heavy glasses focus on an imaginary point behind me. Then he speaks in a pleasant-sounding baritone: 'Don't fight. Try to get along again, after all you're friends. Jonathan, you know very well that you cannot be in the meetings of the executive committee because you haven't been elected to the executive committee. That's why you have to remain outside. And you, Aaron, are needed on the committee. Come on, we want to bring the meeting to a close.' He turns around and skips back into the apartment followed by his loyal assistant.

You will pay for this, you Zionist make-believes! Especially you, Itzig[1] Polzig. He makes me wait outside the door like a Jewish haberdashery pedlar. I will do your Sinai in.

But how, damn it? If I just throw tantrums these bastards will let me dangle in the air like just now. What else can I do?

For starters, go in there, otherwise you will really be standing outside the way Polzig and associates would like you to. I throw open the door. To the right is the meeting-hall which the Jews in Schwabing use on holidays. Opposite that is a small office in which at present the élite of Munich's religious Jewish youth is assembled. Next to it is our 'meeting-room'. This is where the Jewish women come on holidays to chat while the men pray or at least pretend to.

Arale Blau immediately started to go wild when I accused them of blowing our money. That indicates that there must be something to it. We pay two marks membership fee each month. That adds up to about 25 marks per person per year, times 20, that's about 500 marks. You don't hear or see anything of this money. Eli Zeitvogel has told me that these bastards go out for dinner once in a while – now I finally know who pays the bill! Just wait, I'll completely wreck their dinner.

---

1. Allusion to the Jewish character Veitel Itzig in Gustav Freytag's anti-Semitic novel *Debit and Credit* (1855).

In the meantime one by one the gang files into the room. Peter and Carlo are already there, too. I steer toward them. 'I have had it once and for all with Polzig, Arale and the other wankers.'

'What's happened?' Carlo's dark bear eyes widen.

'Today Polzig and Arale wanted to lock me out just because I dared to ask about the whereabouts of our membership fees.'

'And?' Peter smiles.

'And! And! And!' I have to control myself so that I don't start screaming again. 'I've had enough of these tactics once and for all.'

'Me, too. But what do you want to do about it?'

'New elections! Right away!'

'And what is that supposed to achieve if I may ask? You know just as well as I do that everyone on the executive committee has at least one friend who votes for him plus himself, plus some idiots. That means, these bastards have a majority for eternity even if there were elections every week.'

'Had a majority, my friend, had one,' I shout excitedly. 'Do you really believe that a single person is going to vote for this gang if it gets out that they have embezzled our membership fees and spent them on food?'

'How did you find that out?' asks Carlo.

'Very simple, my son, by thinking about it. Have you ever thought about what happens to our membership fees, all in all 500 marks per year?'

'No.'

'See! These bastards count on that and use our money to eat, drink and fornicate.'

'Not bad, *reb yid*,' you can hear Peter murmur.

'So?'

'Today we must force a debate on the fundamental principles in the course of which we will touch upon the question of money; this will completely isolate the crooks, and then we'll have to push for new elections immediately.'

'But we were supposed to discuss the immigration into Israel today,' Carlo interjects.

'We are supposed to, but we don't want to. Today we will turn the "Sinai" into something else. Instead of immigration into the Promised Land, which no one believes in any more anyway, it'll be the question of the beloved money.' My voice is high and clear.

'But how are you going to go about this?'

'Let us handle it. I have a very definite idea about it.' Peter is smiling to himself.

In the meantime Polzig has made his entry into the meeting-room, followed closely by his brood, Arale, Miri Katz, Fanny Friedländer and Henry Nelkenbaum. Polzig sits down, briefly collects his thoughts and calls out above the subsiding noise: 'My dear friends, it is a quarter past eight already. We must begin because today we have a very full agenda ahead of us.' He clears his throat several times: 'My dear friends, today is perhaps the most important meeting of the year. Today, as you certainly all know, is about the *Aliya*,[2] immigration into Israel. Many of you have already completed half of your studies, so now it is time to plan step by step for the *Aliya*.'

'Mr Polzig, allow me this question, why step by step and not right away?'

'Because Israel needs experts who will help build the land and not students who will only cost the taxpayers money.'

'I understand, a new version of reparation payments: educational assistance.'

'Rubinstein, don't interrupt!'

'I have to, Mr Polzig! Because you preach Zionism with limited liability. Go make something of yourself so that you can give something to Israel. First the highschool diploma, then university, then a little bit of practical experience on the job because one does not want to go to the Promised Land with empty hands and as you stated "be a burden on Israel's taxpayers". In the meantime one has turned forty, in most cases one has a family and a business. Do you seriously believe that anyone would still go to Israel then? Just look at our parents.'

Before he can make a sound I continue with my sermon. 'The kind of Zionism which you and the likes of you preach, Mr Polzig, is actually a perversion of Zionism. By means of your Zionism-as-preparation you ease the Jews' bad conscience about living in Germany instead of Israel.

'Zionism means immigration into Israel, no ifs or buts, without preparation and simmer-down preparations. Most of all without professional Zionists who instead of furthering immigration into Israel go to the Diaspora, live a good life there and as it turns out systematically prevent immigration into Israel with their babbling.' Everyone sits paralysed. Until now not one of us has dared to question Polzig's authority openly, now I have denounced him as a hypocrite and a parasite. Polzig's face is pale, his large hands open and close constantly. He moves his mouth, but no sound can be heard. Finally he gurgles: 'Disrespectful lout . . .'

---

2. = ascent, i.e. into the Promised Land.

'Just a minute, we won't get any further by using insults.' Peter makes little effort to suppress his grin. 'It seems to me that there is a lot to what Jonathan has just formulated. For example, no one would deny that our parents have no thoughts of emigrating to Israel even though for twenty years they've been subjected to a constant stream of Zionist propaganda. It is therefore understandable that one should look for more effective ways. The plan to act immediately seems to me to be worth a try at least. As a first step I therefore propose that the "Sinai" donates 500 marks to Israel.'

'I think Peter's idea is far out and I am in favour of sending the money to Israel to the Zionist organization tomorrow already,' Carlo spurts out.

'That's not a bad proposition. So ask your parents before the next meeting whether they agree because every one would have to donate twenty marks.' Polzig has recovered visibly, the colour has returned to his face, just his eyes are still wandering aimlessly through the room.

'There is absolutely no reason for collecting donations, Mr Polzig. For one and a half years we have been paying a monthly two mark membership fee, that's about 500 marks per year. We have no expenditures, so we should have 700 marks in our group's account from which we should immediately transfer 500 marks to Israel.'

'I'll ask the executive committee to discuss this issue during its next meeting.'

'What does this have to do with the executive committee? The money belongs to all of us!'

'Rubinstein, I won't tolerate your lack of discipline! You won't let anyone finish their sentence, insult everyone and think that everyone has to do what you demand. You cannot force the group to do what you want. You've made a proposal. Well, I am in favour of having those authorized to do so discuss it and come to a decision. You alone cannot make decisions about the group's money.'

'Excuse me, Mr Polzig, I think that before we debate the proposal of an immediate Zionist act in the executive committee we should first assess the prerequisites. Do we indeed have 700 marks in the group's account, as Jonathan maintains, or is it less than that, which would mean we would not even be in a position to transfer 500 marks. In short, what is the current account balance?' Peter is oozing with responsibility.

'I will put this question, too, on the agenda of the next meeting of the executive committee.'

'Nothing is going to be put on the agenda of the next executive committee meeting! I want to know right now how much money we have in our account,' I yell.

'If you use this kind of tone with me once more, I will expel you from the "Sinai",' Polzig shouts back.

'Excuse me, but threats and insults really won't get us anywhere. I simply asked about the account balance. And one should be able to answer such a simple question without a meeting of the executive committee,' Peter goes on relentlessly.

'Exactly, I would like to know how much money we have in the account, too,' Carlo shouts. The rest of the guys are slowly getting restless as well, they're starting conversations with the people sitting next to them.

'How much money do we have, Henry?' Polzig finally asks.

'I would first have to look in my files,' Henry Nussbaum answers.

'It's not a matter of every single penny, do we have 500 marks or not?'

'I cannot tell you without my files. For the next meeting I will try to do an audit.'

'You're not supposed to do an audit, you're supposed to tell us how much money we have. No ifs or buts. No lame excuses, files and embezzlements, and right away!'

'You are not a policeman, Rubinstein, you can't just interrogate people!' Polzig is turning red.

'Mr Polzig, it's not a matter of interrogating anyone, we simply would like to know whether we have enough money in the account or not. And I believe a treasurer should in fact be in a position to answer a straightforward question like this without further ado and on the spot.' How come Peter doesn't have any trouble remaining calm while I am almost going crazy?

'Henry, finally tell us how much money we have, or there is going to be an accident,' Carlo rages.

'I don't know exactly.' Nelkenbaum is sitting up straight on the edge of his chair.

'Then tell us inexactly, but right now!'

'My dear friends, it cannot go on like this. We want to discuss immigration into Israel today and don't want to hear about the balance sheets.'

'Not us, you! All you want to do is discuss. We finally want to take concrete steps. As a first step we want to donate 500 marks. For this we have to know if we have enough money in our account.'

'Rubinstein!'

'Mr Polzig, do me a favour and don't always try to get us off the subject by threatening to expel me. You won't bring about the *Aliya* to Israel that way, either. We want to act. Don't try to stay our hand constantly, but help us. See to it that we finally know how much money is in the account.'

'Henry, perhaps you should try to tell us how much money we have in the account.' Why not right away, Itzig?

'We do not have 500 marks in the account.'

'How much then?'

'That's none of your business, Jonathan. I'm not accountable to you.'

'You're wrong, my dear Henry, this money belongs to the entire group, it's not your private property.'

'So, how much money do we have in the account? I would like to know that, too.' Mary Heilmann seizes the opportunity to take revenge on her ex.

'Can we please find out how much money we have in the account?' Moritz Kleiner, too, wants to be on the side that's right.

'I can't tell you exactly, about 150 to 200 marks.'

'In the past months we have paid 700 marks in membership fees. Where did the remaining 500 marks go to?'

'That's it, Rubinstein! We do not want to hear a financial report tonight, but to talk about Zionism.' Polzig's face is getting even redder.

'This is exactly what we don't want. We want to practise Zionism, or at least start to. A first step towards this is honesty. I would finally like to know what happens to our money, and I am certainly not the only one in the room,' I yell.

'That's what I think as well.' See there, Ruthi Seelig has realized, too, who is the stronger tonight.

'Will you finally shut up? Either we talk about immigration to Israel tonight or I'll break off the meeting.'

'You can break off whatever you want. I'm standing here insisting on the motion that the treasurer be forced to report right away on where the membership money went.'

'I'm not going to let this happen. No one is going to be forced to do anything, least of all by a lout like you, Rubinstein.'

'We're not getting anywhere like this, since the treasurer either doesn't want to or isn't able to give a report I move to hold new elections. The executive committee would then be obliged to present a financial report by the time of the next meeting,' Peter declares calmly.

'I'll second that motion!' Stupid he is not, this Aaron Blau. Kept his mouth shut all along and waited. Now that practically everything is decided he's trying to switch sides and go with the new majority. Let Henry ride it out alone. But you won't get off that easily, Arthur. You pigged out like the others. You always let me know that you were on the executive committee and I wasn't. 'Those opposed to elections next Tuesday, please raise your hand.'

'This is not within your jurisdiction, Rubinstein. In order to pull the carpet out from under any malicious insinuations I am in favour of holding new elections during the next meeting. I ask those who are of my opinion to raise their finger also.' Don't waste your energy, Polzig. You've lost. You won't leave me standing outside the door any more.

Only Henry Nelkenbaum has the guts not to raise his paw. 'Except for one abstention everyone is in favour of new elections next Tuesday. I ask all of you to show up. I would now like to adjourn the meeting. Good night and shalom.'

Was the fact that you had to stand outside the door for two minutes worth all that effort? Yes, because at some point the kettle had to boil over. I could no longer stand this hypocrisy and the constant humiliations by Polzig and his lackeys. Most of all – here I can pay these guys back. But in school I am alone.

6

The Underling*
Rafael Seligmann[1]

'As you all probably know in a few months the anniversary of the beginning of the Second World War is going to take place. I believe this should be an occasion for us to think about the changes that have occurred in Germany since this event.'

She does not even look at me. Yesterday she whined[2] at me, now I don't exist for her any more. Instead she indulges in deep historical contemplations. You are supposed to feel that I still exist.

'The only difference I can discern is a noticeable increase of influence by the NSDAP within the government. While thirty years ago it was only the chancellor who belonged to this party and the secretary of commerce did not belong to a party at all, at present the chancellor as well as the secretary of commerce are former party members.'[3]

Isolated gurgling sounds and laughs combine into a liberating roar of laughter as soon as I have finished. Some others, too, now want to demonstrate their wit.

'But the *Führer* was a better rhetorician than Kiesinger.'

'Hitler was more energetic.'

'Better a moustache than the fur of a badger.'

'I won't suffer your provocations, Rubinstein.' So there, now you have to look at me, to deal with me. 'Not to mention the, to put it mildly, wisecracks. I would like us to have a discussion that is to the point.'

---

* 'Der Untertan', from *Rubinsteins Versteigerung* (Frankfurt-on-Main: Eichborn Verlag, 1989), 83–8.

1. There is a novel by Heinrich Mann with the same title which describes the rise to power of what could be called a proto-fascist personality (*Der Untertan,* 1916).

2. The crush on the teacher mentioned earlier had led to a visit by Jonathan to the teacher's home in the course of which things almost happened between them.

3. Kurt Georg Kiesinger, chancellor from 1965 to 1969, had been a member of the NSDAP.

I raise my hand. 'Despite all the persecution back then there was a movement in opposition to Hitler. On the other hand, the leader of the opposition today, Mr Scheel,[4] can hardly be called an adversary of the Nazis – at least he wasn't one 30 years ago.'

Again there is a wave of laughing, yelling and catcalls in the class. Hilde plants her hands on the teacher's desk and shouts, as soon as the noise has subsided a little, with a high and clear voice which betrays the effort it takes her to control herself. 'As you wish, gentlemen. During our first session I offered to teach this class in the form of a discussion. Some of you, if not the majority, on account of intellectual immaturity seem to be getting provocation confused with discussion. I am of course willing to conduct a traditional German class according to the roles which you seem to prefer, with the teacher leading and the students following.'

'Conduct.'[5] For Heavens sake! Why do Germans, whether on the Left or on the Right, always have to 'conduct' something?

'In this way you voluntarily submit to the role of underlings. It seems fitting in this context that this past week we have thoroughly discussed the book *The Underling* by Heinrich Mann. We still have a little less than one class period at our disposal, which we will use for an in-class writing exercise. So during the next forty minutes please commit to paper your opinion regarding "A contemporary reading of Heinrich Mann's novel *The Underling*".'

These guys really do as they're told – even after this uproar. This could only happen in Germany. Hilde is right, perfect underlings. I am going to scribble down exactly this kind of bullshit:

4. Head of the Free Democratic Party (FDP) at that time. The scene takes place sometime between 1966 and 1969, the time of the so-called Grand Coalition (*Große Koalition*) between the Social Democrats (SPD) and the Christian Democrats (CDU). The 'Grand Coalition' had been formed in response to a perceived threat to the constitution posed by the student movement and the first major economic crisis after the Second World War. Many, of course, saw this very act as one step in the direction of a totalitarian government. The Free Democrats, as the smallest party representing the smallest percentage of voters, were not part of the government, but were supposed to act as the checks and balances to this overwhelming majority. Together with Willy Brandt Walter Scheel later on formed the first coalition (in 1969) which did not involve the Christian Democrats, Kurt Georg Kiesinger's party, from which the chancellor had been elected ever since the founding of the Federal Republic. Walter Scheel later on served one term as president.

5. The German word *durchführen*, 'to conduct', is related to the word *Führer*.

The Underling

Jonathan Rubinstein 13b
In-Class Writing Exercise
A Contemporary Reading of Heinrich Mann's Novel
The Underling

The assertions of the novel *The Underling* by Heinrich Mann are as relevant today as they were almost sixty years ago. Because of their upbringing in their parents' home and in school the German people always need clear orders which they will carry out without protest and to the full satisfaction of their superiors.

This assertion by Heinrich Mann will be as true one hundred years from now as it is today. The reason: Those who are trained to obey by their parents and teachers, those whose will has been broken, are themselves only able either to obey or to give orders. In this sense one generation after the other in Germany is brought up to make 'good' underlings – ad infinitum.

I walk up to the teacher's desk and put the piece of paper on it, turn around without looking at her, return to my seat, sit down, then finally look at her. Hilde is reading with concentration or at least pretending to. At last she lifts up her head and says in a neutral tone: 'You are not very optimistic, Rubinstein . . . I would like to talk to you briefly after class.'

Holy shit, she sure does have class, and me, the idiot, I have blown everything. Wet-in-the-pants, wanker, eunuch, coward.

When we are finally alone she sits down next to me. My heart is pounding.

'Jonathan, why did you have to make such a scene today? Do you want to endear yourself to Pauls, Bauriedl and their crowd?'

'They can kiss my arse. I wanted you to look at me. Eventually, you did so – after I raised my hand.'

'It's probably obvious to you that these tactics of yours ruin my class?'

'Why didn't you look at me?'

'Because what happened yesterday has taken such a toll of me that for the time being I wanted to avoid having to deal with you.'

'Is that so? Do you think our meeting hasn't taken a toll of me, too? I constantly have to think about what an idiot I was to let myself be stupefied by your appeals to reason.'

'I have to thank you for that.'

'For that? Why?'

'Because it would have led to endless complications, and our energies wouldn't have sufficed in the long run.'

'Do you think it's less complicated now?'

'If we restrain ourselves and are reasonable, yes!'

'Reason, restraining yourself – and you let other people read *The Underling*!'

'I don't have the strength for a relationship with you. You can say I am a coward or have the soul of an underling like all Germans, but I simply can't do it. I'd rather have myself transferred to another school than participate in this soap opera any longer.'

'Soap opera?'

'Yes, damn it! Soap opera, or call it what you like, I simply cannot handle it. May I remind you that the burden in our relationship is distributed unequally? If our relationship were to be found out you would have to fear almost nothing at all. Perhaps switching schools in the worst-case scenario. I on the other hand would lose my job, would be slapped with a lawsuit and left an outcast.'

'So, an outcast.'

'Yes, go ahead and make fun of it. I know what you think about this society, you just wrote it down very succinctly. You're probably even right. Most certainly! But I just happen to be living in this country. I am a German whether I like it or not, and whether you like it or not. I can't simply go to Israel like you and leave everything behind me. Besides I also very much doubt that Israel's society would tolerate a relationship between a teacher and a student.'

'That wouldn't be necessary. The Yiddish *mammes* would have stoned you long before then.'

'Well at least you've not lost your sense of humour.'

'No, but I would like to be with you.'

'I can't do that. At least not now. You only have a few months until graduation. We'll see about it then. Not now!'

'I need you now, not in a few months.'

'Jonathan, not even if you beat me to death. I can't, at least please try to understand me.'

Her entire face, her neck and the area around her neckline is covered with big rosy spots. Indeed, the old lady can't, me neither, damn it. I take my schoolbag, get up and walk out of the room.

Reason, discipline, cowardice disguised as altruism have made you into the perfect German-Jewish underling, Rubinstein. Spontaneous feelings of desire are immediately suppressed. I'm certainly the right person to make fun of German underlings.

7

Why I Am Leaving This Country*
Lea Fleischmann

At some point I decided to quit my teaching job. It happened when I worked with the job trainees. Neither the principals nor the government officials nor any presidents or executive orders could have moved me to give up the battle voluntarily. It was the weakest member of the school system who made it clear to me that my place in the world was not among them.

With a lot of energy I get involved in the education of the trainees at the Geschwister Scholl School, hairdressers, bakers, butchers, seamstresses. I immerse myself in the masses of German people and swim in the problems of people who have revealed their essence to me and which I would pity from the bottom of my heart if I did not know that they represent a dangerous weapon if one knows how to use them. These people were never a nation of poets and thinkers, they don't think but execute, their souls have been made slaves, and like slaves they love power and respect strength. Pity and kindness are alien to them because they have never known pity and kindness. These people have hit others and at any time they would attack weaker ones again because they themselves have been hit constantly. Parents hit their children, teachers hit their students, employers hit their employees, and strength hits weakness.

Jews and foreigners believe that the Germans behave badly only towards them, but this is not true. They behave even more badly among themselves, even less intransigently, with even less understanding. They all behave towards foreigners as they do towards their own children, towards their own older people, towards themselves. Those who are not tolerant towards their own children cannot be tolerant towards foreigners, those who never experienced tolerance do not know what is meant by it.

---

* 'Warum ich dieses Land verlasse', from *Dies ist nicht mein Land – Eine Jüdin verläßt die Bundesrepublik* (Hamburg: Wilhelm Heine Verlag, 1992), 193–205.

Let's look at Bärbel. She is a trainee hairdresser in her second year. Faultless make-up, the hair done up nicely. She is 17 years old. The kind of girl that one sees every day by the hundreds of thousands. And now let's look at Maria. An Italian in the same year. Maria's appearance, too, fits our concept of a hairdresser-to-be. Two young girls who have the same taste in fashion, who look at the same magazines, who even voice similar opinions. It is important to both of them that they can go out at night, both are in love, both dream of a life of bliss. But there are fundamental differences between the two, differences which one cannot see at first.

Maria is not allowed to go out at night and if she is, then only with her older brother. She doesn't even think about the pill because she is supposed to enter marriage as a virgin. Bärbel's parents are a little bit more enlightened. She can bring her boyfriend home, can go out with him and is able, as she herself says, to talk to her mother about everything. She doesn't talk to her father because she doesn't know what she is supposed to talk about with him.

'Foreigners', Bärbel says, 'are like us. One should not make any distinctions. There are nice foreigners and ones that are not as nice.'

Let's go back ten years in the biography of Bärbel and Maria. It's seven o'clock at night, and Bärbel's mother says to her: 'The Sandman[1] is over, you have to go to bed now.' Bärbel does not want to go to bed yet. She is not tired and would rather watch TV.

'I want to stay up a bit, mom,' she begs.

'It's late already, Bärbel, you have to go to school tomorrow,' the mother says. 'Go upstairs to your room.'

'But I don't want to,' Bärbel starts to whine.

'You go to bed now; it would be even better if you decided yourself when to go to bed,' the mother scolds her.

Bärbel's whining gets louder, and the mother hits her in the face.

'Go to your room, off with you!'

At the same time, seven-year-old Maria is still running around on the street and romping about with other children of foreigners. No one thinks of ordering them to go to bed. It makes no difference to anyone whether they go to bed at nine or at ten. It is normal in Italy for children to stay up late and go to bed when they are tired, and they brought this custom with them to their new home. Maria doesn't have to lose a fight with her parents every night because no one fights with her.

1. 'Das Sandmännchen', a popular German children's programme on air in the early evening.

Let's go back even further. Five-year-old Bärbel is sitting at the table and is trying to spread jam on to a piece of bread with a spoon. The spoon drops out of her hand and she spills some on her pink dress.

'The hands of a fool soil the table and the wall,' the mother scolds her and gives her a slap on her fool's hands. 'Can't you be more careful. We put on this dress just a little while ago.'

'A fool's hands, a fool's hands,' the brother laughs and walks all over Bärbel's five-year-old soul. Bärbel looks at the red jam stain and is terribly embarrassed, just as if she had committed some awful crime.

Maria spills things on herself, too. All five-year-old girls spill things on themselves, but Maria's mother doesn't say a thing since she doesn't want to insult her kid on account of a stain. Cleanliness is not the most important thing to her, and she couldn't care less whether Maria walks around with a stain on her dress or not.

Both mothers are tired out by their work and have headaches.

'Please be quiet, Bärbel,' her mother says. But little Bärbel is not quiet. 'Bärbel, be quiet.' But Bärbel makes some noise with a rickety toy car.

The mother takes the toy car away from her and hits her. 'There, and now you'll be quiet.'

Bärbel starts to scream, and her mother gets even more upset. She thrashes the child and takes her to the other room. 'This is where you will stay, and just watch out if I hear the slightest sound!' Little beaten-up Bärbel sits in the room alone and cries silently, very silently so that her mother won't hear anything. And later on mom is still upset with her and doesn't talk to her.

'You've not been a good girl, and I don't talk to nasty girls. Tonight I'm going to tell daddy about the way you acted up.' Bärbel tries to be a good girl and to be obedient and to do everything that her mother wants so that she won't be angry and won't tell daddy.

Maria makes some noise, too.

'Be quiet, Maria!' the mother screams.

But Maria won't be quiet. The mother gets upset and starts to thrash Maria. Maria starts to scream so loud that the walls echo it back. The mother stops and starts to kiss the child all over.

'Please stop crying, Maria, stop it.'

Maria screams even louder in order to show her mother that she has hurt her. And her mother continues to caress and kiss the child to calm her down. Maria's mother has never heard of such a thing as consistent pedagogy, and, even if she had, she would reject that kind of consistent pedagogy as too cruel for her little Maria.

When Maria's father comes home at night from work he takes his little daughter in his arms and kisses and hugs her, and Maria comes running towards him from far away every night.

When Bärbel hears her father at the door, she gets scared because she knows that he is going to scold her terribly again because of this afternoon. She is even more afraid of him than of her mother.

And so the two girls grow up. Bärbel who is always good, quiet and clean, and who is constantly being criticized for something, and Maria who is noisy and is not constantly being ordered around. Both girls see a laughing child on the street with a dirty jacket and a messy face. 'Yuk,' Bärbel says. 'Look how dirty that child is,' and she finds it repulsive, and the child is repugnant to her. Maria on the other hand doesn't even see the dirt, but she hears the child laugh.

Bärbel rejects anyone who is different from her, whether it is a foreigner or a German. Just as she learned from her mother, who rejected her when she deviated from what was allowed. But, because most Germans have been brought up like this and only a few foreigners had to suffer through this kind of inhuman upbringing, a lot of Germans are quiet, clean, inhibited and repressed while many foreigners are relaxed, funny, impulsive, emotional. And Bärbel cannot stand this.

Bärbel is a hard-working girl. She is obedient at home and at work because for years she was made to feel: only those who are good and obedient won't get hit or scolded.

'Those who won't listen will get to feel it,' was father's standard response. And she does listen now. At work she has to tolerate her boss's bad moods; he constantly nags her and finds fault with what she does. And just as she didn't contradict her parents so she doesn't contradict her superior. She tries incredibly hard and thinks, I hope he will be satisfied with my work, I hope he will like it.

Yesterday she dropped a little bottle of colouring, and this made a stain on the floor which she could not scrub off in spite of all her efforts. She scrubbed and scrubbed, she started to sweat, her heart rate went up, I hope he won't notice the stain, I hope the stain comes off. It did not come off completely, and the boss's keen eye spotted it quickly.

'Who did this?' he asks in an upset tone.

'I did,' says Bärbel, shaking. 'A little bottle of black colouring slipped out of my hand.'

'Why can't you be more careful? I will deduct the colouring from your paycheck, and I will file a claim with the insurance for the stain. If the insurance does not pay I will have to approach your parents.'

Bärbel stands there crestfallen.

How am I supposed to explain this to my parents if the insurance does not pay for the damage, she thinks, and in her mind she hears her mother say: 'The hands of a fool soil the table and the wall.' Bärbel is always tortured by fear of doing something wrong. She has a boyfriend and takes the pill. But the fear won't let go of her even in bed. I hope I am doing everything right, she thinks. She cannot enjoy sex. She doesn't even like it. She cannot get rid of the thought that she might be doing something wrong and that he won't like it. She doesn't know that he is afraid, too, and is also trying to do everything right, just the way it was explained in the magazine. First caressing, he doesn't know how long, then kissing, then fucking. Sometimes facing each other, sometimes from behind. And both of them climb out of bed feeling empty. Was that the right way? They can't talk about it, and even if they could talk it wouldn't help. Bärbel can't give herself over to feelings.

Bärbel lives according to a plan, and anything which messes up this plan causes her problems. Sunday is her day off, and this day, too, is planned in detail. She sleeps one hour longer than on other days, has a leisurely breakfast, straightens up her room, helps her mother prepare dinner. At one o'clock exactly the food has to be on the table. In the afternoon she goes for a walk or watches TV, and at night she goes to the disco.

Bärbel's boyfriend is unemployed. He has nothing to do the entire day and doesn't know what to do with his time. Ever since he became unemployed he has been drinking. Just like Bärbel he has learned to do only what he is told, just like her he depends on directions. He has no clue as to what else he could do except look for work. But he doesn't find work, is frustrated, unhappy, he can't get a grip on himself. The others despise him and he despises himself. And he complains about everyone. About bosses, the government, foreigners.

'It's time for a strong man again,' he tells Bärbel. 'A little Hitler', the epitome of German strength. 'He would make a clean sweep of everything. Of this mob of foreigners and these filthy rich Jews, of these weeds in the government, of terrorists and unemployment.'

'You're right,' Bärbel says. 'My father says the same thing. These terrorists[2] should be lined up against a wall. It's time for a little Hitler, under him there were no such things.'

A lot of little Bärbels say and think the same thing: 'It's time for a little Hitler.'

---

2. The 1970s were a period of frequent terrorist attacks by the Red Army Faction (RAF). See also the next footnote.

The order of things gets a little disturbed, and right away the masses wish for a little Hitler, call for a strong man.

'Look at that,' I say to myself. 'You have learned your lesson well. You must be kidding if you say the Germans have no historic consciousness. Your history bears fruit in secret. The official representatives of the German people can tell me what they want, you have told me better.'

Privately I never had problems with the Bärbels. They are tools without a will of their own, you can do with them what you want. They don't contradict, they don't ask, they do what the authorities tell them. They seem to me like a mass of dough which you can form according to your whim. You only have to be strong and strict.

'You are too soft,' the Bärbels told me at the beginning. 'You have to handle us with more strictness.'

They couldn't bear the fact that I did not admonish the blabbermouths, that I didn't discipline the forward ones. When I was strong I was good. And I was strict and they respected me.

And slowly I understood that the Germans are not a strong but a weak people. A collective of timid and well-mannered individuals who don't trust in their own faculties and only wait for someone to tell them what they have to do. The strength of the Germans is a façade behind which hide fear and feelings of inferiority. The façade does not crumble because among them they adhere to certain rules. The subordinates do not attack the authorities. If the students attacked the teachers they would realize how little there is behind these apparent know-alls; if the teachers turned against the principals they would learn what miserable creatures most of them are; if the people rose up against the politicians then quite a few of these puffed up, autocratic windbags would lose their masks and an awkward timid creature would appear.

Then I'd had enough of the Bärbels. We go on an excursion, it is already dusk, and in front of me two girls are telling each other jokes. One joke was about Jews who are burnt. Something to die laughing over. I could have confronted Bärbel. She hadn't meant it in a mean way, she would say. She would be so sorry, and her fear of me would grow. Or I could have tried to provide information in class. A lesson in history with pictures and documents. 'Terrible,' the Bärbels would say. 'Oh, how awful.' But there is no point to all of this. Bärbels don't have compassion, they can't suffer with others. When Bärbel sat alone in the room back then, beaten up by her mother and left alone by everyone, no one had any compassion for her. And she will beat up her own children and treat them without mercy. Where did she ever experience mercy for the weaker one? Quite the opposite. Every sign of humanity they interpret as weakness, and weakness in their eyes is something bad, something to be despised.

It has become clear to me that I have no business among the Bärbels. This is not my people, this is not my country, I am not a martyr, and the salary and that little bit of security with the claim to a retirement pension are not worth giving up a part of my life to the Bärbels for. I am also unable to help my German friends who are fighting for changes in the educational system. Why should it be my job to bring more humanity to the German educational system? Let them work out their own way of living their lives, I am no revolutionary and no fighter.

The word Holocaust is what finally finished me off.

In the rich German language for years no word could be found for the industrial extermination of people, for the murder of innocent individuals, for horror as such. Now a word has been found: Holocaust. At least no one understands this word, it does not sound too bad, one cannot really have any associations with it.

And all of a sudden the German people remember particulars, minor points, details which they have denied for forty years.

'We did not know anything,' this is what I heard again and again, and then suddenly, as if by a miracle, people are remembering in this country. Somehow the memory of the Germans seems to work differently from ours. The witnesses at the trials for mass murderers are time and again reproached for not being able to remember exactly. Innocent murderers are acquitted because of this; on the other hand the Germans are all of a sudden remembering events which they claim not to have perceived before.

I am reminded of an argument which I had with my mother eight years ago before I became a teacher. 'It is not true, mom,' I say, 'that the German people knew about the murder of the Jews. You are wrong.'

'I am not wrong. Today they claim not to know anything, but the murder of millions could not remain a secret.'

'Mom, that's not true. Why don't they admit then that they knew about the extermination of the Jews? This is after all a democratic country with democratic people in it.'

'These are not democrats. These are small miserable followers of orders, and the most ridiculous ones and the ones who got trampled on the most were the greatest butchers and would butcher again if someone gave the orders.'

'You don't know the Germans. I have gone to school here, I am going to the university, I have German friends. You are simply stubborn and full of prejudices.'

'Listen, my daughter. For five years I had to live with them. For five years I have studied their souls, day in, day out, and I watched them, for five long, fearful, unhappy years which ate me up, which made an old woman out of a young person full of the joys of life. The Germans are people who shit in their pants when they see a uniform, who inform on others out of fear. Everybody is afraid of everybody else, and the dumber they are the more brutal they are. And they make sure themselves that they remain dumb.'

'But mom, my friends are not like that.'

'Germans such as your friends, there were some like that back then, too. There were those few who were in the concentration camps with us and suffered with us. There were a few in the resistance, but not nearly as many as they now try to convince the world of. And you can be sure of one thing, those who showed some humanity back then, who were in the resistance, they have the biggest problems again today. Those who are not like the German masses are being excluded and prosecuted by them. It doesn't make any difference whether they call themselves democratic today or not.'

'You don't have a clue, mom. The perspective of the past makes you see everything distorted. The Third Reich was a big misfortune into which the German people stumbled.'

'We stumbled into this misfortune because we didn't attack them with our bare hands, because we permitted trials to be held after the war in which the victims made their statements as witnesses and were afterwards humiliated and humbled, because we did not spit in their faces after their verdicts in the Auschwitz trials and because we held out our hands to them.'

'Mom, how have you been able to live here? Why didn't you leave this country?'

'How was I able to live here, you ask? You should have seen me after the war. I was a wreck, a wreck that was still alive. There was no one in the entire world who belonged to me and to whom I belonged. No family, no friends, no acquaintances. And it was no different for your father. We were too weak to be able to leave, to be able to re-establish ourselves in another country. And later on I wondered why I should leave in any case. That's what they would like to see. First they finish us off and then we disappear. It's not that simple. The Germans have to listen to what I think of them, and if they don't like it, let them expel me or lock me up. If they use a few Jews in order to clear themselves of the past, then they also have to put up with what I think.'

I didn't believe her. I found her to be unjust. I had got to know the Germans as nice, polite people, and everybody protested that they hadn't known anything, and that if they had known they would have tried to help.

And now? After forty years the filth rises to the surface again. All of a sudden one can hear everywhere: it's true, we knew much more than we admitted to in the years after the war. The church didn't really rebel so much against the persecution of the Jews as it was so fond of telling everyone, and there was indeed very little resistance among the German people. People even approved silently or with cheers of what was being done to the Jews and the gypsies. But we, we are not to blame. The historic circumstances are to blame.

Grandmother, the circumstances shot you and gassed your children. It wasn't the Germans. It was the historic circumstances and the totalitarian ideology. You cannot be angry with them anymore, you cannot even accuse them of anything.

'It's true,' they say, 'you are right. We actually committed all these atrocities, but this awful ideology under whose spell we had fallen was to blame.'

How do you like that? Even this little bit of shame which they had hidden beneath the lie of their ignorance is not necessary anymore. Fantastic. Of course they do not ask: Who creates the circumstances? Why do other people have catastrophic economic conditions and still remain democratic? Why do others have more terrorists and yet do not keep everyone under surveillance with such perfection?[3] Why are there millions of dissidents in other countries who are not being excluded from civil service jobs?[4] The Germans forget to ask themselves why they are

3. Fleischmann is referring to the events in the wake of several terrorist attacks and kidnappings in the early 1970s most of which were committed by what was usually referred to as the Baader–Meinhof Gang, who called themselves the Red Army Faction. The state, as some saw it and how it was intended by the terrorists themselves, overreacted and thereby showed its 'true', that is fascist, face. On the one hand, Fleischmann seems to be attacking the state for exactly this kind of totalitarian tendency, on the other she must be referring to left-wing models of explanation of the Holocaust when she talks about those who always blame a certain set of historical circumstances.

4. The reference is to the so-called *Radikalen-Erlaß* banning any members of parties or groups which are 'not in agreement with the Basic Law of the Federal Republic' (i.e. communist, socialist and fascist groups) from positions in the civil service. This is, however, not a recent phenomenon, as Fleischmann seems to imply, since the very large civil service sector in Germany was created (by Bismarck, among others) precisely with the intention of binding this sector of society in loyalty to the state.

so timid, pedantic and relentless when it comes to obeying laws and why they weave themselves such a tight net of laws, executive orders, regulations and instructions, systematically restricting their freedom.

'Man has been created free, he is free,' this is what Schiller[5] says. This is true, but German education and upbringing make a slave of him, a person receiving orders, an underling. And because the slave needs instructions and the recipient of orders needs orders they constantly long for new regulations so that nothing remains within the jurisdiction of one's own responsibility. Being good and obeying orders, this is what they learn year in, year out, day in, day out, and every hour.

The few who see this and try to counteract it are intimidated and marginalized by the masses and their representatives. Responsibility in Germany involves carrying out directions with painstaking accuracy, personal responsibility is not in demand.

Today I quit my job. I have quit my service to the German people. The end of one German civil servant.

I do not know what kind of life I am headed towards, but I know the kind of life I have left behind. A life boxed in by laws and regulations. It surprises me that after five years of working in the school I have come up with the courage to put an end to this kind of work. One is so perfectly secure in this position that over the years one becomes more and more afraid to flee this security system and to stand on one's own two feet. Life is fixed, regulated and standardized. Thirty years from now around Christmas time there will be the Christmas vacation, twenty years from now in the summertime one has to administer exams. Year in, year out, the same, nestled into desolate, flat-tasting security.

If I ever teach again it won't be in a German school. I will not listen to phrases expressing understanding for foreigners and Jews any more, I also do not want to have compassion for the students, I do not want to teach the German people anything, and I don't want to change them.

For five years my mother lived among Germans, and for five years I lived with them. It is enough.

---

5. Friedrich Schiller (1759–1805), author and historian of the *Sturm und Drang* and classical period in German literature and in terms of his philosophy a representative of subjective idealism, which in this context means that such ideals as freedom are part of every human being. The responsibility of the individual is to realize them to their fullest extent.

8

Heimat? No, Thanks!*[1]

Henryk M. Broder

When I delve into a topic that is new to me, my first step is usually to look up the central concept in the dictionary: '*Heimat:* a territorial unit experienced subjectively by individuals or collectively by groups, tribes, peoples, or nations in terms of a feeling of a particularly close bond' is what I find in Mayer's. This dictionary also lists a number of variants and combinations of *Heimat,* for example *Heimatkunst* [folk art]; *Heimat-museum* [museum of regional history]; *Heimatschein* [certificate of domicile] – a peculiarity of Swiss communal law; *heimatlose Ausländer* [homeless foreigners] – apparently doubly cursed, first as foreigners and then as people without a *Heimat*; *Heimatschutztruppe* [home defense militia] – a subdivision of the territorial army of the Bundeswehr intended to protect our *Heimat* if things get serious, which makes one wonder what job the rest of the army has if war *per se* is nowadays construed as a defensive operation.

Even the most tentative approach to the concept of *Heimat* leads one more into the wide realm of ambiguity than to the desired clarity. The word and its background seem highly suspect. There is something stifling, provincial, stale about it; it is redolent of farmhouse kitchens, homemade brandy, and cow barns. Willy-nilly I associate it with peasant costumes,

---

* From *Jewish Voices, German Words: Growing Up Jewish in Postwar Germany and Austria*, ed. Elena Lappin, trans. Krishna Winston (North Haven: Catbird Press, 1994), 80–101, with the permission of the publisher.

1. The title is a reference to the slogan of the anti-nuclear power movement in West Germany (and Western Europe in general): 'Atomkraft? Nein Danke!', which became one of the most popular bumper stickers. It can be argued that the West German environmentalist movement provided the postwar generations of Germans with a new sense of home or *Heimat* after most other things connected with this concept had been abused by the Nazis. The anti-nuclear movement and other environmentalist concerns allowed these generations to reconnect to a feeling of pride about the area in which they grew up while at the same time it provided them a chance to protest against those generations of Germans whom, to a certain extent justly, they suspected of having been involved with the Nazis.

half-timbered houses, and shooting matches; apparently my concept of *Heimat* is rural. I might be mistaken, objectively speaking, but this is not a random association. I am reproducing images and impressions that have been conveyed to me as embodying *Heimat*.

It's no accident that *Heimatkunst* and *Heimatdichtung* [rural literature] are not the offspring of cities and metropolises, that the very words have a robust, all-natural sound to them, like 'home slaughtering' and 'volunteer fire department'. And if a *Heimatdichter* from Berlin or Munich is mentioned, the stress is not on the urban origins of the writer in question; no, the accidental circumstance that he lives in a city becomes secondary to the dialect in which he writes or the district where he lives, in short, to something one can easily get a handle on. To that extent, the concept of an urban *Heimat* artist is a contradiction in terms and at the same time an attempt to impose something homey on an environment associated with decadence and alienation, the wish to be able to discover a bit of rural idyll even in the middle of the asphalt jungle.

The sense of *Heimat*, as differently as it may come across, is conveyed through the way people define themselves out of and through the surroundings in which they appear. They're not there by chance, or if they are, then they want to belong there, want to be accepted. Nor have they moved there for better living conditions; on the contrary, they've remained true to their *Heimat*, often taken burdens and hardships upon themselves so as not to betray their *Heimat*. One can compare the sense of *Heimat* with those Russian nesting dolls; it can be separated into smaller and smaller units. A German may feel lost in France, a Rhinelander in Hamburg may feel as though he's in a foreign country, and a person from Cologne who grew up on the left bank of the Rhine may refer to the parts of the city on the right bank as if they lay on the other side of the moon.

I know hardly anyone who lives where he was born. There may be such people, but in my milieu it's more the exception than the rule. From this perspective I consort with nothing but people who lack *Heimat* or have been expelled from their *Heimat*, who at most can claim a *Heimat* they've chosen, a second-choice *Heimat*.

I was born after the war, in 1946, in Katowice. Both of my parents had been in concentration camps and numbered among the fewer than 10 percent of all Polish Jews who survived the so-called Holocaust, an unbelievable stroke of luck, especially when one considers that my older sister also escaped, hidden under mattresses in the house of a petty-bourgeois Polish family. Twelve years after the war, in 1957, my family moved by way of Vienna to the Federal Republic of Germany. My sister, who was a Zionist at the time, was the only one of us who went to Israel.

Heimat? *No, Thanks!*

For me, leaving Poland was a move, nothing more. At the age of eleven I'd developed neither a sense of *Heimat* nor other emotional ties. The only thing that caused problems for me and made me sad to go was that I had to leave my dog, an old dachshund, behind; he was given away. For my parents it was a little different. My father came originally from Galicia, my mother from Cracow. Both of them had been shaped by the surroundings in which they'd grown up, he by the shtetl and she by the culture of the Austro-Hungarian colonies. But with the war, my father's shtetl had disappeared, and Cracow had long since ceased to be a suburb of Vienna.

Nonetheless my parents did not find it all that easy to leave Poland. The persistent Polish anti-Semitism helped them reach a decision; they moved to Germany primarily for linguistic reasons. Both of them had grown up with the German language and did not want to live in a country where they could not make themselves understood. In Israel, with Polish, Russian, German, and Yiddish, there would have been no language problem either, but that was a country somewhere in Asia with a terrible climate, and in any case, so many Jews in one place wasn't a good idea . . .

The first years in the Federal republic were relatively free of problems. I can't say we had found a new, a second *Heimat* of our choice – it was and remained a provisional solution of unspecified duration – but I don't think our situation was so much different from that of a family that had come to the Rhineland from East Prussia, for example. At times I felt as though I were on another planet. When Carnival broke out in Cologne, an event that occurred as regularly as Easter and therefore just as inevitably, I felt like Captain Cook visiting some strange, primitive tribe. There I was among all those natives, who became jolly on command, rocked back and forth to the music for hours like autistic children, and laughed at jokes I didn't even understand. At Carnival, especially during the so-called Wild Days, which one has to take literally in Cologne, it became clear to me: this isn't my home, there are worlds between these primitives and me.

On the other hand: whenever I got back to Cologne from a trip, and the towers of the Cathedral appeared on the horizon, whenever I crossed the Rhine after several hours on the Autobahn and saw the Old City lying before me like a postcard, kitschy and beautiful from a distance, I did have the feeling of coming home. Some nerve was touched, a sentiment stirred in me. One could live with this ambivalent attitude – being happy to return to a place where I didn't feel comfortable – especially since Cologne has a major geographic advantage: it's close to Holland. And thus an excursion to Maastricht could satisfy two needs: the need to run away and the need to return. Without my being conscious of it, the whole thing was a Jewish joke, transformed into reality, whose punch line went:

'You're better off keeping moving.' As often as I could arrange it, I kept moving. It wasn't just a longing for distant places that motivated me, but an enjoyment of changing places, of movement for its own sake. One might say this is a typically Jewish characteristic. If there is something like a mass soul, a collective character, a behavioural pattern that marks a particular group, then Jews have a nomadic trait as part of their set of common characteristics. The exodus from Egypt, the forty-day wandering in the desert, occupy a central role in the Jewish psyche. For three thousand years that event has been celebrated annually at Pesach, as if it had occurred only recently. Moving away, moving, emigrating, giving up a place of residence, looking for another – these are normal occurrences for Jews that have been repeated over and over again in the course of history. Ahasuerus, the Wandering Jew, is still roaming around. But the idea of a person who has been expelled and damned to eternal unrest and life without a *Heimat* is a non-Jewish idea. It originated in the New Testament and can be found since the beginning of the seventeenth century in numerous writings and legends, stylized into a sinister figure of horror.

It's pointless to debate whether character determines one's life circumstances or the other way around. In any case, Jews have always had a fairly flexible relationship to stationary existence, even in areas where they've been settled for a long time. The possibility that a pogrom might erupt at any moment led them to develop certain habits that took the looming danger into account. It was best to have everything portable. A little pouch of gold and diamonds could be taken along more easily than a house or a piece of land. Material things that weren't useful were not important. A bed, a chest, a table had to be not beautiful but practical. Learning was important, food was important, family cohesion was important. The lack of aesthetic refinement, whose consequences one can observe today in every second Israeli home, and the emphasis on abilities a person can put to work anywhere, such as abstract thinking and skill with one's hands, were both cause and effect of that mobility that is considered typically Jewish and that, in the form of a negative stereotype, constitutes the image of the rootless Jew, Ahasuerus. For Jews, *Heimat* has never been a territorial concept.

It was the poet Heinrich Heine who spoke of a 'portable fatherland'. Some of its components were religious heritage, tradition, a way of life. Whatever Jews needed for feeling at home they always had with them, if necessary in the bags they kept packed in case they had to flee. Whether in Lemberg or on Long Island, the candles were always lit on Friday evening to mark the beginning of the Sabbath, at Pesach matzoh was eaten everywhere, and on Yom Kippur the fast was observed. The thought that

Heimat might include a piece of land of their own did not occur to Jews until the second half of the last century, much later than with other people.

'The people give us sovereignty over a piece of the earth's surface sufficient to the legitimate needs of our people, and we shall take care of the rest,' Theodor Herzl wrote in 1896 in 'The Jewish State: An Attempt at a Modern Solution of the Jewish Question'. Nowhere was rejection of his ideas as resounding as in the Jewish milieu, which resisted with all its might being transformed from cultural nation into a territorial one. The Jews took several approaches. An orthodox minority behaved as though the Enlightenment and emancipation had never taken place; they made a point of continuing their lives as if in the ghetto, even after the ghetto walls had come down. A secular minority saw in the Jewish question neither a social nor a religious question but a national one, which had to be solved with political means, 'in the council of the civilized peoples', as Herzl formulated it; this was to be one of the functions of the Zionist movement. The majority of Jews in Germany attempted to establish a symbiosis of Jewish and German culture; these were the 'German citizens of the Jewish faith', who wanted to differ from their Christian fellow citizens only in religious practice. Thus at the beginning of the century Jews had three different concepts of *Heimat* to choose among: a spiritual one, in the sense of a portable fatherland; a national one, in the sense of Zionism; and a 'symbiotic' one, in the sense of assimilation.

We know which course history chose. All attempts at assimilation proved futile; the desperate struggle to be recognized as good Germans was merely the prelude to the greatest catastrophe in Jewish history.

'Jews have lived on German soil for more than a thousand years. Common fates and participation in German intellectual life have created an intimate bond between them and those of another faith. German is our language, German our intellectual formation, German our culture. Germany is our fatherland, and German Jews are indissolubly tied to it . . .' These words stand at the beginning of a pamphlet issued early in this century by an anti-Zionist committee to which a few dozen prominent Jews belonged – doctors, manufacturers, government officials, judges, lawyers, bankers, businessmen. 'The Zionist movement mistakes the communal feeling of those united by origin and belief for national feelings; for the German Jew there is no Jewish national feeling – he is a member of the German cultural community and therefore his national feeling is German, like his language. By contrast, the Zionist movement's goals lie outside the German fatherland and thereby undermine the political, economic, and social position of the Jews,' the pamphlet goes on, and its signatories assert that they want to reveal 'to our people the danger posed to us and our children by the pursuit of Zionism'. The pamphlet concludes with the words, 'Anyone familiar with the nature of nationality and national feeling knows that the German Jew belongs to the German people. Anti-Semitic injustice has not been able to rob us of our love for the fatherland. We do not want Zionist agitation to jeopardize our struggle for our rights. German Jews are struggling for equal rights because they are not foreign elements but German citizens – by language, culture, education, and sense of *Heimat*.'

To these German Jews it was perfectly clear where they belonged, where their *Heimat* was. It was clear to them that the Zionist 'Jewish nationalist movement posed a serious danger to the German Jews', and that 'overcoming Zionism' was an 'existential question for German Jews'. At the beginning of this century the German Jews, who had committed themselves so emphatically to the German language, culture, and education, and to the German sense of *Heimat*, could not imagine that this very commitment contained a threat to their existence.

Another document of German-Jewish love for the *Heimat* is even more shattering and astonishing to the present-day reader. On March 30, 1933, just before the Nazi boycott of Jewish shops in Germany, the official newspaper of the Central Association of German Citizens of the Jewish faith carried the front-page headline: 'We 565,000 German Jews Solemnly Protest.'

What were the German Jews solemnly protesting on March 30, 1933? The emerging measures the Nazis were adopting against the Jewish population? Anti-Semitic speeches and threats by party functionaries? Neither nor. They were protesting against the charge that they were encouraging anti-German propaganda abroad.

'Unrestrained atrocity propaganda against Germany is raging in the world,' began the solemn protest in the central Association's paper, and it continued: 'We German Jews are as deeply affected as any other German by every word spoken and written against our fatherland, by every call for a boycott. Not under compulsion, not out of fear, but because certain circles abroad are besmirching the honour of the German name, are harming the land of our fathers and the land of our children, we have risen without delay to protest. At home and abroad we have denounced the lies being reported about Germany and the new government . . .'

Although the German Jews came to the defense of German honor, they were held responsible for the anti-German propaganda.

People charge that the campaign of hatred and lies emanates from the German Jews. They say it would be appropriate for the Jews to rebuke the liars but that the German Jews do not want to do this. Before all of Germany we 565,000 German Jews solemnly register our protest against these unspeakable charges. The German Jews have not instigated anyone in Germany or the world, directly or indirectly, to these shameful libels or to any action against Germany. The German Jews have, to the extent of their ability, done their utmost to render impossible any insult to their *Heimat*, any offense to the government, any harm to the German economy.

The solemn protest concludes with the resigned pathos: 'Before God and man we stand justified. With dignity and courage we shall endure the pitiless measures of Germans against Germans on the soul of our *Heimat* . . .'

To repeat, that was March 30, 1933. At that time, German Jews worried less about their own future than about the threat to the reputation of their *Heimat*, to whose defense they came and for whose honor they spoke up. Even the more clever and prescient among them were filled with a love of *Heimat* that in retrospect seems like an exercise in masochism.

The philosopher Theodor Lessing had already left the German Reich at the beginning of March 1933, after being attacked for years by super-patriotic students and the nationalist press. He sought refuge in Czecho-slovakia. There he wrote for the *Prager Tageblatt* and delivered a series of talks and lectures that was brought out around the middle of 1933 by a German-language publishing house in Prague. Even in exile, indeed especially in exile, Lessing insisted on being German, although he denied having anything in common with the Germans who had the say in Germany at that time:

> If the language spoken today in Germany is German, then I have never been a German. And if the spirit of today's leaders is the German spirit, then it is as little suitable for me as for Goethe or Kant to be a German. 'Land that we love, you should beg our forgiveness or never have our ashes,' Coriolanus said before he left his homeland. So, too, we German Jews leave our *Heimat*. No armies behind us? No! That is not how it is. Behind us the army of our forefathers, Abraham, Jacob, Moses. But behind us also all German guardian spirits. Leaving Germany with us are all those who have a home in our hearts, and would perhaps have a home nowhere on earth if not in us: Goethe's wordly-wise, lucent humanity, Schubert's comforting song, Dürer's loyal childlikeness, Hölderlin's hymnic blessedness . . .

The guardian spirits that Lessing thought were following him must have stayed home. On August 31, 1933 he was murdered by two paid Nazi assassins, who did not have Goethe's humanity or Hölderlin's blessedness in mind, but the price that had been placed on Lessing's head by the Nazis – 80,000 Reichsmark. Lessing became the first victim of the Nazi's lynch justice after their seizure of power. His books had already been burned in May 1933 in the great purge.

Yet one cannot assume that the German Jews experienced their first identity crisis with the outbreak of the Third Reich. Or that they hadn't begun to think about their relationship to their German *Heimat* until 1933, under the sign of the swastika. What today is glorified by many as the time of German-Jewish symbiosis was a very one-sided love affair. 'To be sure, the Jews tried to have a dialogue with the Germans,' writes Gerschom Scholem, 'from all possible points of view and positions, demanding, pleading, imploring, obsequiously and indignantly, in all tonalities from touching dignity to godless indignity . . .' – but: 'They were speaking to themselves, in fact one was shouting louder than the next.' The only ones who took the Jews seriously as partners in conversation, Scholem remarks cynically but aptly, were the anti-Semites, 'who did answer the Jews, but not helpfully'. German-Jewish literature provides numerous examples of this conversation Jews carried on with themselves, which the Germans at best listened in on. One of the most gripping examples can be found in Jakob Wassermann's essay, 'My Way as a German and Jew':

> Recognition of the hopelessness of any effort turns bitterness in one's breast into a fatal convulsion.
>
> It is futile to beseech the people of poets and thinkers in the name of its poets and thinkers. Every prejudice one thinks has been laid to rest brings thousands of new ones to light, as carrion yields maggots.
>
> It is futile to offer one's right cheek when the left has been struck. It does not make them at all thoughtful, it does not touch them, it does not disarm them: they strike the right cheek, too.
>
> It is futile to counter raving cries with words of reason. They say, What, he dares to answer back? Gag him!
>
> It is futile to try to provide a good example. They say: We know nothing, we have seen nothing, we have heard nothing.
>
> It is futile to seek shelter. They say: The coward, he is hiding, his guilty conscience is driving him.
>
> It is futile to go among them and offer them one's hand. They say: What is he up to with his Jewish pushiness?
>
> It is futile to be loyal to them, whether as a fellow combatant or as a fellow citizen. They say: He is a Proteus, he can seem anything.
>
> It is futile to help them throw off the fetters of slavery. They say: He must have made a tidy profit doing that.

Heimat? *No, Thanks!*

It is futile to detoxify the toxin. They will brew a fresh batch.
It is futile to live for them and to die for them. They say: He is a Jew.

Wassermann's 'My Way as a German and a Jew' appeared in 1921, at a time when most Jews were firmly convinced they would be accepted as German citizens of the Jewish faith. Since 1848 Jews had participated more and more in German political developments, and many had achieved positions of high and even the highest rank: Eduard von Simson, raised to the nobility by the Kaiser, president of the National Assembly in 1848, then of the North German Reichstag of 1867, of the German Reichstag, and also the first president of the Supreme Court in Leipzig. Many, in their devotion to their German *Heimat*, became tragic figures.

The Jew Alfred Ballin, an adviser to Kaiser Wilhelm II and a proponent of the Kaiser's policy of building up the German fleet, committed suicide in 1918, filled with despair at Germany's defeat in World War I. The Jew Walther Rathenau, who had organized the supply of raw materials for Germany during the war, and after the war represented the Weir Republic as foreign minister, was murdered in 1922 by a German nationalist. And it was a Jew, the constitutional expert Hugo Preuss, who drafted the outline of the Weimar constitution. Yet a German writer as successful as Wassermann could sum up his experience with the people of poets and thinkers in the resigned statement: 'It is futile to live for them and to die for them. They say: He is a Jew.'

In the middle of Germany, Wassermann was a native without a *Heimat*. He spoke German, wrote German, thought in German, and yet a barrier existed between him and the rest of the German people. This may be something experienced particularly often and intensely by Jews, but it is not an exclusively Jewish experience. When, for instance, there is talk of 'homeless' intellectuals or leftists, that is, those without a *Heimat*, this is not a reference to people who have no permanent residence, who sleep under bridges and roam the land like vagabonds. These are people who do not belong; of course, who belongs is decided by those who have the say in their *Heimat*. Aside from all attempts to define *Heimat* territorially, to make it a characteristic that determines who are fellow countrymen, *Heimat* designates an ideological arena, a spiritual state, a kind of mental congruity, in short, a community of the like-minded. What follows is that wherever there is a *Heimat*, there must be people without a *Heimat*. Not refugees, who maintain their dialect and their folklore, but those who are not admitted to the community of the like-minded or have been driven out of it.

Heimat is always restrictive. It fences people in, and therefore also fences people out. *Heimat* requires not only clear but also clearly visible conditions. Therefore *Heimat* is almost automatically identified with country, village, and town, with morality and decency, with a network of relationships in which everyone knows everyone else, where no one steps out of line or out of his role, where the most powerful group coherence exists. The city, by contrast, stands for decadence and confusion, for anonymity and individuality, and especially for plurality. Marginal figures and outsiders who wouldn't stand a chance in the country can live in the city and survive. The more urban a metropolis, the more pluralistic it is, but that also means that it poses a stronger threat to souls in need of harmony and addicted to *Heimat*.

In a blurb for Fassbinder's 'garbage' play, the playwright Heiner Müller writes as follows: 'Fassbinder's *Garbage, the City, and Death* depicts in large, glaring images the devastation of a city, through the example of a victim's revenge. The city is known as Frankfurt. The instrument of revenge is real-estate speculation, with all its ramifications. The distortion of human relationships by treating them as commodities demonstrates the Biblical wisdom that the first fratricide, Cain, was the first builder of cities . . .'

This is as pretentious as it is confused, and even as a Biblical allusion it's only partially correct. But it sounds like a prophecy: He who murders his brother is also capable of building a city. In these few sentences an entire panorama of blood-and-soil mythology is presented in contemporary dress; history is unfurled from behind, so to speak: building cities perverts human relationships, speculation is an instrument of revenge, and revenge, one knows, has something to do with Jews and the Old Testament. Thus one piece of Biblical wisdom is linked to another.

The connections are clear. In classic anti-Semitic propaganda, too, the city was always portrayed as a Jewish monstrosity, while the village represented Aryan innocence. Here the morass, there the productive field.

In 1981 a publishing house in Hamburg issued a book by a writer who was no longer young. This man presented himself to his readers sometimes as a 'writing cultural worker', sometimes as a 'nationalist Communist'. The book was entitled *Germany – An Attempted Homecoming*, and the title carried a sketch of a peasant parlour in lovely, warm pastels. The author, we learn from the blurb, had an 'extraordinarily happy childhood under Hitler', later lived in Frankfurt, Berlin, and Hamburg. The sketch on the title page must refer to his childhood, if to anything. But what is the title supposed to mean?

Heimat? *No, Thanks!*

The author is no returnee from prisoner-of-war camp, emigration, or banishment. He never went to sea or lived abroad. In the physical sense he cannot return home. Something else must be meant: a return to the bosom of the larger whole – let us call it the *Volksgemeinschaft*[2] – a collective from which the author excluded himself for a time on the basis of his political orientation. And this return, called a homecoming, takes place through a symbolic door, above which hangs a sign saying 'love of *Heimat*'. The blurb informs us that this is a book 'that risks the tension between love of *Heimat* and the horror that *Heimat* once generated and still generates'.

So love of *Heimat* is a sort of house of horrors. One shivers a little, but wouldn't miss the experience for anything. This belated home comer does not want to commit himself unreservedly to love of *Heimat*. He questions his ambivalence, and then at the end of the exercise he says, Well, why not? Thus love of *Heimat* serves as the formula on the basis of which the members of the *Volk* community can come together, a lowest common denominator for collective identity. Since love of *Heimat*, as the author just quoted assures us, is a 'spiritual state', it becomes a question of sharing this condition with as many members of the national family as possible. For, in contrast to national awareness or even nationalism, love of *Heimat* is not discredited, but is seen instead as a harmless emotion. One loves one's *Heimat* as one loves one's family, one's language, one's garden, one's pets. But even those who argue this way occasionally admit that something more is at issue with love of *Heimat*. 'As a German I am sufficiently lacking in a *Heimat*,' writes a young left-wing author, who regrets not his outward but his inner lack of a *Heimat*, 'to see it as my task to put down roots, to try to establish links with German history, even if it be the worst of all possible histories, and at the same time' – watch out! here it comes! – 'with the silent majority of Germans, to whom we will otherwise not get close in a hundred years . . .' Translated, this means that the rediscovery of *Heimat* as a spiritual state creates the link between leftists without a *Heimat* and the silent majority; this rediscovery constitutes a simultaneous homecoming and bridging, after all other attempts at rapprochement, such as class for socialism, for disarmament, or for involvement with the Sandinistas,[3] have proved unsuccessful. One

---

2. This term was used by the Nazis to refer to an imaginary whole of society, thereby ignoring or blurring existing religious, ethnic, social and cultural differences.

3. Broder is referring to the various attempts on the German Left to create a 'mass basis' for their attempts at reform or revolution and lists three typical attempts at doing this: convincing 'the proletariat' of the necessity of a revolution by selling the appropriate newspapers or by distributing leaflets, appealing to people to resist 'US American

might also say: when appealing to class consciousness or international solidarity fails, love of *Heimat* comes into play as *ultima ratio*.

Where there's a *Heimat*, there must also be people without a *Heimat* – people who are refused permission to belong or who renounce belonging: not belonging to the language, the culture, or the same tax bracket, but to that diffuse mixture of pretentiousness, sentimentality, and aggressiveness that also goes into love of *Heimat*. The author who wanted to try to approach the silent majority with the help of this very instrument describes in the same connection what 'is annoying about Henrik Broder and Lea Fleischmann': that they 'turn the historical tables and now exclude us, as people with whom there is simply nothing to be done'.

This is a revelation of praiseworthy unambiguousness. The historical sword is pointing in the right direction when the Jews are marginalized by the Germans, as is fitting, but it's seen as a piece of particular chutzpa when the situation is the other way around, when it's the Jews who separate themselves from the Germans. That shouldn't be allowed – *quod licet Jovi non licet bovi*. A young German leftist would rather cosy up to the silent majority, which doesn't want to know anything about him, than allow a couple of Jews to turn the historical tables and for a change do what they've always had to take from others.

The longer I focus on the concept of *Heimat*, the more obscure it becomes to me. I really don't mind when a person loves the pounding surf of the North Sea or the fragrance of the forest after a storm. That isn't the problem. But those who suddenly and unexpectedly discover their love for their *Heimat* remind me of shareholders in a company who give themselves preferred shares and then justify their action by insisting on their irrepressible love for the stock market – at a time when these shares happen to be going up. Love of *Heimat* is first and foremost a means for creating and preserving the *Volk* community, for bridging contrasts and containing conflicts. That precisely those who until recently were busy analyzing social relations have now switched to the field of love of *Heimat* must be considered one of the curiosities of this transitional period, and *ex post facto* downgrades their exercises in classless society and proletarian internationalism to the status of intermezzos in their revolutionary cabaret.

I don't know when it began or who started it, but at some point in the 'we're somebody again' movement, the question of nationalism was posed in the so-called progressive camp. People said one couldn't leave concepts

---

imperialism' by resisting the deployment of American missiles on German soil, or appealing to international solidarity in the fight of Third World countries for independence.

like *Nation, Heimat, Volk* to the rightists; the leftists, too, or the part of society that considers itself leftist, had to fill these formulas with content. (At this time the debates over whether an alternative *Bild-Zeitung*[4] could be published were already forgotten.) True, the Nazis had abused this terminology and used it for their own purposes, but that didn't mean one could remove *Heimat* or *Volk* from the political dictionary! What sounded quite plausible at first soon led to a new form of repression and rationalization. Where the rightists babbled that the figure of six million was a lie – they wanted to get out from under the historical shadow of the mountains of corpses at Auschwitz – the leftists were attempting to unload the burden of history by displacing the guilt.

'Overcoming our German past consists in solidarity with the Palestinians!' A young German leftist reduced to this brief formula his attempt to, as he put it, 'sneak away from German history'. Either strategy served the purposes of a reconciliation with oneself, restoring a 'spiritual state' in which it was possible not only to speak the words *Heimat, Volk*, and *Nation* without shame or embarrassment, but also to rehabilitate the associated period in history. And as always when the question of nationality is raised in Germany, the Jews came up. Even as shadows of their former selves, they stand in the way of the 'Germans' becoming good again', as Eike Geisel calls it. German self-discovery always used the Jews as a catalyst, and it still does.

The blessing of having been born late, to which Chancellor Kohl likes to allude,[5] corresponds at the other end of the political spectrum to the one-sided declaration made by the Frankfurt Schauspielhaus in conjunction with the Fassbinder play[6] that 'reconciliation should and must come about', whereupon the Jews who refused to step forward and be reconciled were reproached for having rejected the outstretched hand. Deputy Fellner demanded that the Jews show more understanding for the sensitivity of

4. Mass-circulation daily paper with sensationalist reporting and orientated at the political Right. Its price is artificially kept low by its publishing house, *Axel Springer Verlag*, in order to keep the circulation up. It was one of the targets of the students' movement of the 1960s because it was felt that its portrayal of this movement was one of the causes of the escalating violence during demonstrations and other events.

5. *Die Gnade der späten Geburt*, a phrase coined by Kohl to point out the fact that the majority of Germans living in Germany right now, including himself, are too young to have been involved in the atrocities of the Nazi regime. It was perhaps also meant to end any discussions of the collective guilt thesis, but of course only renewed them.

6. Rainer Werner Fassbinder's play *Garbage, The City and Death* (1981) had been produced by this theatre, which started a heated debate about the portrayal of Jews in this play, among other reasons because Jews were represented as having a hand in shady real-estate deals, something which obviously alludes to existing stereotypes and prejudices.

the Germans and not always make demands. And a member of the audience called out to the Jews who had occupied the stage, 'Don't always bring up your Auschwitz!' A mayor from a town on the Rhine made the cheap crack that to balance the city budget they should kill a few rich Jews. On a considerably higher intellectual plane, a well-known liberal theater critic said much the same thing when he called for unmasking the role played by Jewish capital. When a group within the leftist party Alternative List demanded demonstrations against the visit of Shimon Peres, the Israeli prime minister, on the grounds that this was important 'for the establishment of German identity', they were taking up an old tradition.

Jews have always helped Germans develop a sense of unity and solidarity. Even the Alternatives' identity still depends on this vehicle. The common practice among German nationalists of counting Auschwitz, if it is even acknowledged, among the 'war crimes of the Allies' is supplemented in leftist circles by the observation that the Israelis will do to the Palestinians what the Nazis did to the Jews, and the use of the expression 'final solution to the Palestinian question'. Thus the victims of yesterday are made into perpetrators of today, and the perpetrators of yesterday become the moralizing referees of today. This is what Jürgen Habermas[7] has called 'the decontamination of the past'.

And that belated literary home comer I mentioned recently wrote in a review of my book *The Eternal Anti-Semite* that one shouldn't hold my lack of sound scholarship too much against me, for one should ask oneself how the German 'revenge-foul would have looked, assuming Jews had murdered six million Germans'. One reads this sentence, stops short, reads it again, and sees that one is not mistaken. The Germans killed a few million Jews, and forty years later a Jew writes a book about German anti-Semitism. This is seen not only as revenge, arising from the well-known Old Testament spirit of vengeance; it is a *revenge-foul*, an unfair, nasty blow below the belt, against all the rules of sportsmanship. Six million dead against one book.

This fellow member of the *Volk*, from the leftist-nationalist side of the *Heimat* stage, considers it pure happenstance that it was the Germans who killed the Jews; he thinks it could easily have been the other way around. What if the Jews had killed six million innocent Germans, he asks; how would we, the Germans, have behaved afterwards?

I am happy to respond to that. If we're going to play this old game of comparing apples and oranges, let's at least think it all the way through to

---

7. A well-known social and political philosopher, perhaps best known for his book *The Structural Change of the Public Sphere* (Frankfurt-on-Main: Suhrkamp, 1962).

the end. If history hadn't gone the way it did, but the other way around, if the Jews had subjected the Germans to a holocaust, then even forty years after the attempted final solution there would be neither political nor human relations between Germans and Jews. No Jew would be allowed to step onto German soil, and no German would allow a Jew to say that there should and must be reconciliation. The Germans would not consider any Jew's late birth an extenuating circumstance, and they would not allow any Jew to give them advice as to how they, the Germans, should behave toward their minorities. There would be no debates over collective guilt, collective shame, collective responsibility; every Jew would be held responsible for what happened, and no Vatican Council would exonerate the Jews after two thousand years. No Jewish theater would dare to schedule a play that dealt with an exploitative German someone had forgotten to gas; and such an undertaking would certainly not be able to be justified with a declaration that the closed season was over. No one would say it was time to draw a line under the past; and if a Jew suggested that one merely had to kill a few rich Germans, it would cost him not only his job but his head as well. The Jewish state, if there were one at all, would not be a respected member of the international community, and no Jewish politician would have the courage to tell the Germans that they shouldn't carry on so and should be considerate of the Jews' sensitivities and not always be reminding them of the past. And no one would think that paying money would put the whole business to rest once and for all . . . This would be more or less the state of affairs if history had turned out the other way.

Heimat, to return to our starting point, is not a geographical entity, not a place one can find on the map; *Heimat* is a spiritual state. Reacquiring *Heimat* is, therefore, a return to an inner condition in which the home comer is at one with his surroundings, is reconciled. A person who characterizes himself as without a *Heimat* suffers the opposite: he lives in dissension with himself and his surroundings. It's understandable that such a condition cannot be tolerated in the long run, or must result in serious damage.

The Jewish concept of *Heimat* did not envisage a harmonious relationship to one's surroundings, for those were almost always and everywhere hostile to Jews. So what mattered was to preserve and perpetuate one's tradition. There was no need to restore a spiritual state that had been thrown out of equilibrium, for in spite of persecution and suppression, or perhaps precisely because of it, the Jews' inner balance hadn't suffered any damage, aside from those who abandoned their Jewishness or assimilated; these were people who wanted to escape not only from religion, but also from the shared fate of the Jews; among them one can observe that phenomenon for which Theodor Lessing coined the expression 'Jewish self-hatred'. Not until they received recognition as citizens with equal rights did Jews feel obligated to manifest their devotion and loyalty to their external *Heimat*; they transformed themselves from Jews into Germans of the Jewish faith.

'The noblest German blood is that which was spilled for Germany by German soldiers. To these belong as well the 12,000 casualties of German Jewdom, which thereby in turn passed its solemn and admirable blood test in the German sense . . .' is what it says in the preface to a volume commemorating the Jewish soldiers who died in the First World War. The book was issued by the Reich Association of Jewish Front Soldiers in 1932. The definite proof of being a German was the privilege of dying for Germany. By doing that, 12,000 German Jews had passed the blood test in the German sense.

That misunderstanding is now history, although there are a few Jews in the German army again, and the chairman of the Central Council of Jews in Germany, a reserve officer in the Bundeswehr, explains: 'I see it as my task to present the correct picture of Germany, its citizens and parties, whenever the tendency to paint the "bad German" on the wall arises . . .' This reminds one of the position taken by the Central Association of German Citizens of the Jewish Faith in March 1933, which also defended Germany's reputation against those who would have slandered it. The chairman of the Central Council was rewarded for all his loyalty by being urged by a Bundestag deputy to consider whether his own behaviour might not be stirring up anti-Semitism in Germany.

But these are marginalia, small points noted in passing. The actual Jewish problem with *Heimat* answers to the name of Israel. After a gap of 1,900 years, the Jews have had, for almost forty years, a piece of land where they are sovereign. This is a historical accomplishment whose value cannot be overestimated. But at the same time it is a fact that causes the Jews problems and places new burdens on their spiritual state.

About a quarter of the Jewish people live in the Jewish state, our 'historical *Heimat*', as we say. To have this homeland is sufficient to most: three-quarters of all Jews prefer to stay in the Diaspora and say the prayer 'Next year in Jerusalem' every year at Pesach, although they could come this year if they really wanted to. One may ask whether the Jewish state maintains a large Diaspora community of potential citizens, or whether the Diaspora, for insurance reasons, maintains a state just in case worse comes to worst, which everyone hopes will never happen but knows one can't dismiss. The simple fact that Israel exists protects the Jews in the

Diaspora from greater discrimination and persecution, but at the same time thrusts them into inner crises and external conflicts.

Many have a guilty conscience because they don't live in Israel, and they compensate with a 'love of *Heimat*', i.e. long-distance Zionism, which often takes on embarrassing features. Others, in turn, compulsively distance themselves from Israel, so as not to come under the reputation-damaging suspicion of being Zionists. To this inner conflict is added the reproach by others that they have divided loyalties. They teeter between the country in which they live and the country with which they feel solidarity or from which they distance themselves, but with which they are in any case emotionally involved. But even when they make up their minds and settle things once and for all, that is, stay or go, the dissonance does not cease. When a German television station does a feature on the topic 'Do the Jews have a future in Germany?' Jewish existence in Germany is treated as a problem, and the question is directed not just at temporary residents but also at those Jews who by staying have already supplied an answer. On the other hand, those who just a short while ago were shouting 'Jews to Palestine!' don't like it either when the Jews follow their orders, because now it's a matter of combating the imperialist-expansionist ideology of Zionism. And finally, our Arab relatives are right when they ask the question why someone born and raised in Brooklyn should suddenly turn up in Hebron and declare that this is his true homeland, and from now on he must live in the city of the patriarchs, for otherwise the two-thousand-year history of suffering will have been in vain.

To discuss the political and practical implications of Zionism as it is actually practiced would be a topic worthy of separate treatment. But one thing can be said: with the establishment of a Jewish state, a particular set of problems caught up with the Jews which left them only one choice: between wrong and mistaken. It would be wrong, unthinkable, to give up this state. It would be mistaken and not doable to dissolve the Diaspora, to settle all Jews in Israel. So we're stuck with the Jewish state here and the Diaspora there, and the split personality in the middle. We can reflect on the tension between a spiritual and a real *Heimat* and also on the question as to whether the latter doesn't exist at the expense of the former. There is no solution to the problem, but problems aren't there to be solved; they're there to be worked out.

For six years now I've been living in Israel with a German passport. To many, who like to have things neat and tidy, this may seem inconsistent, but it's far less inconsistent than living in Germany with a membership card for a Zionist organization in one's pocket and one's suitcases under the bed. I admit I'm making it easy for myself. I've withdrawn physically and spatially from the alternatives of becoming an alibi-Jew or a Jewish Michael Kohlhaas in Germany. Germany is very stressful for a Jew; it can be tolerated and liked, much better from a distance. In Israel, as a Jew but non-Israeli, I have a privileged status. I live in the country without having to wrestle with the difficulties its citizens have. So I pick the pleasant things from both sides. Perhaps that's what makes my German leftist friends without a *Heimat* so furious with me: they, too, would like to get out, if only they knew where to go. Walter Boehlich recently described me as a Figaro who is sometimes here, sometimes there; one never knows just where he is. Apparently I've violated the commandment of belonging somewhere which Walter Boehlich firmly espouses from his living room in Frankfurt. He garnishes his super-clever analysis of my gypsy-like way of life with a few anti-Semitic digs, reproaching me, among other things, with 'meddling' in the affairs of the Federal Republic. He's right: if the Jew escapes from the anti-Semite's blows, he shouldn't make a stink from the other side of the fence.

If you ask me whether *I* have a *Heimat*, and where it is, I reply in classic Jewish style: evasively. I think I have a *Heimat*, but can't localize it. It's the odour of gefilte fish and potato pancakes, the taste of borscht and pickled herring, the melody of the Hatikva and the sound of the Internationale, but only when it's sung in Yiddish by old members of the Bund in Tel Aviv on the first of May. It's the Marx Brothers' night in Casablanca, and Ernst Lubitsch's to be or not to be. It's Karl Kraus's *Torch* and the autobiography of Theodor Lessing. It's a spot on the Aussenalster in Hamburg, a little stairway in the old harbour of Jaffa, and the Leidseplein in Amsterdam. Isn't that enough?

The big problem with *Heimat*, it seems to me, is that a person is expected to choose one. It would be better simply not to have one. Or best of all: to have a whole lot of them.

Part III
Afro-Germans: Black and German –
a Paradox

The question one immediately wants to ask when one hears the word 'Afro-Germans' points directly to the dilemma of this group: wherever they go in Germany their presence never fails to elicit from their compatriots the question 'Where are you from?' Furthermore, if the individual being addressed answers in perfect German 'I am from Hamburg, but grew up in Munich' the questioner will not stop until he or she has established the link to Africa. Afro-Germans are constantly asked to explain their existence. Being German and being black just does not seem to go together in the minds of most Germans. In a country where citizenship is based on blood relations rather than birthplace, this seems to hold a certain immanent logic. At the same time, however, it demonstrates how such a concept of citizenship can lead to racist thinking in people who would not consider themselves racists. What is more, it also demonstrates how oblivious many Germans are to the history of their own country, though it is true to say that often this is not entirely their own fault but the fault of the educational system. Germany's colonial past and its post-colonial repercussions are frequently not part of the school curriculum.

There are roughly four historical circumstances which have led to the presence of Afro-Germans in Germany. Germany, entering the race for colonial possessions rather late, had four colonies in Africa: Togo, Cameroon, German Southwest Africa (= Namibia) and German East Africa (= Tanzania). A few black Africans came to the German empire during this German colonial period (roughly 1884 to the First World War) as members of the local élites in order to be educated in the German school and university system (on the assumption that they would assume roles of leadership back in the colonies). During this time, some were also brought to Germany to be exploited as circus and carnival attractions and as subjects for medical experiments.

The next group of Afro-Germans came into existence as a consequence of the First World War. The Treaty of Versailles put the Rhineland, a piece of territory situated between France and Germany, under the control of France, Britain and the USA for fifteen years. Naturally, a part of these occupational forces consisted of the black soldiers of each of these three armies. And around 800 children were born to black–German couples during these years. Immediately and in part at least because the presence of black soldiers was perceived as an attempt by the allies to humiliate the Germans, a derogatory term was coined for these people: 'Rhineland bastards' (*Rheinlandbastarde*). What is more, long before Hitler even came to power, there were calls to subject these persons to forced sterilizations so as to prevent these 'products of racial disgrace' having any children. By 1937 about 400 such forced sterilizations had been performed.

The outcome of the Second World War once again brought black soldiers to Germany as part of the occupation forces, mostly as members of the US Army. About 3,000 children of African-American–German couples were subsequently born and the term 'occupation babies' was invented for them. As Helga Emde's contribution in this chapter indicates, this group, too, had to suffer under racist and xenophobic sentiments. The children were seen as the descendants of the intruders on to German soil, while their mothers were considered traitors or *Amiliebchen* (*Ami* is short for *Amerikaner, Liebchen* means 'darling' or 'my love' but also has the connotation 'whore').

Finally, during the forty years of Germany's division into the Federal Republic and the German Democratic Republic (1949–90), some black Africans entered the Federal Republic in pursuit of academic and professional degrees. The Nigerian physician Chima Oji, for instance, spent many years in West Germany earning two doctoral degrees and raising a family. He is married to a German and has returned to Enugu in Nigeria, where he runs a hospital. The two texts in this chapter are excerpts from his autobiographical account *Caught among Germans*, which covers the two decades from the mid-1960s to the mid-1980s. Apart from Oji's Afro-German perspective on life in West Germany during these years, the text also offers detailed insights into the everyday life of this period. The title of the book is derived from the German expression *Unter die Räuber gefallen* ('Caught among thieves'), which conveys the meaning of having been robbed of one's last penny. Obviously, Oji is not referring to material matters here, but rather to aspects of his identity. The cover of the German paperback edition shows the image of a German shepherd dog superimposed on the silhouette of a black person's head.

Further Africans came to West Germany as a result of political persecution in the country of their origin (for example from countries such as Biafra in the 1960s), while, on the other side of the border, blacks came to East Germany as representatives from 'socialist brotherlands' such as Cuba or, for a certain period, Angola. What it means to be East German and black is expressed in Gabriele Willbold's poem in this chapter. She was born in 1962 and is a resident in gynaecology in Cottbus.

As this brief sketch shows, the question 'Where are you from?' in the case of Afro-Germans would have to be answered in almost as many different ways as there are Afro-Germans. Afro-Germans do not have a common history, and yet they are all subjected to the same curiosity on the part of their white German compatriots, for whom, in a predominantly white society, a different skin colour is still something sensational (and perhaps alarming). The majority assigns an ambiguous status to this group, vacillating between bestowing extra attention on what seems exotic and rejecting what is perceived as different. At the same time Afro-Germans are constantly reminded of the fact that they live between two cultures. Africans in Germany who are only visiting or are definitely planning to return to their home country often object to how 'European' these Afro-Germans have become. The white German majority, on the other hand, constantly reminds them with questions as to their origin, for instance, that on the basis of their skin colour they do not perceive them as 'Germans'.

Since there is no ethnic group either inside or outside Germany on which they could model their identity, Afro-Germans have started to articulate in their own voices what it means to be Afro-German. The Ghanaian-German May Ayim, who was born in Hamburg in 1960, was crucial in providing a forum for the articulation of Afro-German voices. Prior to her suicide in 1996, she lived in Berlin, where she worked as an educational specialist and speech therapist, a poet and an editor of *Showing Our Colors*. Her work deals with racism within educational and therapeutic settings.[1]

The texts in this chapter trace the history of Afro-Germans from the immediate postwar period to the consequences of German reunification for this minority and thereby present an account of these roughly fifty years which is markedly different from the official descriptions of this period. While most of these texts are clearly autobiographic, one should not overlook how the act of putting one's own life in writing transforms the individual experience into something bigger. The texts provide perhaps the first building blocks for formulating a common history of Afro-Germans that is always careful to account for the diversity within this group.

---

1. See May Ayim (Opitz), 'Die afro-deutsche Minderheit', *Ethnische Minderheiten in der Bundesrepublik Deutschland: Ein Lexikon*, eds Cornelia Schmalz-Jacobsen and Georg Hansen (Munich: Beck, 1995) and May Opitz, Katharina Oguntoye and Dagmar Schultz, *Showing Our Colors* (Amherst: University of Massachusetts Press, 1992).

9

An 'Occupation Baby' in Postwar Germany*
Helga Emde (age 40)

I was born in March 1946 in Bingen-on-the-Rhine as a so-called occupation baby. According to the few stories from my mother, my father was stationed in Germany as an American soldier at the time. That was about all I knew of him. My father was very dark, and I came into the world as a so-called mulatto. Since my mother could say absolutely nothing about him, I don't know him and wasn't able to have any contact with him. Nor do I know whether I have any American aunts, uncles, or cousins. It hurts a little that a whole part of my history is in the dark.

I grew up in a time that was still strongly marked by Germany's National Socialist past. My childhood wasn't very different from that of other children except for the fact that I'm Black. I'm the only Black person in the family. My mother believed in an awful saying: 'If you say A you must also say B.' For her that meant that she had brought a Black child into the world and she now had to own up to it. It was practically a kind of self-punishment. She demonstrated her 'owning up' by seeing to it that I lacked nothing. I was stuffed like a pig! Nothing was denied me. In retrospect I really hold that against her. Instead of stuffing me with food perhaps she could have fed me with something quite different. Love, for instance. My sister was a delicate girl, you could almost say skinny. She got what she needed for her development, not just food but love, too. We competed a lot with each other. Neither in my childhood nor as a young adult did I have the good fortune to come into contact with other Blacks in my surroundings. There just weren't any. As a child I only saw Black

---

* 'Als "Besatzungskind" im Nachkriegsdeutschland', from *Showing Our Colors – Afro-German Women Speak Out*, eds May Opitz, Katharina Oguntoye and Dagmar Schultz, trans. Anne V. Adams, foreword by Audre Lorde (Amherst: University of Massachusetts Press, 1992), 101–11. English translation of *Farbe bekennen: Afro-deutsche Frauen auf den Spuren ihrer Geschichte* (Berlin: Orlanda Frauenverlag, 1986).

soldiers, and I ran away from them in fear and terror. This clearly shows that I must have internalized the prejudices and racism of my surroundings at a very early stage. Black meant frightening, strange, foreign, and animalistic. For, how else can you explain that I didn't perceive my own blackness as such? That I looked upon a Black man's smile more as a flashing of teeth than as smiling? Of course I wasn't allowed to have anything to do with Blackness. But the idea, the devastating idea of actually belonging to this group was still there!

Black means unworthy of existence. And that's exactly how I felt. I always stayed in the most remote corner; I was shy and timid and felt lucky to be asked to play with the other kids -and how! I felt unworthy of existence. I couldn't afford to be conspicuous or else I'd be noticed, not as a sassy little girl but as 'Nigger', 'Moor Head', 'Sarotti-Mohr'.[1] I couldn't afford to be conspicuous at any price, but already I was 'big and strong' for my age. I was not supposed to stand out and yet was noticeable to everybody with my kinky hair and my black skin. Not infrequently people had the audacity, even in my mother's presence, to 'marvel over' my hair, that is, to touch it and to give free vent to their delight at the feel of horse hair. What my mother was feeling, I don't know. But it always seemed to me that she somehow felt flattered. Maybe she was getting attention in that way. But we never spoke about it. Almost daily, people marveled at my good German accent and at the same time asked where I came from. Often I considered myself 'cute' or exotic, but never as a person with feelings. I had to learn to suppress my feelings, to put things out of my mind and not always be vulnerable and easily hurt. Words like 'Nigger', 'Sarotti-Mohr', 'Nigger Kiss' or 'Moor Head' – I heard these terms as a young child and quite frequently.[2]

Sweet tasting insults. For after all, what child doesn't like to eat sweets? I loved them and was always ashamed to ask for 'Moor Head' or 'Nigger Kiss' in a store. In school I had a girlfriend who always carried around a lot of pocket money. After class she would often invite me for a 'Moor Head snack'.

1. The ads and packaging of the chocolate with the brand name Sarotti showed a black child in stereotypical 'Moorish' clothes. For the reference to 'Moor Head' see footnote 8 on p. 103.

2. The translator of the book from which this passage is taken uses the word 'nigger' to translate both the loanword from English into German and the German word *Neger*. In everyday usage the latter does not have the openly racist connotations and has been translated by this editor elsewhere by the English 'negro', which also conveys some of the awkwardness of the German word.

Oh yes, another thing: In school choir they had a song I could not bring myself to sing with them – 'Blackish brown is the hazelnut, blackish brown am I, too'. As soon as I would hear it I would become flushed with shame, thinking that all the other pupils would point at me. It was torture for me.

'. . . as white as I could be'

A white person is beautiful, noble, and perfect. A Black person is inferior. So I tried to be as white as I could be.

When I was about thirteen I started to straighten my 'horse hair' so that it would be like white people's hair that I admired so much. I was convinced that with straight hair I would be less conspicuous. I would squeeze my lips together so that they appeared less 'puffy'. Everything, to make myself beautiful and less conspicuous.

At fourteen I graduated from eighth grade and then took a two-year training course from nuns in a children's home. My time with the nuns didn't do very much to increase my self-esteem. My life was nothing but restrictions, religious restrictions: every morning getting up early to go to 'Holy Mass'. And shame on me if I was bold enough to ask to sleep late once in a while since my duties started later. Then automatically I was an 'ungrateful, spiteful godless little person', who should have been happy at the chance to lead such a good clean life.

Sexuality was, of course, taboo. It goes without saying that you couldn't talk about it either. You couldn't even wear a short-sleeved nightgown in the hottest part of the summer. It was simply a fact that woman is shameless. When I reached puberty the only instruction on sexuality I was given was that from then on I had to keep away from men. As though I had tried to get close to them before!

I felt fragmented, confused, and disoriented, without an identity of my own. And my mother was incapable at this time or at any other time of supporting me, of sharing this experience with me, or of enlightening me. Rather, she seemed glad that I didn't bother her with all these problems. Probably not so much because it was troubling to her, but more because her own prudish upbringing hadn't prepared her for any of this. My fears of being Black and of men were rooted deep within me. What better way to protect myself than with a fat, unattractive body. I ate myself into a regular cage of protection. It was a vicious cycle: I wasn't supposed to stand out – but I was big and fat. Was supposed to be inconspicuous – but I was big and fat and Black. And to top it all off, I was a girl.

My existence in the male world often seemed to me like one long running of the gauntlet. I remember going for a walk with some girlfriends. We had barely passed a bunch of workmen when right away there was the remark: 'The Black one, that's the one I want . . ' Inside, I froze into a pillar of salt. I felt hurt and humiliated, and even now when I write about it I feel anger and hatred toward those men who only looked upon me as a walking sex object.

After my home economics training I worked for two years as an aide in a children's home, and then at eighteen I began my nurses' training. My nurse's uniform suddenly provided me with an identity and a role. Since childhood I had been trained never to show my true feelings, always smile and keep my mouth shut. So, on the hospital stations I soon became a ray of sunshine for the patients. There it didn't matter how I really felt. I was simply the little exotic girl. People constantly said things to me about my differentness, and that used to make me feel pretty bad. As long as I was a trainee it was okay, but after my exam I worked in the Frankfurt-Höchst Municipal Hospital and was given only the dirty work to do. I had to clean up but was given no responsibility. They even had the audacity to assign me to frequent night duty, which almost nobody liked. But on the night shift I suddenly became responsible for several stations at once.

On day duty it happened now and then that a doctor on the station would see me and ask if anyone else was on duty. In his eyes I was nobody! So, am I really nobody? I am a German, I was born here, but yet I'm different. A Black woman. A mixture of black and white.

I felt degraded and discriminated against. As before, I had no contact with other Blacks, mostly because I would have preferred to deny my blackness. It wasn't enough that I belonged to a minority; I also felt lonely and isolated. In my own life I repeated the story of my mother's life in every way. My first boyfriend was a Black soldier, and I had a baby by him. At the beginning of this relationship I harbored very ambivalent feelings: on the one hand I was very happy and even proud to have a boyfriend – at least in this respect I didn't have to be an outsider – and on the other hand I had the secret fear of being even more conspicuous. After this relationship was over, I had to 'ban' everything Black from my life, at least for the time being.

At twenty-three I got married – to a white man. A year and a half later our child came into the world. We are a very mixed-looking family, with very different shades of color. At last I felt that I belonged and that I had a bit of recognition out there in society. A white man at my side, this could certainly provide me with some security, even if it still meant that only white counts.

maj. spouse

With my husband I sought something that I was never able to find, namely solidarity. There was a lot he couldn't understand, simply because he was white. He didn't experience the many subtle abuses and hostilities that his company – and unfortunately my own – caused for me. Over and over I would hear from him that I was too sensitive. That's just not a basis for a life together.

And then there were the relatives. My husband's sister, during the course of her psychoanalysis, came to the conclusion that my blackness frightened her and that my personality was too strong for her. Since then I've recovered from the pain that caused me for she was my closest friend for many years.

A good Catholic aunt of my ex-husband and of his doctor-therapist sister voiced the opinion, without ever having seen me, that 'I could never be faithful to D (my husband) anyway, because anyone who had ever slept with a "Negro" just couldn't.' So, what am I supposed to say?

Just Be a Housewife and Mother

edu.

When my children were still small I began to feel unsatisfied, over-burdened, caged in, hungry for education. My need to catch up, particularly with respect to education, started to become stronger, for practically all our friends and acquaintances at that time were university students or had already completed their university education. And every time the discussion came up about my needs, I encountered a lack of understanding. Nobody knew how to take what I was saying. Why did I want to further my education? Why go back to school? Why do anything at all to get away from my housewife's existence?

I considered myself ignorant and uneducated. But my friends' answer was that I wasn't ignorant, I knew how to do a lot of things, and I really ought to consider what being a housewife and mother meant. This was their way of trying to 'build me up'. But actually they were neither supporting nor encouraging me, but rather restricting me to the role of mother. At the same time I was giving them the feeling that they were something special. In debasing myself I was raising the status of my educated friends and offering them the opportunity to do 'developmental work' on me. Even my husband didn't take me seriously. For him too I

attn.

was not an equal partner, but his wife to be shown off, whose presence automatically made him the center of attention wherever he went.

My relationships, with our friends as well as with my husband, really became tense and strained when I finally decided to go back to school. I

restricting

began by preparing myself in evening and weekend courses for the high-school equivalency exam. Of course I was still working part-time, for we still needed money. I worked as a district nurse and then later as night-duty nurse in a Frankfurt hospital, and yet my sense of dissatisfaction was becoming increasingly noticeable; I was simply a frustrated housewife and nagging mother.

When the lease on our house on the outskirts of Frankfurt ran out, I pushed hard for us to move back to Frankfurt, as a chance to escape my isolation a little bit. For I felt like I was in a prison, like I had absolutely no contacts with the outside world. My kids had their friends in nursery and elementary school, and my husband could enjoy his little house in the suburbs because he worked in the city and had colleagues from work. After a long hard search – don't forget that I'm not white and for this reason most landlords turned us down – we found a nice apartment practically in the center of town. This move was a real break for all of us: the children went to new schools, in a different environment, and I had found a new job in a rehabilitation center for the mentally handicapped, working with people who had just been released from psychiatric care and had to learn to adjust to the outside world again. At the same time I was preparing myself for my exams in the evenings and on the weekends. I was petrified of failing and the only words of encouragement that I heard from my husband were that if I flunked once I could take it over again. But I didn't flunk, and as a matter of fact I got the same grade that my husband had gotten when he took his equivalency exam a year earlier. I applied to the university for admission and enrolled. Throughout my undergraduate work my husband could not accept the fact that I had to study too, to do some reading or write a paper. He would keep me from studying with a very subtle form of 'love', often asking me to go for a walk with him, or to sit and have a cup of coffee with him ... I was becoming increasingly assertive, defending myself against his 'love' – which felt like shackles – and against his feelings of competition. The whole time I was at the university, I worked at least two to three days a week and also during semester vacations. My husband couldn't throw it up in my face that he had to finance my education. Plus I had my household and my children to take care of. Of course there was no question of my husband taking on equal responsibility. Or maybe he did feel responsible but he didn't do half as much at home as I did. Sure, he'd go shopping or run the vacuum cleaner, but that's not taking one half of the responsibility.

Whenever I would tell my mother-in-law about my studies she would only say: 'And what about the household?' How could I have gotten the idea that I had the same rights as others?

univ. status

Suddenly the roles shifted. No longer was I the ignorant little exotic girl, now I belonged to that revered group: university students. And nobody knew how to react. The more equal I became with the others, the more strained our relations became. A couple of friendships soon petered out. Just like that, that quickly. My white sister even said once that I really wasn't entitled to a place at the university and that I was taking the place away from younger people and that in fact I already had a career.

Fortunately, I didn't let anyone deter me. I continued at the university and felt unbelievably good in the role of student because I belonged to 'that group', even though I never really had the chance to enjoy my student life. I carried too much responsibility on my shoulders. The only ones who were happy about my success at university were my children. They supported me in every respect. When I had to study and they were quiet, that in itself was a great form of support.

I was getting deeper and deeper into a crisis situation, a marriage crisis and also an identity crisis. In order to give myself more clarity and distance from these unresolved issues, I decided after completing my teacher's certificate, to take a trip to southern Africa. So I went. On 24 December 1983, I flew to Zimbabwe for the first time, to stay with friends for two months and share their lives.

'I can say "Yes, I am black"'

Prejudice? Yes, what is prejudice? It's seldom open and direct, but usually very subtle and often covered with a veil of friendliness.

assump- tions + stereotypes

For example, I enjoy listening to music, and it's often hard for me to sit still while I'm listening. But if I express myself, like if I want to dance, then automatically that means: 'You've got music in your blood, so you must know how to dance.'

Of course I must be able to sing too, because all 'Black women' sing fantastically, especially gospels and spirituals. Just think of Ella and Mahalia! And not only can they sing but – in spite of their physical size – they can move to the rhythm.

It was a long journey to find my 'self' in this white system of relationships. Alongside my studies I began reading about all kinds of different ethnic minorities, and delved deeply into the issue of National Socialism and the Jews in the 'Third Reich'. I felt then, and still do, very close to those people.

My circle of friends consists of people of different nationalities. I have since made many African friends. I enjoy being with them, and even seek them out. In their presence I feel comfortable, secure, accepted, and not like a foreigner. But again and again just when I get to feel 'at home' with them, I come to the painful realization that ultimately I don't actually 'belong' among them either.

The 'white world' is more familiar to me. I grew up among whites, although among them also I don't feel like I belong, but am rather a minority. My sons have it easier than I – they are not alone with their differentness; they have me.

An African friend once told me this anecdote: Once when he went out for a walk, he encountered a woman with a child, who excitedly pointed at the 'Negro'. He leaned over to the child and asked where he was born. – 'Here,' that is, in Germany. He continued: 'So you're a German?' The child answered yes. 'You see,' he explained, 'I was born in Africa, so I am an African and not a "Negro".'

He considers the word 'Negro' as negative. This conversation really made me reflect and also made me envious, because this Black person was able to refer to his identity in a very natural way.

I have dark skin, too, but I am a German. No one believes that, without some further explanation. I used to say that I was from the Ivory Coast, in order to avoid further questions. I don't know that country, but to me it sounded so nice and far away. And after this answer, I didn't get any more questions either. Germans are that ignorant. I could tell people any story I wanted to, the main thing was that it sounded foreign and exotic. But no one ever believes that I am German. When I respond to the remark, 'Oh, you speak German so well' by saying 'So do you,' people's mouths drop open.

It's only recently that I have been able to feel more comfortable in my brown skin and come to terms with my blackness. After a long hard struggle through psychoanalysis, I can say, 'Yes, I am Black.' I can accept the white part of me as well as the black part and without feeling any breaks between them. Most of all, I am thankful for the unending patience of my therapist who stayed by my side on this rocky journey in the search for my Self, my identity, and my roots.

The Revolutionary

no mother, I tell you I've
renounced your god
– i'm a revolutionary
i know i'm hurting you all, that's the only reason i'm marrying her,
the black girl, who does not fit in with us
– i'm a revolutionary

look, i'm leaving her already – i'm going in order to fight. please
take me back, for you all can be proud of me
– i'm a revolutionary
i know what i owe to you all, to you, too, mother, that's why i'm
coming back
– but i'm your son. forgive my revolt.
but from today on i'll choose my underwear, mother.
– that's the price you have to pay.

The Cry

because poverty makes you inventive, i always had things to play with.
and friends. lots. scads.
they played with my things and broke them.
ran away. and i was alone again.
why?
let me in!
i want to belong to you, but they were just gone.
Sarotti Mohr, Moor Head.

why are you ashamed?
why do you feel sorry for me?
why are you torturing me?
Nigger.

let me be like you.
look i'll straighten my hair,
make my lips thin and put on pretty clothes.
Exotic girl.

i'm a human being, a female person, don't you understand me?
Sex.
you all make me unequal.
housewife and mother.
Nooooo. please, doesn't anyone understand me?
Sure.
all of us. but stay as you are and don't change.
no, no education, where will we be then???
but understand me, i want to be equal.
but please not like us!
you don't belong to us.
HELP they want to stone me and
They're almost succeeding.

10

Caught among Germans*
Chima Oji

Bitter Honey

In December of 1971 I was in the middle of preparing for my preclinical state board exam (*Physikum*). Even the Sunday before Christmas I had pored over my books from morning till night and crammed for this exam; outside it had been pouring with rain from dawn to dusk; and both of these things had got to me. Tired of studying, I was fighting against the temptation to indulge in a pleasant change from my routine. Right, that record was still sitting there which I had borrowed from the disc jockey of the Tenne, a disco in Münster, because I wanted to tape it. To return it to him would be a welcome excuse to go downtown for a little while and drop in at the disco. And if I was going to go there anyway it wouldn't make much difference if I stayed for a beer as well.

Shortly before 11 p.m. I arrived at the Tenne; I dropped off the record and checked things out. I saw a girl I liked on first sight. On second sight I asked her for a dance which she didn't refuse. I wanted to continue the conversation which we had started while dancing, so I wanted to buy her a beer. We both felt attracted to each other and she accepted my invitation to a Christmas party. Then it was time for her to go to the train station so that she wouldn't miss the last train which would take her back to her home town, a midsize city not far from Münster. She lived there with her parents. I gave her and her girlfriend a ride to the station and promised to call her at the office the next day.

I made good my promise on Monday afternoon; I also wanted to discuss the details of the Christmas party with her. Trying to appear open-minded and straightforward she asked me very diplomatically to pick her up at home before the party because her parents probably wouldn't like it very much if she went to a party – a party in the big city no less – with someone

---

* *Unter die Deutschen gefallen* (Wuppertal: Peter Hammer Verlag, 1992), 115–21 and 247–59.

they didn't know at all. As a sort of preventive measure it had occurred to her that I would not be a stranger any more after I had picked her up at home. I didn't have anything against this and we agreed on a place in the city for our rendezvous which was easy to find, from where she would escort me to her parents' house. That's why my eyes nearly popped out of my head when on Christmas Eve around noon Barbara – that was the name of the girl – showed up in the lobby of my dorm where she had asked for me. I showed her upstairs to my room, and there she told me over a glass of apple juice about the reason for her surprise visit.

On Monday morning she had told her mother that she had met a student in Münster who had invited her to a Christmas party. Her mother was immediately on the defensive, saying: 'Those who do not visit their parents at Christmas must have come from so far away that they cannot go home at all.' Did she already have a foreigner in mind? At the very least her words revealed that she didn't like her daughter's date at all. In order to change her mother's mind Barbara had come up with the idea of asking me to pick her up at her parents' house.

She wanted to prepare her parents slowly and carefully for the person she had met because it was perfectly clear to her that they would have some difficulties accepting a friendship with an African man as something normal. But that very night her family got into a heated debate after she had delicately conveyed to her parents that she had a date with a black man. Her parents at first didn't want to believe her, the idea was too alien for them to grasp immediately. Finally they did understand that the whole matter was not a joke and proceeded to get very agitated about it. Right away they forbade their daughter to meet with me; and from that moment on they could not be persuaded to think the whole matter over again and to depart from their first angry and hasty decision.

'I won't have a negro in my home!' The answer her father gave to end the unwelcome debate to his own satisfaction was brief but unambiguous. Thus any further arguing over this matter was left to mother and daughter. The majority of points the mother brought up against our date were born of unreasonable, partially unconscious fears, which, however, were so firmly entrenched that they made her inaccessible to any attempt at countering them. She was not willing and perhaps not able to consider whether her very general trepidations applied to the special case at hand: that her daughter had met an African student whom she liked and whose invitation to a party she would love to accept. After all, not much more was at stake yet.

Her deep-seated fears were so strong that she was not even able to see this harmless event in isolation. Rather, she reminded her daughter of what had happened to those German women who had got involved with prisoners of war during the Second World War – they had been pilloried, their hair had been cut off, the men had usually been killed. With these nightmares from the times when the brutes reigned she tried to intimidate her daughter – and in the final analysis herself, too. She turned a deaf ear to Barbara's attempts to convince her that this type of brutal harassment was a thing of the past.

But her fears had their roots not just in the past; rather, her main concern was very much orientated towards the present, and in fact did not reach much beyond her own front door, that is: 'I don't want to think about what the neighbours would have to say about this!' Indeed, the fear of malicious gossip put her in a state of panic, and she pictured the shame which Barbara's liaison with a negro would bring upon the family. I would like to add that a few years later the daughter of a family in the neighbourhood had a relationship with a Turk, for all to see and over an extended period of time, and that today the daughter of another neighbour is married to an Italian, with whom she had been friends from early on.

In this regard, I am reminded of a story which Barbara once told me. In her home town, in which numerous companies have their head office, there had been many 'guest workers' from early on; towards the end of the 1960s they were mainly Italians, who, for the most part without their families yet, had been put up in run-down houses, where they eked out a dreary existence in the company of other men. Back then, Barbara knew a number of very young girls who preferred to have their first sexual encounters with these Italian men – of course all in secrecy on park benches at dusk or in the dark entrance ways of the guest workers' homes. They never went out into the open with the men they preferred; they even avoided being greeted by them downtown. And of course at home and with their neighbours they kept up the appearance of being proper and inexperienced. They gossiped about their secret adventures only with their peers and behind closed doors, where they might even brag about them ('Tonio really gave it to me!'). Of course after they had amused themselves enough, these girls turned to 'well-mannered' German boys, to whom they got married later on. And who would still remember today her exciting past with 'hot-blooded' Italians? I believe this story illustrates the prevailing double standard with regard to the 'problem of foreigners' of that city and others much better than words of explanation, the double standard of which one of the victims was Barbara's mother.

But back to the impossibilities of understanding between mother and daughter. The mother was afraid of everything and everyone: she was afraid of the reaction of neighbours, relatives and acquaintances; afraid that her younger children wouldn't be able to go out on the street any more without being pointed at – afraid, that is, of having the family's reputation as a whole go to ruin; and she was afraid for the moral conduct of the younger siblings, who would be corrupted by Barbara's bad example.

Part of her anxieties was a consequence of the common attitude among her generation, a hostility towards sexuality, as in her worry that I wanted to exploit Barbara sexually and would leave her afterwards, perhaps even with a baby. The epitome of this worry was her fear that no proper German man would want to have anything to do with Barbara after she had slept with a negro because she would have acquired the irrevocable reputation of being a 'negro's whore'.

The fight in the home of Barbara's parents over her acquaintance with me couldn't be resolved that night. Rather, the atmosphere in the house was ruined by very bad vibes for the entire week before Christmas because for days Barbara wouldn't give up hope that she could change her mother's mind. But she came up against a brick wall with her despairing entreaty for them to at least let me come by their house. Shouldn't the parents at least get a first-hand impression of me before they condemned a friendship which had not even really started yet? Her boundless disappointment condensed into helpless rage – in the course of this process she used all the means available to her: she begged, flattered her parents, tried to talk them into it, to convince them by reasoning, rebelled, cried, yelled. But the result of all her efforts was a complete ossification of their position until she was told that it was enough already and no more objections would be tolerated. The topic had been thoroughly discussed and was not to be brought up again.

The whole soap opera took place at a point when the Social Democrats, who were in power at that time, had not yet put into law their intention to lower the age at which one attained majority from twenty-one to eighteen. Being just about nineteen she was bound to obey her parents for more than another two years. She had to defer to their opinion, and did so for example by really not talking about the matter any more; but she did not have to give in to the supreme power of her parents, for example by giving up meeting me – there was another way! And she was not ready to put up with a situation without resistance in which a human being was rejected and turned away because of his skin colour. Therefore she decided to find a way which would allow her to prevent my coming in vain to her home on Christmas Day.

But to realize this courageous resolution proved to be an almost impossible undertaking because she hadn't written down my address or my phone number; she remembered the sound but not the spelling of my name; and of my casually uttered comment 'I live out there in Wilhelms-kamp,' she could make no sense as someone who didn't live there. But against all these odds she managed to find me. And there she was, around noon on Christmas Eve, in the lobby of 'Münsterland Hall', where she had come by asking passers-by and where she immediately ran into me. Back then I admired the courage and will-power of this girl, and a lasting and close relationship developed between us which is still intact today after a long marriage.

But for a long time to come our love would be overshadowed by the strained relationship with Barbara's parents. For several months Barbara was forced to keep our relationship secret from them, but then everything within her impelled her to stand by me for all to see. There were further intense arguments in her parents' home, into which both sides put a great deal of emotion. What her daughter 'had got into' was too strange and therefore dangerous for the parents to ever really comprehend and thus to approve of. This showed in her mother's fears, which she expressed in sentences like: 'Aren't you afraid when you wake up in the morning and see this black man next to you in bed?' or: 'It might very well be that among his crowd he is a decent human being, perhaps even a very decent one; but not among us. He just doesn't fit in with us!' Her motherly worries about the future of her daughter (and her children) also found an outlet time and again: 'Those poor kids who will be the outcome of this, what is to become of them?' Of course her mother was also simply haunted by the fear that through me she would one day lose her daughter to some far-away place, and this fear she formulated as: 'You will fall to pieces in that climate, you won't be able to stand it!' Similarly she was able to predict: 'Perhaps he assimilates and adopts European ways of living as long as he is here, after all he has sufficient education which allows him to do so. But as soon as he's back home – I can vouch for that – he'll fall back into his old customs and habits. And then you will go to the dogs!'

Barbara's last hope was that through being separated from her parents geographically she could soften the hardened positions back home to a point where there could be some kind of *rapprochement* between the two differing opinions.

Very soon there was the opportunity for exactly this because in a short while she was to begin a pre-professional training programme (*Fachober-schule*) in Münster, and for many young people that was a reason to leave home for the first time.

Bone of Contention

A young mother had gone swimming with her little son to a nearby lake. The heat of summer had driven many city dwellers out into the country to seek refreshment in the cool waters of the lake, and so the woman had to look for a while before she found some space near that part of the lake where the depth of the water was appropriate for kids. She was approached by an older gentleman, who had already been tracking her with his eyes while she was looking for this spot. He greeted her with emphatic friendliness and remarked: 'What a cute adopted kid you have.' 'Oh, thank you, but actually this is my own son, I did not adopt him,' the young mother replied. Immediately the expression on the man's face clouded over, he turned around and looked at those around him as if he was checking out his audience. Then he exclaimed: 'Look, people, what happens when a female[1] gets mixed up with a negro!'

This scene took place at a swimming lake in the province of Salzburg in Austria in 1989. An Austrian friend of ours and her little son had been the victims of this denouncement, which sounds a lot like a relapse into a very inhuman era.[2] And it is only one example of how the rejection of a black/white love relationship intensifies when it occurs to such a couple to get married and have children. In Germany and elsewhere in Europe, the couple is exposed to this rejection among the family of the person whose home this culture is, among closer friends and acquaintances, mostly among strangers in public places and, once the relationship is made official through marriage, also by government offices. From among my acquaintances alone I could list numerous examples.

The parents of a girl who several years ago wanted to marry an African in Münster responded by saying: 'We would prefer a white garbage collector to this black physician.' The parents of another girl, pharmacists from the Ruhr area, literally did not survive the shock which the marriage of their daughter to an African inflicted upon them. They committed suicide together. A young woman got married to a man from Ghana after a friendship of many years. She and her parents had already fallen out several years earlier on account of this relationship; originally they had offered to give her a car if she and this man split up. But when she had her first child the grandparents refused categorically to even look at the grandchild, and the woman found out through her brother that their mother had remarked: 'Well, while they're little, they're still quite cuddly.'

1. The German derogatory use of *Weib*.
2. That is, 1933–45.

Some years ago friends of ours, a German–Nigerian couple, wanted to have their daughter, who had been born before the wedding, declared legitimate. But the officer in the Bureau of Vital Statistics first tried to impede their application with the words: 'It's really not that simple, after all there are plenty of American barracks around here!'[3] The German wife of another Nigerian man went to the immigration office after the first year of their marriage to get her husband's residence permit extended. Because the way it works is that a spouse from abroad first gets a residence permit for one year after marriage to a German and only if they are still married is this paper extended for another three years. Only then are you eligible for permanent residence. The couple is thus forced by the system to lead a probationary marriage. And the officer in charge did indeed ask the woman: 'What? Are you still married?' (And this was before the time when there was a lot of talk about the so-called fake marriages of foreign asylum seekers to German women.) Towards the end of the 1970s a quote by the head of the Münster immigration office got some publicity among insiders. On various occasions this man had uttered in front of witnesses the following *faux pas*: 'This kind of foreigner is ready to marry any German woman no matter what she looks like – and even if her arse is right in the middle of her face – the main thing is he can stay.'

[handwritten margin note: marriage residence]

This time around I was spared; that is, my wife and I experienced no hostilities when we decided to get married in 1976. Of course I, too, just like the other foreigners, would have had to produce the 'Certificate of Marital Qualification' – documents from home which, among other things, were supposed to prove that I was not already married to anyone there. All my papers such as my birth certificate etc. had been destroyed in the war with Biafra, and so the respective Bureau of Vital Statistics felt it was sufficient that a relative stated under oath that I was I and had no wife at home. The Nigerian Embassy certified this statement.

But it is not so easy in all cases to get this Certificate of Marital Qualification, and the degree of difficulty seems to vary from one office to the other and can even depend on the good intentions of the particular officer. By the way, in the wake of all the uproar which the discussion about 'fake marriages' had caused, the requirements were made more difficult: all the evidence now has to be produced in the country of origin of the foreign spouse, and for many concerned this brings with it great difficulties and might even be impossible. But the requirements had always been different in each case according to the country of origin of the candidate because German institutions paradoxically take into account

---

3. The implication is that the child's father could also be an African-American soldier.

the local law of the country of the husband when they issue the Certificate of Marital Qualification, even though people get married in Germany under the jurisdiction of its own marital law. In some cases even a certificate of sexual potency is required. The person who is about to get married has to (and I know people who had to go through this) bring in some sperm, brought along from home or produced by masturbation in the doctor's office, which is then investigated regarding its fertility. With this you can prove a man's fertility – but his sexual potency?

After I had submitted the papers required in my case, there was nothing in terms of bureaucratic hurdles standing in the way of our marriage any more. But in our case, too, there was a confrontation at some office, although that was much later in Freiburg after we had already been married seven or eight years. My wife wanted to take care of some business at the immigration office – I believe it was about my permanent residence. For the spouse from abroad and his German family this document means much more security with regard to staying in the country. Without it the family always has to face the risk that the spouse from abroad can some day, for whatever reason, be expelled after all, so the authorities naturally try to make getting this document as hard as possible.

For her visit to this office Barbara had to present the registration document[4] from the Freiburg government office for the registration of residents in order to show the residence of the family, and the stamp with the date on this piece of paper was unfortunately somewhat illegible. In addition, as it later turned out, the Freiburg immigration office had misplaced our file, which it had received from the city council of Münster after we had moved. For some inexplicable reason they had sent the files to the agency of the county where my wife was born, where it had been collecting dust ever since. But then an officer at the immigration office dared to claim that Barbara was not actually living at the address on the registration document, that she had forged the document in order to establish a 'common domicile' for 'the husband'.

But back to the topic of marriage: my in-laws, for whom the order of the world had collapsed when her daughter had met me and decided to go ahead with her friendship with me, had managed to accept our relationship; they had nothing against our marriage any more.

But when our daughter was born there was a new onslaught of experiences with the racism of the people in our very own sphere of life. These were incidents during which our child or my wife as the mother of

---

4. The German *Anmeldebestätigung*, the record that one has registered with the local police after having moved to this town or region.

a 'negro child' became targets of prejudice and discrimination. Over the many years which I had spent in Germany derogatory remarks had of course been made about me, too, on the streets and elsewhere. For example, during the time when the TV series 'Roots' was broadcast for the first time I could hear 'Kunta Kinte, Kunta Kinte' at every street corner. Words like 'negro' or even 'maroon' and 'oh, is he ever black' had been daily occurrences in those years. I got used to them, I actually learned not to listen to them any more. But I remember two incidents when I was with my little daughter when I was called names like this. Once – Enyi was still a baby – I was carrying her on my arm as I went shopping for something in the neighbourhood. A bunch of children playing in the streets came running towards me from a driveway with toy guns in their hands; the kids yelled at the top of their lungs: 'Look at the nigger with his child, we are going to shoot him now.' Enyi was too small back then to be able to understand what this was about. But the other time she was two years old and understood exactly what was being said. I was holding her by her hand walking though the city with her. A German family was crossing the street and was following us for a short stretch. All of a sudden the father said to his son (and by no means the other way around): 'Look, a gorilla.' The boy laughed wildly about the joke his father had made. But the mother protested and made it clear that she didn't think much of jokes like this one. Enyi asked me: 'Dad, did you hear what the man just said?' I pretended not to have heard and she repeated it for me. 'I think he means you,' she added. 'It doesn't matter. I think it would be nice to be a gorilla because gorillas are very happy animals. But I guess this man doesn't know that.' I didn't say anything else because I wanted to give her a chance to process what she had heard. The next morning she told her mother about it. She answered that this must have been a very stupid man.

These encounters in which our child became the 'bone of contention' for our fellow Germans mostly occurred out on the street or in other public spaces like on the bus or when we went shopping. It became apparent to us that they were more frequent when Barbara was alone with the child than when I was with her or when all three of us were together, and that strangely enough they became less frequent the older the child got. Members of all social strata and all age groups, men, women and children, couldn't hold back their prejudices against the 'mongrel' or against the woman who had 'got involved with a negro' and had begotten this 'shame'.

There were differences in the manner in which these people voiced their prejudices and in how far they went in doing so. Some people just stared at the child or her mother, others turned up their noses at them or shook their heads before they went on their way. Some simply bent down to the child to touch her – to caress her, to fondle the soft black curls or even to put sweets into her hands. They did that without addressing the child's mother first or establishing eye contact with her.

My wife experienced exactly this kind of behaviour as particularly bothersome and usually resisted it. In German society acts of tenderness among strangers are simply not the norm! Other kids, white ones, were not being touched, she could see that with her own eyes. Over and again it was only our child which stirred complete strangers to express their attraction without respect for personal space. Barbara was of the opinion that respect for the personality of a child, no matter how little she was, prohibited such bodily contact with strangers. Because it didn't matter to the ones doing the caressing whether the kid wanted to be caressed or not, so that by ignoring boundaries against the will of the mother such acts were akin to rape. But simply for sanitary reasons alone for a long time she didn't like it when just anybody wanted to fondle her child.

But she would only 'really get to know' these people when she dared to protest at their behaviour and tell them not to touch her child. Without exception they became obnoxious and accused her of being arrogant. Once when Enyi was just seven or eight months old it happened again that a stranger on the street suddenly bent over the stroller to caress the child. Barbara conveyed to her that she did not desire this. The woman, a lady in her forties, was indignant, called the mother arrogant and the child 'so cute nevertheless'. And then she asked in an acidic tone: 'So, do you have a daddy for her?' Barbara lashed back at her: 'What business is it of yours? I hope you have a daddy for your kids, too!' This unexpected attack, which, after all, implied doubts about the woman's own sexual respect-ability, must have hit her pretty hard because it took her some time to pull herself together. In the meantime Barbara had pushed the stroller on and had reached her destination, the pharmacy. But immediately after she had gone inside, the door opened and the woman stuck her head in and said as if trying to redeem herself: 'I have seven children and two fathers for them!' With great presence of mind Barbara responded: 'Then I sure hope there is a father between them for each one of the children.'

This episode in the pharmacy had a funny little sequel. Back then my wife was on the pill and sometimes she forgot to get the prescription in time before the beginning of the next month. In the pharmacy (the same one which she had just now frequented) the staff was disinclined to give her the medication without any fuss even though she promised to give them the prescription later on. They would first call her doctor to cover their backs by his approval. Barbara was in this kind of situation when she came into the pharmacy this time. The pharmacist had overheard the brief exchange between the two women. Politely she inquired what had been the cause for the quarrel. 'Just imagine, she asked me whether I had a father for my kid.' 'Well, really!' the pharmacist answered and went to the door as if she wanted to have a look at the woman. On the way back she glanced surreptitiously at the stroller because up until then she hadn't seen the child. 'That's really outrageous! But isn't the little thing cute?' she added as if to calm my wife down. After she had installed herself back behind the counter Barbara told her what she wanted. Immediately and without any objections regarding the missing prescription the pharmacist went to get the medication and handed it to her without further ado!

Most of the time passers-by would – in passing, so to speak – utter spontaneous remarks about the child, starting harmlessly by shouting things like 'Oh, how cute!' 'Oh, how sweet!' 'Look there, the little negro! Isn't she sweet!' which could be interpreted as the expression of a certain kind of joy about seeing the pretty, exotic-looking child, but there were further, less friendly-sounding comments like 'Look there, a negro!' 'Is this a negro or a negress?' which God knows was not really a big shift in tone. All these utterances had one thing in common, they were not addressed to my wife directly but were said after she had already passed them. The people who made themselves heard in this way did so in a clumsy and inconsiderate manner, showing impoliteness in the register of their voices, the focus of their gaze and their gestures. They were in the immediate vicinity of my wife and my child, they stopped for the purpose of saying these things, pointed their fingers at the child, turned around conspicuously or stared at mother and child with impunity. And even the most harmless-sounding of these comments were not always meant as harmlessly as they at first sounded and as many people liked to claim they were. Barbara could easily 'prove' this by telling Enyi in any particular case: 'Look at what a cute kid *they* have! Isn't she sweet?' In those instances the passers-by, who right before had felt so self-assured, would react with dismay, become insecure and walk away.

Then there were those people who addressed my wife directly about the child. They did so almost exclusively with the following two sentences: 'What a cute kid she is! Did you adopt her?' If she answered that it was her own child, inevitably the following response would ensue: 'Well, it isn't really so bad!' perhaps supplemented by the sentence: 'It's not the poor kid's fault.' But there was also a minority who then said it was wonderful! The question about the adoption sometimes took a more indirect form: 'What a cute kid! She looks exactly like the adopted child of my sister.' If Barbara objected to the word 'bad' in such cases, she had always to witness the same uniform behaviour displayed by the fondlers when they were told that their caresses were not welcome: the people asking the question became angry and accused her of arrogance, or they became insecure and sometimes perhaps even started to defend themselves. But one thing became clear through the frequently asked question about the adoption: no matter what motives a German couple in any particular case might have when it decides to adopt a child from the Third World, society will always judge this step positively, indeed it even improves the image of the respective family. But if it turns out that the exotic-looking child is a biological child, then they have to emphasize: 'It isn't all that bad!' The real message of this statement is plain to see, and is its opposite: it is bad!

Children, too, asked Barbara the stereotypical question after they had looked at Enyi intensively: 'Is this your child?' In response to the affirmative answer they often went on in a rude tone: 'But he looks like a negro!' Once a girl asked literally: 'Is this one of those negro boys who are out there to be adopted?' And another one wanted to know: 'Where can you get one?'

But again there were people who simply asked my wife with concern and interest whether the child could tolerate the climate in this region or whether she already knew German. Interestingly enough, we usually did not have any trouble with those who put the question this discreetly. They kept up their friendly attitude even after they learned that she was our biological child.

As Enyi was growing up, it sometimes happened that she was approached directly, mostly by other children. At the age of about two, she occasionally would bring home the expressions she had picked up outside, which she would in turn use when she was playing, such as 'Kunta Kinte', 'Are you a German child?' and 'You! Negro!' Once my wife was in the playground with her and she was only just in time to prevent a four-year-old boy from pushing the two-year-old off a wall with the words: 'You, negro, go away!'

Apart from the coarse remarks on the street which I have just described I remember basically three occurrences during Enyi's childhood which came close to racism and discrimination and which I would therefore like to describe here. During the first three years of her life we put Enyi into day care at the day-care centre for students in Münster. One day, one of the nurses there said rather innocently: 'The urine of mulattos is really much more caustic than the urine of German children.' Probably the young woman was not even aware of what nonsense she had just uttered. Nevertheless – or perhaps because of it – I brought up what she had said during the next parents' meeting, simply in order to make people aware of it; after all, she was taking care of three so-called half-breeds[5] and if she should ever make such a remark in front of outsiders they would think of her as a competent source, would adopt her opinion uncritically, and right away a new prejudice would have been brought into circulation. I therefore asked her politely whether she had made this remark, what she had been thinking of when she did and whether she could give any reasons for it. If she could give me a plausible explanation I would be satisfied. She reacted with unexpectedly deep consternation and became so embarrassed that she was not able to defend herself, and she left the room crying. A German father got very upset about this and accused me of suspecting the 'innocent, dear Ingrid' of a conscious racist remark and called it very arrogant.

I didn't think that I had done Ingrid an injustice, but out of diplomacy and a sense of tact I went over to her, tried to calm her down and apologized for having confronted her in front of the other parents and not in private.

When Enyi was three we had to rely on putting her into day care for the entire day because my wife was now in the midst of preparing for the state board exam and I had to continue my studies in Hanover for reasons I could do nothing about. But our financial situation was so bad that we applied for assistance for the day-care fee at the welfare and youth office. We had substantiated our application thoroughly and were therefore very surprised when it was turned down. The author of the letter declining the application had ignored all our reasons for putting our daughter into day care stating that there was no reason to put the child into day care other than to confront her with her 'otherness', and this purpose could be served by a kindergarten[6] as well.

My wife went to the office and asked for an appointment with the case worker, and this time her initiative was successful on two counts. She succeeded in making the officer, who was essentially well-meaning, aware of the prejudice which was at the heart of her way of putting things. The young woman was even very much concerned – she had not meant it like that and had not intended her assertion to be taken that way. She apologized sincerely; during this conversation one on one, Barbara was able to convince her that there were indeed important reasons for putting the child into day care. The application was retroactively approved.

---

5. The German word is *Mischlingskinder*, which does not sound as extreme as the English translation even if this is so, because the word is actually still being used not just as an insult.

6. Which traditionally takes children only during the morning hours.

In our search for a place in a day-care centre we had decided on the Nikolaus Kindergarten, which back then enjoyed a very good reputation, and because apart from Germans, there were also children from all parts of the world and children of bicultural couples in it. Thus, Enyi would not be an outsider there; further than this we hoped that the assortment of international children in the kindergarten would have a positive effect on its educational philosophy.

Then one day Enyi came home with the popular old children's song about the 'Ten Little Negro Kids'.[7] This song has been haunting all German nurseries for a good one hundred years now and wreaks havoc with its stereotype of the child-like negro who is lost in European civilization. Because during the various attempts to survive in this civilization one of the little negroes after the other simply dies. The bad thing is that hardly anyone who passes this song on to a new generation is aware of its dangerous character, which builds prejudice. But even worse is the fact that children learn the lyrics of this song at such an early age that they cannot grasp its sense cognitively; its content therefore becomes second nature to them without their being conscious of it.

Together with one other mother my wife decided to bring up this point at the next parents' meeting. She prepared well for this, she even brought along some informational material because she did not want to put anyone on trial but only to raise people's consciousness. Supported by her friend she presented her concerns, carefully and politely, always trying to avoid giving the kindergarten teachers in charge the impression that she was implying that they had consciously taught the children racist ideas. She supported her points by the informational material, which she had brought along which at least in part she also passed on to the teachers. As illustrative material she passed around some very nice picture-books about Africa. Happily her presentation was received positively by the kindergarten staff, including the manager, a Catholic nun. There was even a certain degree of consternation about having reproduced age-old prejudices as a result of their own ignorance. Deeply concerned, the manager said that she only now understood something which had happened there several years ago, the context of which had never become apparent to her. There had been a black girl in the kindergarten back then who had

7. In English, the song is called 'Ten Little Indians'. The song's title in German is *Zehn kleine Negerlein*. In the course of the ten stanzas of the song all ten children disappear, which is reflected in the countdown of the chorus 'And then there were only nine (eight, seven, etc.)'.

always got sick whenever they had had 'negro kisses'.[8] She had also always refused to eat them. But while the teachers were receptive to the well-intentioned attempts at enlightenment on the part of my wife her efforts were not very well appreciated by the parents. Indeed, she was attacked directly by some of the mothers. They accused her of undermining the good reputation of the kindergarten and the valuable work being done there by putting the staff down and by insinuating racism on their part. One mother said that she didn't perceive the lyrics of such children's songs negatively and that she very much wished that her daughter would continue to memorize them. Barbara then resorted to the very effective technique of turning things around – she referred to the well-known poem about the 'coal pitch raven black Moor' from the *Struwwelpeter*[9] and presented a version in which the victim was not a black but a white boy who was being teased by bad black boys because of his pink 'piglet' skin. This didn't fail to have the desired effect: 'You're right,' the mother said, 'I am deeply touched.'

The debates about the ubiquitous prejudices against blacks in the minds of the citizens of the Federal Republic, which concerned me less than they did my daughter or my wife in her role as mother of a brown child, amazingly enough slowly became fewer as the child grew up. Enyi was occasionally praised by well-meaning Germans for her German, which was already so good, although this might have been based more on ignorance than on prejudice. But there was another incident in Freiburg when Enyi was already old enough to start school. It belongs with those other rude remarks on the streets about which I talked earlier, and it is by itself so indicative of things that I must not forget to mention it here.

Early in the evening my wife and Enyi were coming from downtown and were taking the bus home. Sitting across from them was an old woman who initiated a conversation with Barbara. Abruptly she changed the topic of conversation and said: 'Are you just looking after him at the moment?' as she pointed her finger at Enyi.

---

8. The German *Negerküsse*, literally 'negro kisses', a chocolate-covered marshmallow on a piece of wafer, which is still known by this name even though big supermarket chains like Aldi have these days adopted the term 'chocolate kisses', *Schokoküsse*. A similar concoction, sold by bakeries, is called 'Moor heads' or *Mohrenköpfe*.

9. Popular book of comic-like picture stories and rhymes from 1845 by Heinrich Hoffmann, which was intended to entertain as well as to have a pedagogic effect. In the episode referred to here, a boy gets dipped into a barrel of black ink after making fun of a black person.

'No, this is my daughter.'

'No!'

'Yes it is.'

'No!'

'Why not?'

'But she is so black!'

'What?'

'But so black!'

'Yes, you should see my husband, he is even blacker!'

'No, there can't be such a thing.'

'But it is so.'

'And what do people say about this?'

'What people?'

'Well, the people where you live. Do they let you do this?'

'The people where I live? But that's none of their business!'

'Well, you know, where I live we once had one like that living there, too. We scared her away! Scared her away! We don't want ones like that!'

Hesitating, still searching for words Barbara answered:

'Oh, you can really be proud of what you've done!'

'Yes, and that's what I am. We don't want to have such rabble in our house.'

There was a silence since Barbara first had to digest the last couple of sentences. Then she asked:

'Where do you live?'

'Well, of course, I am not going to tell you.'

'You're right. With the bad conscience you must have you're better off keeping it to yourself and not telling anyone where you live!'

The old woman was so put off by this last sentence that she gave up her seat; rather unsteadily standing in the overcrowded bus she waited out the stretch to the next stop.

11

The Year 1990. Homeland and Unity from an Afro-German Perspective*

May Ayim

For me the past two years have been dominated by rapid political as well as personal developments and changes.

In my thoughts I am turning back the pages to the end of 1989 and 1990, back to the confusions and contradictions, the departures and aborted departures, the memories of things I have repressed and to the new discoveries.

Back then I was moving about as if on a boat rocked by waves. I was so preoccupied with trying not to suffer a shipwreck in the whirlpool of time that it was hardly possible for me to look at the events around me with subtlety and to comprehend them. Looking back I see some of the things only as shadows, others I can see much clearer from this distance. It seems to me that the wall between the two German states was casting its stony shadows far ahead long before it collapsed, precisely into the heads of those who had surrounded themselves by it, had decorated it and had put up with it – into our East-West brains. People from both parts of Germany met like twins who knew about the parents they have in common but had been living separately from each other since birth.

The initial euphoria turned out to be the happiness of two people seeing each other again who for the most part did not know each other, who tried to deny that up till then and from a distance they had been mostly enemies.

In all of the media there was talk of German-German brothers and sisters, about unity and reunification, about solidarity and compassion . . . Yes, even concepts like homeland, the *Volk* and fatherland were suddenly

---

* 'Das Jahr 1990. Heimat und Einheit aus afro-deutscher Perspektive', from *Entfernte Verbindungen: Rassismus, Antisemitismus, Klassenunterdrückung*, eds Ika Hügel, Chris Lange, May Ayim, Ilona Bubeck, Gülsen Aktas and Dagmar Schultz (Berlin: Orlanda Frauenverlag, 1993), 206–22.

– again – being used by a lot of people. Words which in both German states had been used with caution since the Holocaust or had even been taboo and had only enjoyed a continued popularity among people on the political right were passed from one to the other. Times change, and people, too. Perhaps the questions of different time periods don't change much and the people's answers change hardly at all.

The initial enthusiasm of meeting each other crumbled with unforeseen speed and the treacherously regained uniformity soon suffocated under the firm home-made coat of liberal Germanomania. But before that all-German banners and flags were being waved, Germany jackets, T-shirts and stickers were being put on display. In November of 1989 I was amazed at how quickly and in what quantities the most diverse products in black, red and gold made it into the department stores and even to the flea markets, products for which there was a great demand everywhere, and I was not able to explain for myself what was going on at the deeper levels of people's minds and feelings. As it seemed, the white, Christian, German, collective guilt neuroses had evaporated overnight and had in the process torn the past away from the present. Who were the buyers, who were the producers of this freedom offered at sale prices, and for whom and for how many was there going to be room in the lauded new homeland? Who embraced in German-German unification, and who was being embraced, monopolized, disowned? – Who for the first time, who again, who as always?

Within a few moments, unification led to the birth of a new Federal Republic, clad in not particularly new clothes – so far as the old Federal Republic is concerned. The GDR was passed on the right.

When the Wall came down many were happy, others became dizzy.

Deutsch–deutsch Vaterland ... Täusch–Täusch Vaderlan ... Tausch–täusch Väterli[1]

My fatherland is Ghana, my mother tongue is German, my homeland I carry with me in my shoes. When the Wall came down I feared for a

---

1. Editors' note: the play on the similar-sounding German words *deutsch*, *tauschen*, and *täuschen* (which mean 'German', 'to change' and 'to cheat') cannot be imitated in the translation. In addition, the two verbs for 'to change' and 'to cheat' are based on a phonetic minimal pair, the difference in sound between '*a*' and '*ä*'. The three different spellings of *Vaterland* (fatherland) might be an attempt to reflect three dialects: high German (*Vaterland*), Saxonian (*Vaderlan*), and Alemannic (*Väterli*). These three dialects reflect the geographic extension of Germany into the north, east and south.

~~while that I would be buried~~ underneath it. Not much fear or not a big fear, but more than usual.

Since 1984 I have lived and worked in West Berlin and I am at home in this city more than anywhere else. Thanks to my not very well-developed sense of direction I get lost in the streets every day, but nevertheless in comparison with other cities in which I have lived and studied so far Berlin has always been the place in which I have felt fairly secure. In the streets my skin colour does not attract the gaze of others in any particular way, I am not being complimented for my good German every day, and only rarely am I the only black person among an indeterminate number of whites in seminars, at events or at parties. I have to explain my existence often, but not always. I remember times in small West German cities when I often had the impression of being under constant surveillance, of suffering under constantly exploring and questioning gazes. I remember days on which I felt particularly lonely and unbearably exposed and was looking out for black people on the bus. In Berlin, this anonymous city with an international countenance, these impressions in my memory faded fast. During the fall of the Wall and the time afterwards they reappeared in my everyday life as from a dusty drawer.

During the first days after the 9th of November 1989 I noticed that hardly any female immigrants or black Germans could be seen in the streets, at least only rarely those with dark skin colour. I asked myself how many Jewish women were (not) out on the street. A couple of Afro-Germans whom I had got to know in East Berlin the year before accidentally crossed my path, and we were glad to have more opportunities to meet each other now. I was on my own, wanted to breathe in a little of the general excitement, wanted to feel the historic moment and to share my guarded joy. Guarded because I had heard about the pending restrictions in the laws for immigrants and asylum seekers. Just like other black Germans and immigrants I knew that even a German passport was not an invitation to these East-West festivities. We sensed that the imminent inner-German union would be accompanied by an intensified closure towards the outside – an outside which would include us. Our participation in the celebration was not desired.

The new 'We' in 'this our country' – as Chancellor Kohl likes to put it – do not have room for everybody.

'Go away, you Negro, don't you have a home?'

For the first time since I had been living in Berlin almost every day I had to fend off blunt insults, hostile glances and/or openly racist defamatory remarks. I started – just like in earlier times – to look again for the faces of black people on the public transportation and when I went shopping. A girlfriend was holding her Afro-German daughter in her lap on the local train when she had to listen to this: 'Ones like you we don't need any more, we already have more than enough people here.' A ten-year-old African boy was pushed off the crowded subway on to the platform to make room for a white German...

These were incidents in West Berlin in November of 1989, and starting in 1990 there was an increasing number of reports about racially motivated attacks, especially on black people, most of them in the eastern part of Germany. At first, these were reports known only among immigrants and black Germans; official correspondents did not take much notice of the violent excesses. I started the year 1990 with a poem:

Without borders and impudent
a poem against the German mock unity[2]

I will nevertheless
be
African
even if you
would like
to have me
German
and I will nevertheless
be German
even if to you
my blackness
seems improper
I will
go one step further
to the outer limit
where my sisters are – where my brothers stand
where
our
FREEDOM
starts
I will
go one step further and one step
further
and return

2. Editors' note: by adding the letters '*sch*' to the German word *Einheit* (unity) Ayim creates a new word, which could be translated as 'seemingness'.

whenever
I want
if
I want
to stay
without borders and impudent.

Starting with 'Black History Month', a series of events about topics in black history, culture and politics which had been initiated in February 1990 by black action groups in Berlin, a coalition of black groups and individuals formed which among other things published a first documentary account of racist attacks in Berlin and the surrounding area.[3]

In that same spring I completed my training as a speech therapist. I remember not only the nerve-wrecking time of the examinations with sleepless nights and lovesickness, but also the meetings of the black political groups during which we discussed for the first time steps for our self-defence against racist attacks on our organizations and on us as individuals. Between the two parts of Germany contacts among groups dealing with immigration policies and black groups intensified and led to joint activities and parties. I was upset and disappointed that during this time Mandela's release from prison hardly got any attention in the German media. For the first time I respected the invention of cable TV somewhat, because this way I found out that at least not the entire European world was absorbed in self-reflection.

At rallies against restrictions in the laws concerning foreigners and the right of political asylum in spring there were hardly any white Germans. In the 2 April 1990 edition of the *tageszeitung*[4] it said: 'German Leftists were missing at the big rally against the laws concerning foreigners. Too foreign?'

I started to get angry about the East-West parties and events which did not address the North-South dialogue. Even the women's movement discussed and celebrated German-German matters as if Germany were exclusively white and the centre of the world. Conventions and seminars were being organized, with travel subsidies for women from the GDR, without thinking at the same time about the female asylum seekers, who no matter whether in East or West Germany have to live at subsistence

---

3. Black Unity Committee, ed., *Documentation: Racist Attacks in Berlin and the Surrounding Area* (January–September 1990), Berlin 1990.

4. Editors' note: German leftist/environmentalist daily paper published in Berlin. Can be read daily on the WWW: http://www.prz.tu-berlin.de/~taz/heute/index.new.html

level. To proceed in such a way was in harmony with the short-sighted and half-hearted campaigns of solidarity which at the government level were staged by the 'Better-Westies' for the 'poor Easties'.[5]

Looking back I see before me an advertisement subsidized by the Berlin Senate which was shown in cinemas: East German workers on a construction site in West Germany. The voice-over explained that it is the citizens from the GDR who take the badly paying jobs not wanted by the West Germans. The commentator admonished the audience both insistently and congenially to receive 'the people' which had come to 'us' in the past weeks and months with friendliness. Why are they only showing white German men when they talk about compassion between women and men from both parts of Germany? I am very much in favour of calls for solidarity, but not ones which do not mention that the least attractive jobs and those with the lowest wages are taken by migrant workers from European countries and from countries outside Europe. Where is the call for solidarity with those who are most at risk of not finding a job or housing any more or of losing their jobs and their positions as trainees in the course of German-German monopolization and competition? For those applying for political asylum there were no broadly based solidarity campaigns with nice words and tickets at reduced prices. On the contrary, the laws concerning residence and permanent stays in Germany were severely restricted by newly introduced legislation, especially for people from the mostly impoverished extra-European countries, and until the end of 1990 white citizens and politicians from East and West watched the increasing racist violence on the street for the most part without doing anything. The 'willingness to accept' white citizens from the GDR and the hospitality towards them, too, appeared to me to be deceptive considering the behaviour towards their so-called foreign fellow-citizens who, not only in most recent times, have been reminded that the 'boat' is full.[6]

5. Editors' note: the term *Wessi* had been coined originally by people on the Left and in the alternative scene in West Berlin to distinguish between 'native' Berliners and the ones (mostly students) who had 'emigrated' from 'bourgeois' West Germany to West Berlin. After 1989 *Wessi* and the formation by analogy, *Ossi*, were used by a wider sector of the population and by the media strictly to differentiate between inhabitants of the former FRG and GDR. A further play on words created the term *Besserwessis* which is based on the noun *Besserwisser* (know-all or wise guy), an ironic commentary on who set the tone of reunification.

6. Editors' note: allusion to the title of a film about immigration policies in Switzerland with the title *The Boat is Full*, which itself is the quote of a populist slogan in the context of immigration.

The biologist Irenäus Eibl-Eibesfeld,[7] for example, had published an article with the title 'Dangers of Mass Immigration' in which he writes: 'One basically has to be aware of the fact that with each new immigrant admitted one gives up land, and one has to tell the citizens the plain truth because the logical connections are as unclear to them as the possible consequences of a massive biological infiltration.'[8] Characteristically only certain groups of immigrants and 'foreigners' are being noticed and excluded, just as black Germans supposedly cannot be 'real Germans'.

A blonde and blue-eyed woman told me that white Germans have a hard time believing that she is from Brazil. Often she is asked: 'But certainly your ancestors were from Germany?' In Brazil, so she said, no one has doubted yet her Brazilian heritage and her membership in this society. Only in Germany had she started to think about and research the history of her family. She found out that a great grandfather who had died a long time ago had indeed emigrated from Germany to Brazil. If she mentions this piece of information today during one of these 'Where are you from?' conversations the reaction is very often: 'Oh, that's nice that your ancestors are from Germany. How do you feel being in your homeland for the first time?' Black Germans experience something else in this regard.

Afro-German I

You are Afro-German?
. . . oh, I understand: African and German.
What an interesting mix!
You know: there are still some who believe
    the mulattos don't quite make it
    like the whites do.

I don't believe so.
I think: with the right education . . .
    You really have been lucky that you grew up *here*.
    Even with German parents. How about that!

7. Editors' note: Ayim does not mention here that this particular behavioural scientist (born in 1928) has for a long time already cut out a niche for himself on the extreme Right and his studies in animal behaviour have always been viewed with scepticism because of the gross analogies he claims exist to human behaviour. This quote from an obscure publication is not a very happy choice in support of Ayim's thesis. It would have been more effective to quote editorials in mainstream newspapers such as *Frankfurter Allgemeine Zeitung* or *Die Welt*.

8. Irenäus Eibl-Eibesfeldt,' Dangers of Mass Immigration' in *Lutherische Monatshefte* 1, 1981: 34.

Do you ever want to go back?
What? You have never been to the homeland of your daddy?
That's sad . . . Well, if y'ask me:
A heritage like this, that really shapes you.
I for example, I am from Westphalia,
and I think,
this is where I belong . . .

Oh dear! All this misery in the world!
   You can be happy
   that you did not stay in the jungle.
   You wouldn't have made it this far then!
I mean, you really are an intelligent girl.
   If you are really serious about your studies
   you might be able to help your people in Africa: You
   are just the right person for this,
   because they will listen to you,
   while to someone like me –
   there are just such big cultural differences . . .

How do you mean? You want to do something here? What d'you want to
do here?
OK, OK, not everything is hunky-dory. But I think,
everybody should first set his own house in order!

The new German 'We' – An Inclusionary and Exclusionary Place?

As head coach of the German national soccer team Franz Beckenbauer proclaimed about the victory of his team during the world championship in the summer of 1990: 'For years to come no one will be able to win against us. I am sorry for the rest of the world, but this is how it is.'[9] The frightening vision of a Germany which claims 'to have to be reckoned with again'[10] took on more and more realistic features during the year 1990 with the growing popularity of racist remarks and behaviour. At the same time this 'We' I mentioned before remained split into different halves.

9. Quoted according to Norbert Seitz, 'Wir sind das Volk' in *Alles Banane, Ausblicke auf das endgültige Deutschland*, eds. Arthur Heinrich and Klaus Neumann (Köln 1990) p. 163.

10. Editors' note: *Wir sind wieder wer*, a phrase from the years of the *Wirtschaftswunder*, the German 'economic miracle' of the 1950s, reappropriated for German reunification.

The historic moment in which there was, wrongly, so much talk about a 'revolution', could have been a moment of critical reflection about oneself in both parts of Germany and a moment in which both sides could have made suggestions for change. But already at the point when the Wall came down it became apparent that hardly anyone was willing to criticize the old FRG as rigorously or to refashion it as was intended for the GDR. Above all, the people connected to the government primarily thought about realizing political and economic interests and were not guided by humanitarian ideals. Hans-Joachim Maaz, a psychotherapist from Halle, was one of those who asked in 1990: 'Where are the honest politicians of the West who warn and inform us about things that have taken the wrong direction and the troubles of their own system and who do not just smugly offer us their "superiority"? Where are the serious considerations about what should change in the Federal Republic, too, so that a common Germany will be a new chance and not a new peril for Europe?'[11] In the meantime, that is two years after the fall of the Wall, one cannot recognize the face of the former GDR any more: school books, laws, institutions etc. were either made to conform to those of the old FRG or abolished. The ubiquitous glittering neon signs signal that capitalism has found its way even into the smallest village of the five new states, and the 'Trabis',[12] which have long since become a collector's item, give the impression of solitary remnants of days gone by. The location of the Berlin Wall can only be reconstructed with some trouble due to its thorough removal. The number of unemployed people, especially of unemployed women, is going up at a galloping rate. The renaming of streets and the removal of monuments belong to the ideas which point the way and demonstrate how the new perspective on the past and the path of Germany into the future are being charted by those in power. What will we remember, what have we already forgotten? It strikes me that in the process of renaming streets in the new states the names of resistance fighters are frequently being replaced by plant names. As of a short while ago the name of Liselotte-Herrmann-Strasse in Erfurt is now Mispelstrasse.[13] The renaming of the East Berlin subway station from Thälmannstrasse to Mohrenstrasse[14] is a

11. Hans-Joachim Maaz, *Der Gefühlsstau. Ein Psychogramm der DDR* (Berlin 1990) p. 182.

12. Editors' note: reference to the most popular East German car, the Trabant, which features a two-cylinder two-cycle engine and a body design resembling a shrunk Cadillac of the 1960s.

13. Editors' note: *Mispel* = 'medlar'.

14. Editors' note: Ernst Thälmann (1886–1944), communist politician during the time of the Weimar Republic who was murdered in the concentration camp Buchenwald; *Mohr* = 'moor'.

sure sign that racist language and the corresponding mind-set are going to be tolerated and passed on among the white élite of the new republic. This can also be seen when, as yet unquestioned, the street names and monuments in the western part of Germany which glorify the colonialists and which continue to demoralize the colonized are being retained.

In 1990 I felt it was frightening and shocking how 'progressive' Leftists and women in the women's movement were silent about and ignored racism; nevertheless it did not surprise me much. On the one hand, since the mid 1980s there had been more and more discussions about the topic of 'a multicultural Federal Republic'. But on the other, only in some exceptional cases had this had the consequence of changing people's own patterns of living and political work in such a way that a continuous cooperation on an equal basis with immigrants and black Germans had become an indispensable matter of course and that the critical examination of racism had become a permanent effort. The Second Women's House in Berlin and the Orlanda Women's publisher belong to the few auto-nomous women's projects which for years have made an effort to hire immigrants and black women on the basis of quota.[15]

Many white Germans consider racism something exceptional and a special topic. As a consequence migrants, black Germans and Jews are only perceived and included in the context of special events, such as a 'Week of the Foreign Fellow Citizen' or a conference on 'Migration and Population Policy'. This is one of the facets of inconsiderate and subtle monopolization and exclusion. Here is an observation by Klaus F. Geiger of November 1989:

> The correspondent is standing on the Kurfürstendamm,[16] surrounded by people celebrating the fall of the Wall. He first interviews two or three people from East Berlin, is looking for West Berliners as partners for his interviews. Behind him are four or five Turkish Berliners participating in the celebration, young men between eighteen and twenty years of age, they shift from one foot to the other, look expectantly into the camera, they show that they are ready to be interviewed but are not pushy about it. The correspondent turns around in a circle, does not see a person whom he would call a West Berliner, interrupts his search and goes back to the studio. Because today is about the unification of two German territories, about the unification of two populations who are by law German citizens. If the topic of the broadcast had been 'the problems

---

15. Cf. the contribution by Dagmar Schulz, 'Kein Ort nur für uns allein – Weiße Frauen auf dem Weg zu Bündnissen' in the anthology from which this text is taken.

16. Editors' note: famous boulevard for shopping and tourists in West Berlin. Also usually the route for any major political rally.

of foreigners', the young Turkish Berliners would have been considered as interviewees – next to many German experts.[17]

The voices of immigrants, black Germans and Jews were not heard until 1990 during the election campaign in the second half of the year. During this time there was an increasing number of conventions and events about the topic 'racism', which were organized for the most part and sometimes exclusively by white Germans. The latter applies for example to the conference 'Exclusion and Tolerance', which took place in Eindhoven in November 1990. While both black and white academics from the Netherlands and from the Federal Republic were giving papers and were holding seminars about this topic, black women had not participated in the planning and organization of the convention. The composition of the organizational team was therefore changed for the purpose of planning the next convention. Fortunately not just painful injuries remain from some other events, but also productive stimuli for a real cooperation between black and white women.

In a society characterized by racism and mechanisms of oppression the respective real or potential victims are not at the same time the better people. Sometimes I observe in black-white contexts that black women or men are given unlimited time to talk irrespective of whether their contribution makes sense or not. Preferred treatment is appropriate and necessary and an important demand if for example it is a matter of filling jobs. But this must not mean the freedom to do as one pleases. If we want to cooperate and see each other as allies – and this is what I suppose – then we have to take each other seriously and have the courage to voice and accept criticism. This applies equally to blacks and whites when dealing with each other and among themselves. For example, it is not only a particular characteristic of East-West encounters of white people that often a dialogue takes place only if the women and men from the new states come to the negotiating table in the western part of Germany. Black Germans and immigrants, too, have gradually come to understand that you can only talk about a dialogue if the groups in East and West move toward each other actively and at the same pace.

I myself am becoming more and more aware of how certain experiences in this society have moulded me and which aspects of this I want to cancel

17. Klaus F. Geiger, 'Nationalistische und post-nationalistische Diskurse im Verteilung-skampf der Bundesrepublik Deutschland' in Institut für Migrations-und Rassismusforschung, ed., *Rassismus und Migration in Europa* (Hamburg and Berlin 1992) p. 273.

out and which ones I want to keep. I often remember my childhood dreams and experiences and bring back to mind what the adults said in order to look for significant messages; I dig out repressed ideals and examples meant as deterrents. Writing these texts I all of a sudden met my grandmother, who had died in 1990, or, to be exact, the mother of my foster-mother. I saw her in her cosy kitchen and heard her talk to my 'brother'. We loved her, and she always had some sweets for us in the drawer of the cupboard. When I saw her in front of me just now, she was upset about our wild behaviour as children and she shouted halfjokingly: 'You are carrying on like in a Jewish school!' It was not until years later that I cringed when Grandma leaned over her youngest grandchildren with the same words and I understood their meaning. Racist remarks, too, were uttered frequently in our house without people being conscious of it and without ill intent. No one wanted to be anti-Semitic or racist. Everyone detested the atrocities of the National-Socialist past, and it had not been a coincidence that I as the only black child had ended up in this white foster-family. No one in this family could have had prejudices, or could they? Racism and anti-Semitism were some of the disagreeable ingredients of the upbringing I experienced. I am aware of it and I will not rest until I have hunted them down inside and outside of me and have demolished them.

Now we have the year 1992, European unification is being carried out and in a few weeks the anniversary of German reunification[18] is going to be celebrated. Every day we hear about new racist and anti-Semitic attacks, fire-bombs against shelters for asylum seekers and manhunts in East and West Germany – just like last summer and autumn and the summer and autumn before. In many places voyeuristic citizens applaud, loudly or secretly, and politicians show a lot of concern for the reputation of the country but not for the real and potential victims of the attacks. The Secretary of the Interior, Rudolf Seiters, said of the escalating violence: 'The consensus is that these are events which hurt the German image in the world and they are commensurate with clouding and damaging the image of a Germany which is hospitable to foreigners, which we want to preserve at all costs.'[19]

18. Editors' note: the 3rd of October, replacing the 17th of June (the date of the uprising in East Germany in 1953), commemorating the signing of the unification treaty between East and West Germany in 1990.

19. Quoted after Dietrich Leder, 'Medientagebuch' in *Freitag*, October 4, 1992, No. 37.

In his statement of 27 August 1992 Chancellor Helmut Kohl demanded: 'The abuse of the right to asylum must finally find a solution. Part of this is an amendment to the Basic Law.[20] This alone does not solve the problem, but it is an important step towards limiting the abuse of the right to asylum.'[21] During the past weeks the situation of marginalized adolescents, who at the time are the primary agents of neo-Nazi attacks, has been increasingly discussed. Discussions about the causes for the migrations of refugees are being neglected as are initiatives which could end hunger, war and the destruction of the environment in the impoverished countries which are being held dependent on Europe. A tough intervention into the asylum law has to be feared in the near future, and even for those seeking refuge who are allowed to stay, the Federal Republic will not be a place which could happily be called 'home' any time soon. The latter also applies to immigrants, black Germans and Jewish people who have been living here for a long time or all their lives.

The open violence on the streets is in harmony with the words of politicians in leading positions and is partially the implementation of their words. But I am convinced that we – and here I mean all the people in this country who do not tolerate racism or anti-Semitism – are willing and capable of forming alliances. There are examples which we can follow or which we can use as starting points. The action group 'Black Germans', for example, which formed in the mid 1980s from a small group of Afro-Germans, in the meantime has study and contact groups in numerous cities in the FRG. Organizations of immigrants, black Europeans and Jews are working on forming a network of their groups and activities beyond national borders. Since 1987 the 'Intercultural Summer Institute for Black Women's Studies' has been meeting every year, with black participants from all continents. In 1991 the hosts were the black German Women, and the seminars, which went on for several weeks, were held in Bielefeld, Frankfurt/Main and Berlin. The second conference of and for immigrants, black Germans, Jewish women and women living in exile, which took place the same year in Berlin, has to be mentioned as an additional positive example of white Christian secularized women showing their solidarity. Excluded from participating, a great many of them made an important contribution by providing rides, child care, places to sleep and monetary contributions. There can be no doubt: the global and national structures

---

20. Editors' note: *Grundgesetz*; see the discussion of Article 16a of the Basic Law in Chapter 1.

21. Quoted from Tissy Bruns, Klaus-Peter Klingelschmitt, 'Kein Wort der Scham im Bonner Kabinett' in *die tageszeitung*, August 28, 1992.

of dependence and the power relations within our own personal relationships, too, are frightening and destructive, but not at a standstill. We can
make changes!

Blues in Black-and-White

while still and again
some are being cut to pieces and divided and expelled,
those who are and always have been and are supposed to remain the others,
some of the truly others
still and again
declare themselves the only true blue ones
some of the truly others
still and again
declare war on us

it is a blues in Black-and-White
one third of the world
destroys in dance
the other
two thirds
they celebrate in white
we mourn in Black
it is a blues in Black-and-White
it is a blues

the re-united germany
re-celebrates itself in 1990
without immigrants refugees
jewish and black people . . .
it celebrates among close friends
it celebrates in white

but it is a blues in Black-and-White
it is a blues

the united germany
the united europe
the united states
celebrate 1992
the 500th anniversary of Columbus Day

500 years – expulsion, enslavement and genocide
in the americas
and in asia
and in africa

one third of the world unites
against the other two thirds
to the tune of racism, sexism and anti-semitism
they want to isolate us to erase
our history
or to shroud it in mystery
'til it is a mystery

it is a blues in Black-and-White
it is a blues

but we know what's going on – we know
one third of humanity celebrates in white
two thirds of humanity do not participate

12

East German Black*
Gabriele Willbold

EastGermanBlack
means isolation from black people
almost always

means white mothers with bluegreygreenbrown eyes
and light skin
almost always

means
black unknown fathers whose hands do not
protect, warm, comfort
almost always

EastGermanBlack

means
to give explanations for being here
most of the time

means
to speak German without an accent
in SaxonLowGermanVoigtlandBerlin dialect
most of the time

---

* 'Ostdeutsch Schwarz', from *Entfernte Verbindungen: Rassismus, Antisemitismus, Klassenunterdrückung*, eds Ika Hügel, Chris Lange, May Ayim, Ilona Bubeck, Gülsen Aktas and Dagmar Schultz (Berlin: Orlanda Frauenverlag, 1993) 233–235.

means
blondebrownblack
straight curly frizzy hair
most of the time

means
lightdark skin
freckles, sunburn, rosy scars
most of the time

EastGermanBlack

means
dance of the soul without rhythm in the blood
exoticism eroticism
often

means
of course to live BlackWhite
never checkered

means
to live now – Here
with open racist violence and colour-blindness

means
to speak Russian
and Mother'sTongue
and Father'sTongue
rarely

EastGermanBlack

means
to suffer with Thälmann
to know Brahms
to love black Beethoven
to revere black Pushkin
to experience the black Dumas
unrecognized from day to day

means
Young Pioneers and Blue Shirt[1]
Timur Batallion and Member of the Collective
of Socialist Work
almost always

means
to know the history of the German working class
and that of the brother nations[2]
and the Black Continent as a White Dot on the map
almost always

means
to be a child, chocolate kiss[3] and negro baby
man or woman *never*

means
negro, coloured, mulatto
but black German *never*

means
to be quiet
to keep quiet
to be unwanted

EastGermanBlack
I hear often
isn't this a kind of parody?

It is so German in *Coldland* . . .

1. The uniform of the FdJ, Free German Youth, the most important youth organization
in the GDR. The other names in this stanza also refer to mass organizations in the GDR.
2. This was the official way of referring to other socialist countries.
3. See note 8 on p. 103.

Part IV
Ethnic Germans from Eastern Europe: Strangers in Their Own Home

Aussiedler are defined legally as 'German citizens or members of the German people who before 8 May 1945 lived in the German areas in the East, formerly under foreign administration, Poland, the former Soviet Union, Czechoslovakia, Hungary, Romania, Yugoslavia, Danzig, Estonia, Latvia, Lithuania, Bulgaria, Albania or China and have left or will leave these countries after completion of the general procedures of expulsion'. The Federal Republic grants citizenship to those who can prove that they professed to belong to the German people in their home country, through origin, language, education or culture (*Bundesvertriebenen- und Flüchtlingsgesetz*, Article 6).[1]

Before the Second World War, 9 million Germans lived east of the rivers Oder and Neisse within the borders of the Reich. In addition, there were about 8.6 million east of the borders of the Reich. During and after the Second World War, more than 7 million of them either fled or were expelled, but, even after these massive migrations, there were still about 4.4 million ethnic Germans east of Oder and Neisse outside the new borders of Germany. From 1951 to 1988, another 1.6 million migrated to the Federal Republic. The influx of these so-called *Aussiedler* increased immensely in the late 1980s because the political climate east of the Iron Curtain had changed. Their numbers peaked at almost 400,000 in 1990 and decreased again afterwards.

The history of German settlements in eastern and south-eastern Europe goes back to the twelfth century when the so-called Siebenbürgen Saxons settled in the kingdom of Hungary. In the eighteenth and nineteenth centuries, other groups migrated to the area, which then belonged to the Habsburg Empire. Among these were the so-called Banat Swabians, who came from southern Germany and settled in the Banat area. Starting in the 18th century Germans also settled in Russia, invited by Catherine II and Alexander I.

---

1. For history and current problems, see Barbara Malchow, Keyumars Tayebi and Ulrike Brand, *Aussiedler in der Bundesrepublik. Die fremdem Deutschen* (Reinbek: Rowohlt, 1990) and Klaus J. Bade, *Ausländer, Aussiedler, Asyl. Eine Bestandsaufnahme* (Munich: Beck, 1994), 147–74. For a brief English-language account, see Nora Räthzel, 'Germany: One Race, One Nation?' *Race and Class* 23.3 (1990): 31–48.

The fate of German settlements in eastern Europe was considerably changed by the First World War and the end of the Habsburg Empire and even more so by the Second World War and Hitler's expansionist politics. In the aftermath of the First World War, the Banat area, and with it the German minority, was divided between Hungary, Romania and Yugoslavia. In the course of the Second World War, Germans in the Soviet Union lost their rights; they were deported as collaborators and kept as prisoners. The fate of Romanian-Germans was slightly different since Romania was Germany's ally until 1944; this changed after the cease-fire with the allies in 1944 when Romania declared war on Germany. After the war the 75,000 Romanian-Germans who had served in the German army lost their Romanian citizenship and did not return home. In addition a large number of ethnic Germans in Romania were deported to do forced labour in the Soviet-Union; all members of the minority lost their political rights and property, and they had to give up their schools to the state, but they were able to continue instruction in German.

The repression of German minorities in their home countries, together with poor economic and social conditions, the desire to join their families in the Federal Republic and to live as Germans among Germans as well as the longing to participate in the wealth of the West led to the most recent mass migration from the East. By 1989, about half of the Romanian-German population had left for the Federal Republic, despite the fact that migration was not always easy. Ceauşescu , for instance, asked the German government for considerable amounts of hard currency in return for every ethnic German who was allowed to leave Romania. But, with reform and revolution in the 1980s, emigration became easier and the mass exodus continued after the fall of the dictator Ceauşescu and his regime. Today, there are only a few ethnic Germans left in Romania, mainly old people who don't want to move any more.

For many of those who left the arrival in the Federal Republic has, however, not been as easy as expected, life as Germans among Germans not as uncomplicated as hoped for. Often they feel like strangers at home; for they do not have as much in common with their fellow Germans as expected. If they speak German, they speak it with a different accent; they think and behave differently because they have been shaped by a socialization under totalitarian regimes. Their sense of German identity and history, furthermore, is often nostalgic and perceived by many Germans as *Deutschtümelei* or Germanomania.

This chapter focuses on two very prolific writers, who grew up as part of the German community in Banat, Romania, and now live in Berlin. Herta Müller, who was born in 1953 in Nitzkydorf, studied German and

Romanian, and worked as a translator and as a German teacher before becoming a writer. Richard Wagner, who was born in 1952 in Lowrin, also studied German, and worked as a German teacher and journalist in Temeswar. Both were members of the *Aktionsgruppe Banat*, a literary and political group of young writers who were critical both of the Romanian dictatorship and of the German community in Romania.[2] They were both persecuted by the Romanian secret service *Securitate*. In 1984 Richard Wagner, Herta Müller and other members of the group were forbidden to write and publish, a circumstance which led many of them to apply for an exit visa. Müller and Wagner left Romania in 1987.

2. For an account of Romanian-German literature and the political involvement of its authors, see *Nachruf auf die rumäniendeutsche Literatur*, ed. Wilhelm Solms (Marburg: Hitzeroth, 1990).

–13–

The Identity of a Minority is Reflected in its Language*

Richard Wagner

It all begins with an artificial word: Romanian-German. This word refers to Germans living in the territory of contemporary Romania. But hardly any of those designated thus would ever have used this word to refer to themselves; rather, they would have referred to themselves as Banat Swabians or Siebenbürgen Saxons, the two largest groups of the German minority in Romania. Romanian-German is a political concept, which describes something that has existed since 1919 as a result of peace treaties after the First World War. In their youth, my grandparents were still citizens of the Austro-Hungarian empire, Hungarian-Germans. Overnight, without leaving their village in Banat, they turned into Romanian-Germans. If the village had been 70 kilometres further west, they would have become Yugoslavian-Germans. In the peace treaties, the Banat was divided between Romania and Yugoslavia. When my ancestors in the eighteenth century followed the call of the Habsburgs to the Banat, an area which had been liberated from the Turks, Vienna administered this area directly; its official language was German, and Temeswar was an attractive Habsburg provincial town. That was a long time ago.

The attitude of a traditional minority is always one of defence or resistance. Ethnocentrically, it defends its own, that which is threatened and which it perceives to be threatened. Its own, however, is what they brought with them, their origin. Origin is understood as the foundation of identity. A minority is caught in the contradiction of origin and the place where it lives. Culturally, a minority always refers back to its country of origin. The cultural centre for Romanian-Germans was Germany, in the following order: the Germany of the 1920s, the Third Reich, the Federal Republic. Initially, Vienna was still somewhat attractive. Nationalism in

---

* 'Der Spiegel der Identität einer Minderheit ist ihre Sprache', from *Mythendämmerung* (Berlin: Rotbuch Verlag, 1993), 103–10.

central and eastern Europe affected the German minorities in these areas as well. Nineteenth-century ideas were engulfing reality. Fascism is also a product of the peace treaties following the First World War, which were based on the idea of the nation state. The political principle of the time was revision, the cultural principle the rebirth of the nation. The German minorities in the east performed the same business as at the centre, its mother country; and this was in no way different from what the surrounding peoples were also doing.

The Banat Swabians lived in the isolation of a traditional, rural minority for a long time. They did not succeed in creating their own intelligentsia. The bourgeoisie in the administrative centre Temeswar was shaped by Austria and was only minimally connected with the Swabian villages. Most of the intellectuals produced by this peasant people left for Hungary for careers and prestige, but also in order to escape intellectual death in the provincial atmosphere, particularly after the settlement between Austria and Hungary in 1867. At the turn of the century, Budapest was an attractive metropolis, which, because of its creativity, attracted intellectuals from all directions. But it was also the time of disastrous Hungarian nationalism, which was striving for an independent Hungarian nation state within the empire and which made extreme cuts in the rights of minorities. These Hungarian attempts contributed greatly to the destruction of the multi-cultural balance in eastern central Europe. Before the First World War, there were no German-language schools left in the Swabian villages in Banat. The children were forced by overzealous teachers to speak Hungarian even during break; and my grandmother still told us decades later that as a punishment she had to write the sentence: 'Nem szabad nemétul beszélni' (I am not allowed to speak German) a hundred times.

Thus, the unwished-for move to the new Romanian state protected the Banat Swabians from Magyarization and pushed their striving for emancipation forward. The Romanian state, which had doubled its territory, was obliged by the peace treaties to grant wide-ranging con-cessions to its minorities, which made up almost 30 per cent of the population. In actuality, this state was soon in constant conflict with these minorities because, true to its conception of itself as nation state, it tried to undermine their rights again and again.

The identity of a minority is reflected in its language. It is only possible to stabilize this language through cultural background in one's own schools. With the exception of the first years after the Second World War, when they were not officially recognized as a minority (1945–9), Romanian-Germans always had schools in which the language of instruction was German. During the time between the wars, these schools were partly run by the church and partly by the state; by and large, the attitudes of the minority were propagated in them.

But language alone is not sufficient to constitute a minority's identity; it has to be possible for this language to become the instrument of the minority's public sphere. Particularly in this century, minorities have strived again and again to create and extend their own public sphere. The minority's public sphere emerged firstly as a cultural one. In the time between the wars, besides schools, Romanian-Germans had their own newspapers, magazines, their own literature. These received their ideas mainly from Germany or related them to Germany. Improved possibilities for communication also began to break down the Banat Swabians' isolation. Their encounter with modernity, however, became an encounter with the Third Reich, which turned German minorities into its Fifth Column.

The cultural public sphere is only part of the public sphere as a whole; the second sphere that minorities have wanted access to is the administrative one. To different degrees, they have strived for self-government; and self-government has always been at the centre of the formation of a new state; this is not possible in the case of a minority. Thus, minorities have been confronted again and again with their limitations.

The longing for a state remains. In the case of the Banat Swabians this manifested itself once: after the First World War, some of their political representatives suggested an independent Banat state with a proportionate German minority, a formation of four peoples, of Germans, Serbs, Romanians and Hungarians, another Switzerland illusion, which the victorious powers ignored. The Romanian-Germans became a state within the state because of the general political situation of the Second World War. The Volksgruppe of Andreas Schmidt, which had been brought into line ideologically by the Nazis, received special status in a Romania governed by the self-declared Marshal and ally of Hitler Antonescu. This status even allowed the group its own police force. Thus, a culture dominated by the police emerged, which drifted into disaster in September 1944 after the change of power in the Allies' favour in Romania. Stalinism, which was instituted by the Red Army, took care of the rest. Looking back, one can say that the combination of National Socialism and Stalinism destroyed the *Lebensraum* of German minorities in Eastern Europe.

When my ancestors went to the Banat area in the eighteenth century, they proceeded into voluntary isolation. They were emigrants. The course of world history deprived them of their isolation 150 years later. Romanian-Germans got involved with the world; and the result was that my father's generation participated in the Second World War, with all its consequences.

The emancipation's last stop was the Waffen-SS. Afterwards came collective guilt, and for many, both men and women, five years of forced labour in Stalin's Soviet Union.

To live in isolation also means to live under the illusion of being the majority. This illusion was destroyed by contact with the modern world. This contact suddenly made one's identity seem like an option. One thought of it as an option of language, of culture; and finally it was a political option, National Socialism, which captivated the minority.

New isolation ordered by Stalinism was an involuntary one, which was never accepted by the minority. By total expropriation, which Stalinism dictated to the Romanian-Germans, the foundations of their existence were taken away. They were emigrants; they always had a pronounced economic self-confidence. They possessed a certain economic self-sufficiency, which also granted their economic identity continued existence. Without this economic self-sufficiency, they lost their (self-)confidence.

In vain, Stalinism instituted German-language media and schools and talked constantly about the important contribution of national minorities in building socialism. Neither the media nor the schools belonged to the minority. They belonged to the totalitarian state, and they had been instituted for the minority for propaganda purposes. They were institutions of re-education. Their language was not the language of the minority. Even though it was German, it did not address issues the minority felt strongly about. Stalinism had recognized the cultural significance of the minority's institutions; it wanted to use them for intellectual seduction. The content of these institutions, however, was always ambiguous. They certainly caused plenty of harm in people's minds, but at the same time they granted the minority the survival of linguistic self-confidence. Without these institutions, the Romanian-Germans' language would have been limited to home and the street; the language would have regressed into dialect; to a great extent, people would have lost their identity; whole realms would have become foreign-language realms; and today the fate of Romanian-Germans would not be any different from that of Germans in Poland or Hungary, who ended up speaking hardly any German at all. Under Stalinism, Romanian-Germans did not have their own public sphere any more, but they kept the German language.

This was a basic prerequisite for the development of the German minority since the sixties pragmatism of national communist politics in Romania. Back then, a new generation was striving to modernize the Romanian-German minority culture. It would take two generations to achieve this. This work, which also tried to establish a new public sphere, was destroyed by Ceaușescu's dictatorship, which sealed the fate of the minority through absurd repression and emigration to the Federal Republic in exchange for ransom. The revolution in December 1989 did not change the decision to emigrate; rather, the political and economic consequences of this revolution confirmed to Romanian-Germans that they should leave the country.

In the 1960s, we Romanian-Germans possessed an antiquated language, a written language. This language had been dead for a long time; writers of the time lamented that it was a mummified language. The culture of a minority often does not transgress boundaries of folklore. Thus, it hardly develops any creativity, particularly without a public sphere. Innovations are adopted from the centre, but 1950s Stalinism had cut off the Romanian-Germans from their centre. Travel was impossible; long stays in the Federal Republic unthinkable; no publications made it into the country; the only bridge was the radio, with which one could secretly listen to West German stations. Books came from the GDR, but the GDR was quite correctly perceived as the bridgehead of Stalinist power.

The language and reality of a minority are not identical. The minority's language only describes inadequately the shifts of reality a minority participates in. In the 1960s and 1970s, there was a confused debate in Romanian-German literature about the language of dialogue in prose. The most important texts of this debate were often poems, for political, but also linguistic, reasons.

The beginnings of modern Romanian-German literature in the 1960s and early 1970s are imitations, imitations mainly of contemporary German literature. In some respects, at times we lived in a simulation of the centre. Language itself developed as imitation. In the Romanian-German media, a strange mixture of old Romanian-German, West-German and GDR-German came to be used. Austrian words and loan translations from Romanian glittered in between. A minority's language has gaps, particularly in the institutional realm. In colloquial language, names for state institutions were often taken from the language of the state; particularly the dialects were infiltrated by Romanian designations. These words, however, never stayed in the language for long; they were present because of trends. My grandmother, who hardly knew any Romanian, in her old age still said *Varoshaza* and *Ovoda* for city hall and kindergarten. To me, the child in Romania after the war, these words seemed strange.

To the member of a minority, language proves his cultural belonging. Language is his most important sanctuary from the pressure to assimilate. In language, he thinks he is secure, but language also makes him insecure. He constantly feels that it is slipping out of his hands. On the one hand, it is a most private thing, on the other hand, he is forever afraid he might lose it. In contrast to the majority, for a minority today language is the visible expression of an existential threat. Much more often than for the majority, language is not just communication; the communication is often full of holes. The endangered words turn into poems. This is another reason why poetry predominates. Referring to the Federal Republic as the centre uncovered the contradictions. The contradictions between East and West, real existing Socialism and free market economy. The Romanian-German's head was spinning. Words from both Germanies, Romania, Habsburg painted a confusing picture. Romanian-Germans were forced into modernity; at the same time, urbanization of their world was contorted by Stalinism. Modernity made the member of the minority realize his loneliness, which the others perceive as an inadequate existence. More and more often he is exposed to bilingualism. There are more and more experiences in the other language. The member of the minority defends himself against contact with the other. Entry into the German armies of the Second World War was also an escape from the Romanian army.

Again and again, those in power tried to break up the minority's cohesion. Under Ceauşescu's dictatorship, academics were forced to work in other parts of the country; in the 1980s, an (illegal) hiring freeze applying to members of the minority in German Departments was ordered. Already at the beginning of the 1970s, it was said at the Temeswar University that German Studies was not an institution of the German minority. In fact, students of German in Temeswar at the time were almost exclusively Romanian-Germans; German Studies was the secret university of the minority. The struggle of the national communist powers against the minority's cohesion went so far as ordering the playing of Romanian melodies on call-in radio shows and to forbidding the printing of Bundesliga soccer results in the *Neue Banater Zeitung* which was published in Temeswar. It was also forbidden to use German place names in the media.

After the 1970s, the dictator Ceauşescu thought the problem of national minorities was solved; he was striving for a cultural and social melting-pot, for which his ideologues invented the concept 'socialist nation'. After the expropriation by Stalinism, the cultural identity of the Romanian-Germans was definitely called into question by Ceauşescu's National Communism. However, since the dictator also sold his Germans to the Federal Republic in exchange for hard currency, origin seemed the only way out of the dictatorship. More and more people took advantage of it. They came and are still coming into the Federal Republic, where they are undergoing an inconspicuous process of assimilation, called integration. Through emigration, the minority is cancelled out in the centre, which it longed to relate to from far away for such a long time. My generation is probably the last which still has the Banat accent. A whole context for a way of life is in the process of becoming memory.

The Apparent Patience of the Line
Richard Wagner

I wake up; I hear steps. The steps are in the stairwell. Insecure steps. Somebody's going downstairs, holding the handrail. It's not day yet. It won't be day for a long time, and the steps are steps in the dark. I know there is no power. I try it anyway. I feel for the reading lamp, turn the switch. Nothing. During the day, they turn the power off, and at night they do it anyway. Somebody is walking down the stairs, somebody is leaving the house. I feel for the torch. It's always on the table ready to use. I use its light to look for my watch. It's three thirty. I think, he is going out for milk. And already it seems I can hear bottles clinking.

When talking with friends, I say our apartment is strategically located. We live on the fifth floor of a new building. It's a high-rise building with ten floors. Built from prefabricated sections. Tower block, it's called here. The narrow building bulges out in the middle, there is a slight curve. When people talk about our building, they say: Oh, I know! the crooked building, that's where you live. But aren't you afraid it's going to collapse at some point? No, I say, we aren't afraid. The building has a steel construction. It's welded together. Whether it's crooked or straight doesn't matter. We really aren't afraid. We live in a two-room apartment. We were lucky with the apartment. The building was built fourteen years ago. Therefore, we still have parquet floors and large windows. In new apartments the windows are small, and the occupant has to put down his own parquet floor. This cuts down on building costs. The rooms are tiny, and it's never very light in these apartments. In order to be able to read, you need the light of a lamp. But there is no power. Once I saw an apartment without any doors between the rooms. Only an entrance door outside. You walked from the kitchen into the living room, and from one room to the other through the door openings. If you wanted doors you had to put them in

---

* 'Die scheinbare Geduld der Schlange', from *Mythendämmerung* (Berlin: Rotbuch Verlag, 1993), 127–34.

yourself. But how can you get a door? By knowing the right people, by bribing them, with a lot of patience, you could even get a door.

Our apartment is strategically located. When you look out of a bedroom window or from the balcony of the living-room, you can see the rear of a grocery store, a vegetable store, a cake shop and a bar. The stores are situated in the building across the street. Down there, delivery trucks drive up. So we are in a strategic position. When something is delivered, we immediately know. My hearing is very good. I hear bottles clinking, and I know immediately: Now they are unloading milk. Now they are unloading beer. Milk is unloaded at night. You can hear the clinking of the metal containers while you are asleep. In front of the store, there's already a long, quiet line of people. The store is still closed. People usually stand in rows of three, the empty milk bottles in their bags. You have to bring along a returnable bottle; otherwise you can't buy milk. There are people who never leave their house without such bottles and yoghurt containers. The line passes the store, the vegetable store, the cake shop and the bar; it extends as far as the street corner.

The people stand and wait. Nobody says anything. Sometimes, somebody whispers to her neighbour. Everybody is in anticipation. How much will they deliver today? Will it last until it's my turn? There is never enough for all of them. Milk is distributed. Returnable bottle on the counter, money. Full bottle returned. Everybody gets one bottle, two sometimes. Some stand in line several times. The bottles are sealed with thin aluminium. Many are open. You have to look closely at the bottle neck, to see whether it's chipped. Once there were splinters of glass in our milk, a woman said. What am I supposed to do, I have to sell everything, the saleswoman said. It's the same with the beer bottles. When I open one, I immediately run my finger over the inner rim of the bottle neck, look at my finger. No splinter. Or maybe one? If a splinter is shining on my finger, I strain the beer through a cheese cloth. A young woman looks at her watch nervously. I have to go to work, she says, I'll be late again. But what am I supposed to do with the children? They need the milk after all. Three more containers to go, the saleswoman calls. It is like a countdown. Gone, the saleswoman says. The line dissolves immediately.

For a while, milk stamps were used in our city. I was entitled to three litres of milk a month. I went to the store with my stamps, and I had to show my ID. Then there was no milk, and we still had the stamps. At times they were blue, at others red. A large L was on them. L like *Lapte*, milk. We looked at the L, we had the stamps. Then there weren't any stamps any more. Only if you stood in line in front of the store all night did you have a chance. We did not stand in line. Therefore, we hadn't had any milk in six months.

At six o'clock, I went back to sleep. I was cold. I'd woken up from the cold, or from the steps in the stairwell, or from the clinking of bottles. I'd woken up, and I'd been cold. I put on my sweater again. Then I went back to sleep. Fortunately, we have these heavy comforters. Last winter, we bought heavy down comforters. My mother-in-law brought them from the country. Somehow, she managed to get the feathers. I pull the comforter up to my nose, and it's like it used to be when I was a child. Only that there is no fire in the stove. And I can't hear my parents' voices in the room next door; they are gone. Our apartment has central heating. I put my hand on the radiator. The radiator is cold. The radiator is freezing cold. Every morning, when I wake up, I get out of bed and walk over to the thermometer. I have a thermometer on the wall in my room. I check the temperature. Twelve degrees, I say loudly. Yesterday, it was still thirteen degrees. The radiator is cold. I decide to put on my hat; I wrap the scarf around my neck. The radiator cools down the room, my neighbour says angrily. We should take them off and put them outside. He's obtained an electric space heater. But nobody's supposed to know this. When there's power, he turns it on. But since we've had the decree on the standardization of electricity consumption, he can hardly use his heater any more anyway. The electricity meter shows his consumption, and when he exceeds the norm, well, then . . . He curses. People say that a commission goes from door to door and controls whether you are running additional heaters. It's only a rumour. Yesterday they said on TV that you should insulate the windows properly so that no heat is lost. They claimed people were wasting energy.

I turn the switch. There is power. I look at the watch. I go into the bathroom. Since the bathroom doesn't have a window, we keep candles in the bathroom, in case there's no power. Our stock of candles is rather large; our West German friends sent us the candles. You can't buy them; if you're lucky you can find them in church. Once we had a baptism candle. We've a large stock of candles and a large stock of toilet paper. There was a time when you couldn't get any toilet paper. We used paper napkins then, and when they were used up, we used writing paper. We had a large stock of writing paper because of our literary projects. We didn't want to use newspapers. I open the faucet, I can hear a noise. A thin stream comes out of the pipe, and I put my finger in it; cold. There's that noise again; I open the hot water faucet all the way; it's only dripping. But now we're supposed to have warm water. From six to eight in the morning and from eight to eleven at night. But it isn't running. Everybody's faucet is open, and there's not enough water pressure to reach the fifth floor.

I go into the kitchen. I turn on the stove. Usually, the power is turned off at nine o'clock. We have a gas stove with an electric hot-plate, dating from way back. I haven't seen anything like it in the stores for years. We used to cook with gas. Gas from the bottle. Gas bottles are allocated after long waiting periods or you can get them on the black market for three months' salary. The bottles have to be refilled twice a month. Twice a month, the delivery truck drove up. You had to wait three months for your order. Or you talked to the gasman. A hundred lei, and the thing was all set. This is how it was until a year ago. Now it's almost impossible to get gas. Once the truck drives up, half the town gathers immediately. Mr C., the gasman, is the hero of the day. He has a job which allows him to build connections. You can arrange a lot with a bottle of gas. Mr C. lacks for nothing. He stands next to his car in his blue jacket, smiling, as the women from our neighbourhood all talk to him at the same time. He lifts a full bottle from the bed of his truck and picks up an empty one. Women's hands inconspicuously put money in his pockets. He pretends that he finds this annoying. Sometimes, he even carries a bottle into a house. To where the saleswoman from the grocery store lives, and to where his son's maths teacher lives. He has high hopes for his son. Everybody pesters the gasman. The gasman gets annoyed. The crowd is getting bigger and bigger. No, I can't give you any gas without an order form. Don't insist; it's pointless. Take your money back immediately. The gasman is standing on the running-board of his car; he looks hunted. Oh, a policeman. What does he want? Needs something for his relatives. The gasman only distributes legally now. He carries the bottles into the house; he keeps an eye on the policeman. He has to find out what the policeman wants.

I've made the tea; I'm sitting at the kitchen table. The burner is turned on; I put a pot of water on the stove. This keeps me a bit warmer. The kitchen is small. I've closed the kitchen door. When the morning sun shines through the kitchen window, the window-pane turns warm. I put my hands on it.

I decide to leave the house. I do my usual rounds. I'm a writer. I see all of this. I haven't published anything in a long time. I just look at everything. I'm writing less and less. I don't write anything any more.

I lock the apartment. The neighbour from across the hall steps out of the elevator. She's carrying a shopping bag. Downstairs, you can get frozen chicken, she says out of breath. If you hurry, you'll still get one. Don't forget your ID, she calls after me. I go down the stairs. I don't use the elevator. The power can be turned off at any moment, and then I'd be stuck in the elevator. Last week, somebody was stuck in the elevator for three hours, until the power was on again. I leave the house; I see the line behind the store. Approximately eighty people, I estimate. I walk past them. At the bus stop, people wait freezing. Too many, I say. Who knows when the bus will come; and people will already be hanging on to the outside of it; you'll never get on. I prefer to walk. It's cold, but dry. I'm lucky, I live in a manageable city. I live in a part of town from which you can walk to the centre in half an hour. In Bucharest, for instance, I'd be lost. You have to live in a place from where you can walk to the centre, because only in the centre do you still have the opportunity of finding something, of being able to shop. I don't say, I went shopping; I say, I found something, and, whatever happens, I have to get this and that . . .

I step into a grocery store on the way. On the shelves, the usual. Preserved fruit and cans of fish. They have been sitting around everywhere for years. Most of it has probably been spoiled for quite some time. Shelved goods, so that the store isn't empty. Five or six old people are chatting in front of the sausage counter. They've been waiting since this morning. There are three smoked hocks on the hook. I can see the toes. Maybe they'll still bring salami, the old people are saying. Who they mean by 'they', nobody knows. The delivery people or the government. Doesn't matter. It's the same. 'They' have taken everything from us. Maybe 'they' will bring something after all. That's too uncertain for me. I'm not patient. You'll pay for it. Nevertheless, I look around the store. On one shelf, there is sugar, oil, flour. I can't buy this. I can only look at it. Sugar, oil, flour are rationed. I'm eligible for half a kilogram of sugar, half a litre of cooking oil, and one kilogram of flour a month. I can only buy this in the store I am assigned to. My name and address are on a list there. And whenever I shop there, it's recorded. At times they say they don't have cooking oil at the moment, or flour is not available this month. Previously, butter was included as well. A hundred grams. Now butter isn't rationed anymore, you can't get it at all. And officially, nothing is rationed. Officially, it is called an 'order'. I have a permanent order in my store, and I pick up what I 'ordered' every month.

At eleven, I'm in the centre, at the newspaper stand. There's a long line in front of the door. The sports magazine hasn't arrived yet. I pass the people, ask for yesterday's papers. Yes, they're here. I buy two papers from yesterday and one from the day before yesterday, which only arrived today. It's not exceptional that the papers are yesterday's. There's nothing current in them anyway. Why do I buy them? Because I study the regime, I say. Maybe out of habit as well. I'm a writer; I can't stop it. Most people only buy the newspaper for the sports pages or the paper itself. Packing paper is rare.

In the past I used to go to the cinema in the morning. At eleven. I watched the film and then stepped out into the brightness of midday. But then they stopped heating the cinemas; you sat there wearing a coat and gloves, and while the adventure was developing on the screen, you were getting cold feet. And then there was no power any more, and the morning shows were cancelled.

My mother-in-law lives in the country. She has a house and a garden. In the garden, she plants the necessities: potatoes, vegetables, maize for the pigs. Every year, she raises one pig. Half of it's for herself, half of it's for us. Therefore, we have sausage and ham. Don't have to go looking for salami every day. Which doesn't contain any meat anyway, as people say. Only soy. In the autumn, the community commission went to visit my mother-in-law. She had to deliver so much maize, so much chicken, so many potatoes, at government-regulated prices, almost for free that is. If she didn't deliver, she wasn't going to get any more bread. Only those who work are entitled to bread. An old Romanian saying. From the lips of the *apparatchiks* it's an obscene compilation of words. Every day, my mother-in-law stands in line for two hundred grams of bread. This is less than she got when she was deported to Russia after the war, she says. Last time, when she went for oil and sugar, she had to buy a solidarity button. International Solidarity Fund was written on it.

I've prepared everything. The pressure-cooker's on the burner. I'm waiting for the power to come on. At two thirty, I hear the refrigerator humming. That's the sign. Power is on. In an hour, we can eat.

My wife's at school. She's standing at the board, wearing her coat, writing. The children, also in their coats, are sitting at their desks copying what she's writing on the board. At around four, she stops. It's too dark to continue writing. She's not allowed to turn on the light. They are saving energy. The principal walks around the school, making sure that no lights are on. He's satisfied, no window is lit up.

At night, we're at home. We haven't been out at night for a long time. Where would we go? The streets are pitch-black, the buses don't run any more, the restaurants are overcrowded, and they close at nine. What would we do there? The music is so loud you can't hear yourself think, you might be able to eat ocean fish and drink white wine full of chemicals. We stay at home. We watch TV. We watch Yugoslavian TV. With an antenna on the roof, you can receive it in our city. Romanian TV only lasts two hours. Ceauşescu on the news, Ceauşescu in reports, and finally the Ceauşescu who singers sing about in song programs. We stopped watching this a long time ago. We watch Yugoslavian TV. Then we go to sleep.

–15–

Multicultural*

Richard Wagner

There is talk in this country. The talk says: Come here, everybody, we want to establish a multicultural society. I am from the Banat area. It is located in a region where three countries meet: Romania, Yugoslavia, Hungary. Until 1919, Banat belonged to the Habsburg Empire. I experienced the east central European variation of a multicultural region there. There were always several languages around me. The towns and villages I knew were inhabited by members of different peoples. They lived there as if it had always been this way. They worked together, and they lived next to each other. Often separated by streets, separated by festivities and traditions. But they lived in the same town, with several churches, and in a precarious balance, which was disturbed again and again by the politics of the nation states from the outside, first by Hungary, now by Ceauşescu's Romania. But they lived there, and many of them could communicate in more than one language. It was always the distant national centre which pressured them into disastrous homogeneity. I don't know whether these experiences can be transferred. Multiculturalism does not emerge over night; it takes time for it to find its proper course. You know it is for real when you don't have to talk about it. But in Germany? Here it's not even natural for foreign films to be shown in the original language with subtitles. Germans don't have any real experiences with minorities. They have lived with themselves and by themselves. How many Germans speak the languages of their foreign fellow-citizens and not only a foreign language like English?

I came to the Federal Republic two years ago; I belonged to the German minority in Romania, the Banat Swabians; and here, I have been subsumed into the group of ethnic Germans from Eastern Europe (*Aussiedler*), even though there is an essential difference: I have been an opponent of Ceauşescu's dictatorship, and I have worked as such. Since I have always

---

* 'Multikulturell', from *Mythendämmerung* (Berlin: Rotbuch Verlag, 1993), 135–9.

seen myself as German, even in Romania – German is my mother tongue, and as a writer, I have always written in German – I wanted to become a German citizen.

In order to get German citizenship, I needed a certificate of expulsion (*Vertriebenenausweis*), and in order to get this certificate, I had to prove that I was of German origin. In the forms I had to fill out, there was the following category: belonging to the former German armed forces (*Wehrmacht*), Waffen-SS, police, Reich Labour Service (*Reichsarbeitsdienst*) or similar organizations. Membership in the Waffen-SS proves German origin. It doesn't prove anything else. In Berlin, in the Marienfelde transition camp, an official said to me: If you had written what you wrote in German in Romanian, you would have been persecuted just the same. I said, yes. He said, if that were true, I was not entitled to the *Vertriebenenausweis* and therefore not to German citizenship either. The latter I did receive, however, after one year and lengthy investigations by internal affairs.

Ethnic Germans from Eastern Europe are foreigners, too, even if many of them don't like to see themselves as such. Among certain groups of German intellectuals, one encounters a dislike of those ethnic Germans from Eastern Europe (*Aussiedler*) based on their specific view of the world. Recently, this dislike has been extended to East Germans who moved to the West (*Übersiedler*). The common opinion in these circles is: *Aussiedler* are reactionary. Therefore, they are supposed to stay where they are. However, this attitude merely reflects the repression of German history.

I think the Federal Republic has responsibilities towards the *Aussiedler*, not only because of its constitution, but also because of its history. This history is significant because the *Lebensraum* of the German minority in eastern central Europe, of those who are coming here as *Aussiedler* now, was destroyed by the combined effort of National Socialism and Stalinism. The Federal Republic's Basic Law is the result of this history, and its article referring to the *Aussiedler* is just as important as the one referring to asylum.

'Just stay over there (in the East)' doesn't mean anything other than 'Go over there (to the East).' One of the most cynical aspects of our time is that parts of the West German intelligentsia are preoccupied with the future of the idea of socialism and the concomitant fear of upheavals in Eastern Europe. These people think things should remain the way they were, in the stagnation of real existing socialism. It is a dream this intelligentsia is dreaming, but one that it does not want to experience. However, these same German intellectuals are only too willing to accept that the lives of millions of people have been shattered by this experiment.

All this just for the sake of their world-view.

Talk of the multicultural society has also called into debate the Federal Republic as a country of immigration. Well, the Federal Republic has always been a country of immigration. Fugitives, people expelled from their homeland, guest workers, asylum seekers, *Übersiedler* and *Aussiedler* are proof of this.

But the Federal Republic has never understood itself as such and consequently never acknowledged it. And stating it now does not mean realizing it. Rather, it functions as a precondition for boundary demarcation. The idea is to define oneself as a country of immigration in order to prescribe quotas of immigration. The progressive intelligentsia would like quotas for *Aussiedler*. But then one would also institute quotas for guest workers, for asylum seekers, and finally for GDR Germans. For every group in society has its ugly foreigner whom it would like to get rid of. The *Aussiedler* represents for one group what the asylum seeker is for another. Floods of asylum seekers and waves of *Aussiedler* are telling words. And there is a silent consensus in this society. It is essential not to lose one's wealth. For the country's wealth is perceived as a guarantee of one's economic security. The rest of the world consists of economic refugees.

Talk of a multicultural society is the talk of the progressive new middle class, which has built its (post-modern) buildings on the ruins of the ideologies of 1968. Talk of a multicultural society is talk about the good foreigner. But often it only means that a few enthusiastic people can't take their eyes off a beautiful woman from Abyssinia or find black children really cute. Going to the Turkish vendor to buy vegetables, to the Greek or Italian place to eat, is this what multicultural means?

Foreigners don't just add colour; they are part of society. Foreigners are not better than native citizens. They also share the bad characteristics of the natives, from where they themselves are the natives. Most foreigners (*Aussiedler*, guest workers, Germans from the GDR, the so-called *Übersiedler*) are characterized by the pronounced mentality of the emigrant. They are preoccupied with work and settling down, many want to assimilate quickly, not be conspicuous. No prerequisites for solidarity. Egoism writ large.

There is no one foreigner. There are those foreigners who have lived here for a long time already. There is the Greek restaurant owner who declares he doesn't let any foreigners into his restaurant. There are the *Aussiedler*, who are offended when they are called foreigners; they are diffusely German, and it is their tragedy that they are against foreigners, against asylum seekers. There are *Übersiedler* who are against *Aussiedler*, particularly against those from Poland; and I shouldn't forget the Eastern European asylum seekers who argue in favour of sending their African colleagues home and point to their European origin as justification for their own right to stay.

You don't qualify as West German if you have a West German passport, but only if you have a West German past. As long as this is true, the Federal Republic does not have the normalcy of a country of immigration.

In the current situation, it would be necessary to give citizenship to all foreigners who live and work here permanently. But it shouldn't be compulsory. It would be necessary to accept dual citizenship, as has been tolerated quietly in the case of many ethnic Germans from Eastern Europe. I myself still hold Romanian citizenship, not voluntarily however, but because I refuse to sign a declaration of loyalty for the dictator Ceauşescu. Ethnic Germans from Romania sign this declaration of loyalty and are silent.

When I was handed the naturalization document, I also had to sign a form that declared that I was aware of the continuation of my former citizenship. Among other things, it said: 'The authorities of the other state, whose citizenship I still hold, are, at any time on their territory, entitled to treat me as if I held its citizenship. In such a case, for example, their authorities could prevent me from leaving.'

A prerequisite for dual citizenship, however, would be that all other affected nations are accessible for Germans with dual citizenship. This would be a preliminary stage towards a European framework which exceeds the consensus of nation states.

In addition to citizenship, foreigners should be granted minority rights, if they want them. These would include, for example, accredited schools in their own language.

But it is most important, I think, to let them live the way they want to live, and not to constantly give them well-meaning advice.

For a long time, it was fashionable to denounce the Habsburg Empire. The east central European intelligentsia has looked at this empire differently, let's say in a more subtle way. This intelligentsia is often dismissed as nostalgic. Those who dismiss them mockingly, I've noticed, are often Germans and Russians. Central Europe, they say and wave it aside, as if it was the Capuchin crypt and not an idea which they are confronted with, but a musty smell rising up.

Is there really any need for a multicultural society?

I conclude with an ambiguous remark:

Maybe I'm a foreigner (*Ausländer*) who wants to be a native (*Inländer*), but one who is different from you.

16

The Funeral Speech*
Herta Müller

At the train station, the relatives ran alongside the steaming train. With every step they moved their arms up in the air and waved.

A young man was standing behind the train window. The window-pane reached up to his armpits. He was holding a bouquet of dilapidated white flowers in front of his chest. His face was rigid.

A young woman carried an inert child out of the train station. The woman had a hunchback.

The train drove into the war.

I turned off the TV.

Father was in a coffin in the middle of the room. There were so many pictures on the walls that you couldn't see the wall any more.

In one picture, father was half the size of the chair which he was holding on to.

He was wearing a dress and standing on crooked legs covered with baby fat. His head was the size of a pear and bald.

In another picture, father was a bridegroom. Only half of his chest was visible. The other half was covered by a bouquet of dilapidated white flowers, which mother was holding in her hand. Their heads were so close together that their earlobes touched.

In a different picture, father was standing, bolt upright, in front of a fence. There was snow beneath his boots. The snow was so white that father was standing in empty space. He was holding his hand above his head in greeting. There were runes on his jacket collar.

In a picture next to that, father was carrying a hoe on his shoulder. Behind him, there was a maize plant which rose into the sky. Father was wearing a hat on his head. The hat cast a broad shadow, covering father's face.

* 'Die Grabrede', from *Niederungen* (Berlin: Rotbuch Verlag, 1984), 7–12.

In the next picture, father was sitting at the wheel of a truck. The truck was loaded with cows. Father drove the cows to the slaughterhouse every week. Father's face was narrow with hard edges.

In all the pictures, father was paralysed in the middle of a gesture. In all the pictures, father looked as if he didn't know what to do next. But father always knew what to do next. This is why these pictures were false. Because of so many false pictures, because of all his false faces, the room had turned cold. I wanted to get up from my chair, but my dress was frozen to the wood. My dress was transparent and black. When I moved, it made a crunching sound. I got up and touched father's face. It was even colder than the objects in the room. Outside it was summer. Flies dropped their maggots in flight. The village was dragging itself along the broad sand path. It was hot and brown, and burnt the eyes with its glare.

The cemetery consisted of debris. There were big rocks on the graves.

When I looked towards the ground, I noticed that the soles of my shoes were turned upside down. The whole time, I had walked on my shoelaces. I was pulling them behind me, long and thick. Their ends curled up together.

Staggering, two small men lifted the coffin from the hearse and lowered it into the grave, using two crushed ropes. The coffin was swaying. Their arms and their ropes became longer and longer. In spite of the drought, the grave was filled with water.

Your father has many dead men on his conscience, one of the drunk little men said.

I said: That was during the war. He was decorated for twenty-five dead men. He brought several decorations home.

He raped a woman in a turnip field, the little man said. Together with four other soldiers. Your father stuck a turnip between her legs. When we left, she was bleeding. It was a Russian woman. For weeks afterwards, we still called every weapon a turnip.

It was late autumn, the little man said. The turnip leaves were black and shrivelled up from the frost.

Then the little man placed a big rock on the coffin.

The other drunk little man continued to speak.

In the new year, we went to the opera in a German town. The singer sang as shrilly as the Russian woman had cried. One after another, we left the room. Your father stayed until the end. Afterwards, for weeks, he called all songs and women turnips.

The little man drank rye. His stomach gurgled. I have as much rye in my stomach as there is ground water in the graves, the little man said.

Then the little man placed a big rock on the coffin.

Next to a white marble cross was the funeral speaker. He came towards me. He had both hands pushed deep in his pockets.

The funeral speaker wore a large rose in his buttonhole. It was velvety. When he was standing next to me, he pulled one hand out of his pocket. It was a fist. He wanted to straighten his fingers but couldn't. The pain made his eyes swell. He started to cry quietly.

One doesn't get along with fellow-countrymen during the war. They don't let themselves be ordered around.

Then the speaker placed a big rock on the coffin.

Now, a fat man came up to me. His head was like a hose and didn't have a face.

Your father slept with my wife for years, he said. He blackmailed me when I was drunk and stole my money.

He sat down on a rock.

Then a wrinkled, skinny woman came towards me, spit on the ground and said shame on you to me.

The funeral congregation was on the other side of the grave. I looked down at myself and was shocked because my breasts were showing. I was cold.

They all had their eyes directed at me. They were empty eyes. Their pupils were piercing beneath their lids. The men had rifles over their shoulders, and the women rattled their rosaries.

The speaker plucked at his rose. He pulled a blood-red petal off and ate it.

He gave me a sign with his hand. I knew that I had to give a speech now. Everybody looked at me.

I couldn't think of a word. The eyes rose through my throat into my head. I brought my hand to my mouth and bit my fingers. On the back of my hand, bite marks were visible. My teeth were hot. Blood ran from the corner of my mouth down on to my shoulders.

The wind had torn out a sleeve of my dress. It was floating in the air, delicate and black.

A man leaned his cane on a big rock. He levelled the gun and shot the sleeve. When it sank down in front of my face, it was covered with blood. The funeral assembly applauded.

My arm was naked. I felt it become petrified in the air.

The speaker gave a sign. The applause fell silent.

We are proud of our community. Our industriousness protects us against our downfall. We won't let ourselves be insulted and abused. In the name of our German community, you are sentenced to death.

All of them levelled their guns at me. There was a deafening noise in my head.

I fell down and did not reach the ground. I stayed in the air sideways above their heads. Quietly I pushed open the doors.

My mother had emptied all the rooms.

In the room where the corpse had been laid out there was now a long table. It was a table for slaughtering. On it were an empty white plate and a vase with a bouquet of dilapidated white flowers.

Mother was wearing a transparent black dress. She was holding a big knife in her hand. Mother stepped in front of the mirror and cut off her grey thick braid with the big knife. With both of her hands, she carried it to the table. She put one end of it on the plate.

I will wear black for the rest of my life, she said.

She set one end of the braid on fire. It extended from one end of the table to the other. The braid burnt like a fuse. The fire leapt and consumed it.

In Russia, they shaved me. That was the least of my punishments, she said. I staggered about from hunger. At night, I crawled into a turnip field. The guard had a gun. If he had seen me, he would have killed me. The field didn't rattle. It was late autumn, and the turnip leaves were black and shrivelled up from the frost.

I didn't see mother any more. The braid was still burning. The room was filled with smoke.

They killed you, my mother said.

We couldn't see each other any more; there was so much smoke in the room.

I heard her steps right next to me. With my arms stretched out, I felt for her.

All of a sudden, she hooked her bony hand on to my hair.

She shook my head. I cried.

I opened my eyes wide. The room was spinning. I was lying in a ball of dilapidated white flowers, locked in.

Then I had the sensation that the building was falling and emptying its contents out on to the ground.

The alarm clock rang. It was Saturday morning, five thirty.

17

And Still Our Heart is Frightened*
Herta Müller

After my arrival in Germany in 1987, I lived in Berlin for three years. Back then, Berlin was a city in which the wall moved. On many a day, it was located at the end of streets where it could not be found on other days. I was convinced: the wall was moved around on the backs of the animals which lived on the bare strip of land. Rabbits and crows, these animals of those who were shot, scare me as much as the gun barrels. The wall is gone, the animals of those shot escaped into the country. Maybe their hearts were raging in their flight like the hearts of the many who had been hunted before. It was winter back then, and the back country was as barren as the bare strip of ground.

'Foreigner', the word is blunt. It is so neutral and at the same time as tendentious as the tone of each voice that pronounces it. From one person to the next, it can jump from one meaning to the other. From one *intention* to the other. Yet, in its continued neutrality, it is above those it thus designates. A *collective word* for individuals who have come to this country from other places. Every one of them has his *own* story, even though the danger or poverty in his country is the same for thousands like him. When he leaves his country, his biography is his most certain and most fragile property. As a stranger, he looks for substitutes for what his country never gave him or what was taken away from him a long time ago.

Germans who mean well cannot claim the word 'foreigner' for themselves. Steffi Graf and Boris Becker said a while ago: I am a foreigner. In Germany, they are not. And wherever they happen to be foreigners, they hit small balls over the net, watched benevolently by their fans. They are the centre of attention, and shortly thereafter they leave: for home.

---

* 'Und noch erschrickt unser Herz', from *Hunger und Seide. Essays* (Reinbek: Rowohlt Verlag, 1995), 19–28.

Wherever they are foreigners, privilege predominates. Being a number on a winners' rostrum is not the same as being a number in a refugee registry. This is why the well-meaning statement of such celebrities falls flat; it plays down the problem. To a certain extent, they represent Germany to the outside world. More the country than the state. With ample opportunities to be themselves: for the *country* does not pressure them into a victory, and losing does not entail any fear from the *state*. This makes them different from athletes under dictatorships, who toil away in a pseudo-political order and even under real police observation. Their bodies are nationalized. Through their athletes, every dictatorship breeds human beings for winning, soldiers in foreign affairs. Consequently, every loss is reviled as failed state order and every win celebrated as successful state order, and thus abused politically. It was like this in Romania, it was like this in the GDR. It would have been like this in Berlin for athletes from China and Cuba, if the Olympics had taken place here.

The Romanian rower Ivan Pațaichin was world champion for years. Even though he defeated everybody, he carried with him the shadow of a dictatorship whenever he stepped into his boat in the foreign country. And carried with him another shadow: the shadow of childhood. For he came from the Danube delta. His parental home was one of the pile-dwellings, where stepping over the threshold meant stepping into deep water. In this area, hunger was just as excessive as water. Food was not available for picking or slaying above the water. It was underneath, and it wouldn't stay put – it had to be caught: mussels and fish. Accompanied by hunger alone, Pațaichin was put in a boat by his parents in order to catch something to eat. Back then, like all children in the Danube delta, he sat in the boat, so small that not even his head looked out over the edge. As a result it looked as though the boat was striking the oars itself to where reeds and mud surrounded him. A place where you have to row fast, without looking around, surprised hours later because you are still alive. This is where Pațaichin comes from, a place where, back home, in front of the shed, you have *escaped* the great waters once again.

Pațaichin's athletic achievement always meant rowing for food that wouldn't stay put, and he transformed this into a pure art. His rowing passed through hunger before it could become a sport: rowing without need, rowing for the sake of rowing. It moved into a different world; it became a luxury.

The Romanian world champion in gymnastics, Nadja Comaneci, had her Hungarian name made Romanian and had herself pulled into bed by the dictator's youngest son in order to be on a balance beam in the outside world. And the dictator's shadow wavered with her. She became a winner in foreign stadiums – in her own country, however, she remained a subject. Far away from the World Championship's jubilations, '*at home*', she stepped in front of the dictator to express gratitude. And said she won on the balance beam thanks to his leadership and wisdom. After the dictator's son had long since been sleeping in other beds, she disappeared to America. There she was doing commercials for underwear, it was later said.

Wherever one looks: nothing is the same for people from democracies and those from dictatorships. For the ones are children of a country (*Landeskinder*), and the others are children of a state (*Staatskinder*). If children of a country and children of a state do the same thing in the same place, the shadows only fall away in the minds of the *Staatskinder*.

> *I have to admit, back then I was actually inclined to describe Erich Honecker, with all his Saarland attributes and peculiarities, as a fellow-countryman of mine; I went as far as to diagnose his ideas of borders as Saarland aberrations full of symbolic meaning, and I erroneously made the capricious statement, that this is how far it can go with somebody who musters up feelings of home within himself, and pretends that they are feelings of international brotherhood. It ends up as the mistakes of a neurotic arising from repressed counter-will, barbed wire which results from the need to escape, to the building of the Wall arising from a longing to return home.*

Ludwig Harig wrote this. Only somebody who never had to live in a dictatorship could think of the sophistry of reversed local patriotism in the case of Honecker. This sophistry stylizes the imagined pain of the dictator and ignores the real pain of the country. Ceauşescu was a Saarlander, too, if barbed wire and gun barrels are the material of *longing for home*. Fidel Castro, Saddam Hussein, Mobut, Milosevic are also Saarlanders longing for a home of this kind. If a dictator needs a home in his mind, however, the only words for it are: contempt for humanity. This alone is the space he inhabits and furnishes with all necessary means. With feverish ambition, dictators destroy countries and people so that they can pathologically respect themselves as rulers. The deafness of the man who had been Honecker's bodyguard for years resulted from hunting. Honecker used his bodyguard's shoulder to support his gun barrel. Honecker gave him a hearing-aid from the West. And, when out hunting again, he used the shoulder beneath the deaf ear as a support for his gun barrel.

With regard to the antlers around the house in Wandlitz, it occurred to me that the antlers of a young buck, covered with skin, are like fingers that are spread out. That the skin only peels off when the antlers aren't growing any more. That it hangs off the bucks' heads like bloody shreds, as long as the bucks fray their heads. If one needed images to show what dictators destroy in people for ever, then it would be this image that shows what happens in a dictatorship, and not the Saarland one. And that in front of every *socialism with a human face* (*Antlitz*), there was a broad letter, a *W*: a *socialism with a human Wandlitz*. Every dictator succeeds in destroying his bodyguard's hearing. But no dictator longs to return home. Dictators are not imagined foreigners in their own country. Not even dictators who are refugees are foreigners. Whoever takes in dictators treats them as guests of honour. And they are not capable of feeling guilt anyway. They reproach themselves for what they did not do strenuously enough, not for what they did. Deprived of power, the necessity of their own power mania confirms itself even more. Honecker's thinking has remained as hard as the old man's fist, which he held up over his head so often after his fall. Only the fist managed to let the face on top of his old body light up one more time, as if forty years younger.

When standing before the authorities, a foreigner first has to reveal his biography. Instead of believing in it once again and telling it, he has to *reveal* it. This is the opposite of *telling* it. And in view of the opportunity which this presents to him or deprives him of, to reveal is already to question. I remember the time in the reception camp. With a piece of paper in your hand, you go from door to door. The order of the doors is fixed. And the first two doors are the Federal Intelligence Agency (*Bundesnachrichtendienst*). No, this is not written on the doors. On the doors, it says: Examination office A and Examination office B. And the piece of paper in my hand was called *Laufzettel*[1]; its name is at least honest. Many of the doors back then carried the sticker: I no understand German. The German officials thought it was funny; the stickers after all expressed what they were not allowed to say out loud.

Those who are politically persecuted know the price of their flight. The words 'moral integrity' *vis-à-vis* a dictatorship are important to them. Germany has no intention of considering this in the case of refugees. And because of this, German officials do not have a category for it on their standardized forms. When revealing the political refugee's biography, the issue of moral integrity is ignored. However, 'moral integrity' is the reason for the flight. It distinguishes those persecuted from political opportunists

---

1. *Laufzettel* literally means a sheet of paper that walks or that you walk. It refers to a form that you have to take from one office to the next to collect signatures.

and criminals in their country. Moral integrity is the dearly paid-for opposite of political opportunism. It is not touched upon by the objectified version of life contained in the forms. In Germany, it is not an issue, not even in the media. And very rarely in private conversations. The first thing that somebody who has put his life in jeopardy and who has managed to save it through flight must learn in Germany is that from now on the reason for his flight is not worth a question. Instead, a German journalist asks a Bosnian soldier: Did you kill Serbs? This she asks after the survivor told her that from his hiding-place he had witnessed Serbs torturing his grandmother while looking for him. And of how, two days later, they had pulled her out of the yard where he had buried her secretly at night. And of how dogs came by afterwards and fed until they were full. The survivor said he had probably killed Serbs. But that, where he had been, four or five men had been shooting simultaneously; he didn't know whose bullet had hit.

What would the German journalist with her hypocritical sense of morality do in this situation? Not defend herself against murderers?

Biographies of refugees are nothing but countless lived *details*. One doesn't need to know thousands of them; one only has to know what is attendant to a few life stories in order to understand. *Precision* lies in details. Only they can be related and compared with one's own life. Only they step in between unrealistic *admiration* and unrealistic *contempt* of foreigners. For both are prejudices. They talk each other to death. They prop themselves up against each other and make each other necessary.

It made the officials nervous that I talked about the Romanian dictatorship when revealing my biography in 1987. I left a dictatorship for political reasons, and the German officials wanted to hear something as to my Germanness. When I answered yes to the question about whether I would have been persecuted for my attitude even as a Romanian, the official sent me to the police in charge of foreigners. He stated: *either* German *or* politically persecuted. There was no form covering both at the same time. What I told him confused his categories. Maybe Germans have never got into the habit of *asking* about one's personal moral integrity because it intrudes into the life of the one asking. And because even here in a freer country, moral integrity cannot be reconciled with security – without posing a threat to one's life. While the officials, distracted from their routine, pushed the papers back and forth, I had to wonder what would have become of them if they had been in my place. I came up with only part of the answer. And the rest I forbade myself to supply. But the *forbidden* part was not better for them than the part I *did come up* with.

Many people describe the revived self-confident behaviour of the Nazis as a new form of *youth protest*. They bend the words youth protest until they are no longer recognizable. For the young Nazis don't call for social or political changes. They yell National Socialist slogans. They are high-waymen in the name of a superior race. Hunting and killing people changes their lives, lives with which they, quite rightly, are not content. You cannot call something that commits cowardly murders and draws a trail of smoke and blood behind foreigners and Germans who disturb the image of the race because they are homeless, homosexual or disabled a *youth protest*.

But the unanimity by which *the* Germans are associated with character-istics based on the historic pattern of fascism has petrified also into ideology. The pattern asserts that the only posture available to an individual German at any time has been what *his* people did as a result of the brutalization under Hitler. The critical scrutiny of fascism, even in its strictest rejection of National Socialism, takes the individuals' predestin-ation to be part of the whole national character as seriously as National Socialism itself. To define characteristics of Germanness only imitates National Socialism; it is enough in itself; imitating fascism does not go beyond what is self-evident. It is not possible to differentiate because this would go beyond the pattern. People want the pattern to stay self-contained so that whoever repeats it can feel as comfortable as if he were inventing it himself. It is the self-confidence of a maniac. It occupies language and blocks the path to reflection, which – insecurely – wants to try it the other way around.

Society, however, or what we call society for lack of a better word, people that is, *live*. Every day, they talk and move between two opposites. *In between* therefore.

Moreover, what is historically and politically given does not stay that way unconditionally. Otherwise East and West Germans – because of the separation into two states with completely different intentions – would not have moved so far apart in forty years.

In 1970 Uwe Johnson wrote 'The Attempt to Explain a Mentality: On a Type of GDR Citizen in the Federal Republic':

> *Those who left now hardly needed a single current reason, not even all of them together. He was done with the GDR; he didn't believe any of its words; he didn't get along with it anymore; he couldn't stand its voice any more; his trust had gone flat; it didn't work any more: all these are expressions which comment on the dissolution of a personal relationship. Because whoever left the GDR left thinking that he had jilted her like an all too power-hungry and quarrelsome bride, who he wants to hurt after all . . .*

And Still Our Heart Is Frightened

The procedure in German reception camps had a shock-treatment effect. It immunized forever against any dreams of unification: this is how the people who one wants to be united with are treated. One couldn't have expected the entrance ticket to be so repulsive. This injury was hidden; it didn't help it to heal. By the way, they have not come in order to be in the Federal Republic, but in order to leave the GDR . . .

The way East and West Germans deal with each other is not a consequence of unification, but it is as long-lived as the first flight from East to West. Complaints in the East and arrogance in the West, which are described as 'typically German', are typically Hungarian when Hungarians from Siebenbürgern who want to belong to Hungary and 'natural' Hungarians from Hungary meet. And when Romanians from Romania and Moldawia meet, it is typically Romanian. The dealings between East and West Germans are as 'typical' as anywhere else where there is a difference between people who speak the same language. This is not 'typically German'.

I lived in Rome for a year, where I used to shop in a small vegetable store. When I entered the store for the first time, the salesman asked me where I was from. I said from Germany. He was an old man; he had experienced fascism. I greeted him in Italian, asked for everything I wanted to buy in the language of the country. But the sales man only greeted me in German, in a barking tone of voice which chops up every word into syllables. Everything German for him was Hitler. When I left the store, he followed me to the exit, goose-stepping, and said: *Jawoll, alles in Ordnung.*

I didn't have a chance in this store, I *could* not do anything right. For I was not a person. I was nothing but his memory of a bad experience. My ancestors are Germans. His tone forbade any reply. In order to cope with this, I had to find something that gave the injured party the right to behave this way. I found Primo Levi. With Primo Levi on my mind, I could enter the store again and again. But I would have liked to take Helmut Kohl with me every time so that he could never again say that postwar history is over. In claiming this, Kohl erases the revolting memory of those injured by the war. But the Germans don't have the right to declare that suffering caused by the war is over.

Just as nobody today has the right to declare the Stasi debate closed. Neither those who were outside the dictatorship nor those who lived inside it and spared themselves or were spared. The argument that the *crux of the matter* got lost, that opportunism and resistance are often indistinguishable *is not true*. Only those entangled in it want to deceive. They talk about a *hunt* and a *hate campaign* because a shadow has been cast over their existence. The shadow outside causes them more trouble than the shadow inside their heads. But it can't be wrong to wish for oneself and for these others that the shadow inside cause them more trouble than the one outside.

The Stasi victims became victims because they resisted the entanglement – *obviously in the same predicament as those entangled*. They have not lost sight of the crux of the matter: *the distinction between denunciation and refusal*. The victims are not concerned with *opinions* which are open to interpretation. It is *facts* that matter, facts which have occurred *precisely this way*, and *no other*. And these facts have to set the standard in every discussion. Only those who let themselves be deceived by this standard no longer have one.

But there is someone whose name was Uwe Johnson. And there is someone whose name was Robert Havemann. There is someone whose name is Sarah Kirsch. There are Wolf Biermann and Jürgen Fuchs. Hans Joachim Schädlich, Günter Kunert, Walter Kempowski, Erich Loest, Reiner Kunze. And in everyday life, there are many more even if we don't know their names.

One often hears that those who were lucky enough to have been born and grown up in the West are not allowed to criticize. The Stasi debate cannot be closed as long as those who were cheated are investigating the lives that were taken away from them. And as long as the ones not directly affected keep thinking about it. And they have the same right to do so as those who were injured. One doesn't have to live in a dictatorship to judge it. One judges daily anyhow, if one is aware of world news. In condemning the tanks on Tiannamen Square back then, one included oneself without having to be Chinese. Expected that one would be with the demonstrators on the square. Ruled out that one would be sitting in a tank or be part of that government. Nobody has to justify this to himself: to not know this about oneself any more would be to have thrown oneself away morally.

It's the same when it comes to art. The question of whether an artist lives according to his texts has to be allowed. Expecting him to do so has to remain justifiable. As justifiable as it is in the case of all other people.

For, without this standard, we have no choice but to believe when Mielke says: 'I have loved you all'. When Elena Ceauşescu says before her death: 'I have loved you like my children'. When Antonescu says about the deportation of Jews and gypsies (*Roma*) to the death camps in Transnistrien at the trial in 1945: 'In my house, we don't even slaughter a chicken'.

When I try to understand Germany, I necessarily come across myself. In this I am no different from the people who have always lived in Germany. I am different in the compulsion to run into myself here and in the country I left behind *at the same time*. But the two countries are so different from each other that nothing in them and nothing in myself (from back then and from now) can meet without being punished. This is probably the reason why I cannot say anything binding about *the* Germans. Why I can never belong in Germany and why I cannot leave Germany.

In order to explain why my perspective is not similar to the perspective of the natives, I have to relate something that is foreign for them and in the past for me. If I forced my perspective to become similar to theirs, it wouldn't just be in vain. It would also be fake.

Here in Germany, my books evoke two constantly recurring questions. The one: when I will finally write something about Germany. The other: why I write about Germany. In the latter case, my perspective on Germany is considered *wrong* because it doesn't correspond with the one people are used to. The strangeness of it is irritating; one senses illegitimate interference. The second question relegates me to the well-defined: I'm supposed to write about where I come from. In my *second better* life here, feeding on the breadcrumbs of Germany, I have the right to bite and to swallow. But with this formerly empty and now full, but still foreign, mouth, it is proper to keep my mouth shut at least while eating.

In the Eastern European countries, pipes were visible above the ground everywhere, at times barely above the ground, at times arched high into the sky, higher than bridges. They were the image of an industrialization not coped with. Steam rose from them through all the gaps along the streets. The steam flew through the air, torn to pieces: it was the white breath of misery. Understanding this steam as the ghost of a threat was close to reality when one was threatened; it was not perceived as a metaphor. The streets in Germany lack the breath of misery. They run smoothly; bucks leap on traffic signs, they even have antlers on the signs. Covered with skin or peeled off, I sometimes wonder. Telephones accompany the drive in case of an accident. If you are still on your way, still driving, you do *not* need them, *yet*. While driving, it seems to me that you have to escape from them unnoticed. That they are there for those innumerable people who are not on their way any more: those dead in accidents. Here they telephone with the living, who are still on their way.

I don't believe myself when I think this. And yet, I think this again and again as if it were compulsory. This compulsion is only an example of my invisible baggage, of the DOUBLE MEANING of the country left behind.

Then I read in the paper:

Kinkel, in his speech, used nautical metaphors. He said, the ship FDP needed a new helmsman because Graf Lambsdorff will abandon ship in June . . . The convention at Epiphany was the yearly army parade of the FDP in the homeland of liberalism.

'This is where I'm from, this is where my roots are, this is where I want to continue to belong – politics and politicians need a home(land)' . . . It was necessary to reflect self-critically and openly, he said. 'But then one must continue one's trip with a clear destination, staying on course.' It was simple to be liberal in good weather, more difficult in choppy weather, he said. He wanted to help make sure that the FDP doesn't lose its direction in rough seas . . .

The foreign minister said politicians and politics needed a *homeland*. He is thus using the kind of local patriotism that locates Honecker in Saarland. Kinkel's local patriotism cannot be contradicted. Kinkel *is* really deeply at home in Germany. And yet, he uses metaphors from sea travel and moves his language into homelessness. The image of seafaring moves him poetically because he has never been homeless.

Romania is the DOUBLE MEANING for what happens in front of my eyes in this country. German is my mother tongue, but in view of this locality a language that I brought with me. Where I learned it, the petrification of metaphors in politics was very similar. In the same stretching of words, there as well as here these metaphors became involuntarily funny and failed. But still, it was all different: its intention was sinister and aimed at life.

Even common words like *store*, *street*, *hairdresser*, *policeman*, in everyday usage, say something different in the same words because the things these same words named were different. But one cannot learn a language twice: I say the same old words, I speak like I used to speak back then. But I have to see something new in them.

There is no time-lapse of the mind. Even when everything is new to the eyes, one cannot comprehend more quickly. For only while time is running does it pass its details on to you. A foreign place hesitates in the mother tongue, too. Because the mother tongue is familiar to me, it acts as if it was too old. It moves slowly among the new things.

Then, one day, it says in the paper:

In heavy snowfall, home owners are not required to clear the snow and put salt on the sidewalk. It is only necessary to shovel and get the salt bucket out, once the snow has let up. Reasoning thus, the state court in Nürnberg-Fürth rejected a woman's claim for damages in a ruling announced on Wednesday. The woman had asked for 5,000 Marks from the home owner in front of whose property she had fallen during a heavy snow fall and broken her leg. The judges, however, declared that home owners are only obliged to clear the snow with salt 'when these measures promise to be successful, in this case having the effect of stopping slipperiness'.

This search for justice is unimaginable for someone who comes from a dictatorship and a country stripped by poverty. When I read something like this, it becomes a parody without intending to be one. But my laughter comes from fear. Just as I laugh out of fear when, in Berlin, I see two women stop on their walk in front of the wire fence of a garden house. In the middle of the lawn, there is a pond, as big as a mirrored door. And, on the pond, there are three ducks. And one of the two women says: Aren't these ducks from the public park? And the other one says: It should be reported.

German can use 'report' to paraphrase the unambiguous 'denounce'. 'Denounce' can be refined in this language, presumably because it has been used so often. Only someone who simultaneously tones down the word with the deed can spare his conscience. Can turn the word into an everyday word through toning it down. One can after all *report* to one's friends, in the sense of checking in with them on the phone, and no one *reports*, in the sense of answering the phone. But when one *reports* in the Registration, the word *reports* differently to the ears.[2]

When I arrived in Germany, for the first time there was something final for me. It oughtn't to be the spatial distance between the two countries, I thought. That it shouldn't envelop my brain so easily. I hated *home-sickness*, I refused to call the pain that. I could always keep the word at a distance from me. Not the state. To think back often felt like whining to me. I knew that I had left of my *own* accord. But what does it mean when the reason for this wish was an *external* threat. Driven into a corner by the Securitate, I finally took to my heels. There was no closure, it was over because it was cut off.

In the first weeks after my arrival, I was shocked by how sparsely furnished German rooms were. From Romania, I only knew crowded apartments, colourful carpets and tapestries everywhere, the table always in the centre of the room. Dammed-up life wherever you look. The empty

2. Herta Müller plays with the different meanings of the German word *melden*, which is impossible to translate adequately into English. In the original German text it says: 'Man *meldet* sich schließlich auch bei Freunden, oder man ruft bei ihnen an, und es *meldet* sich niemand. Doch im *Einwohnermeldeamt meldet* dieses Wort sich in den Ohren anders.'

rooms here scared me; they provided no security. They made my eyes twitch. Wherever I sat or stood provided no security. What I ate or drank, held in my hand or put in my mouth tasted good but strange. What I said referred to half of me, and I had the impression of disappearing into myself. In Romania, fear couldn't tolerate an empty space in the house. Where there was little, one wanted a lot. Surrounding your body with objects gave you a sense of security. To be able to grasp and to touch what was there gave confidence; for outside in the streets were only individual people being brought into line. Only the objects that you had chased after guaranteed your history. You attached your life to their stable form in order not to lose yourself.

To live in empty apartments like this, one has to be strong inside, I said to Berlin friends back then.

In my room in Romania, which men and women from the Securitate entered and left even when I was absent, there was a poem stuck to the cupboard for years. Sarah Kirsch wrote it in the GDR. When I attached it to the cupboard, Kirsch had long since been expelled from the East.

> *This evening, Bettina, everything is*
> *Just as before. Always*
> *We are alone when we write to the kings*
> *Those of the heart and those*
> *Of the state. And still*
> *Our heart is frightened*
> *When on the other side of the house*
> *A car can be heard.*

This poem guaranteed that tomorrow was another day, that this wretched life would not snap shut and be gone. Every day, I was prepared for something to be done to my friends and to me which would end life. Precisely because of this, the poem both inspired and removed fear. When I recited it to myself, it was frightened by its own lines. I relied on the danger because there was nothing I could do to diminish it. If the death threatened by the secret service was a certainty one day, I thought, danger would pay dearly too. That would be its end. I knew danger wanted to live. *And still our heart is frightened* turned into a guarantee that death was not a sure thing yet. The poem also described how one walked through the apartment or through the open day outside. How one looked out of the window. And why it was better to turn the key only once in the door when you locked up when leaving home: so that the gentlemen of the

Securitate, when they came, wouldn't break the door open. For they came and left just as they pleased. Even if the floor had eyes, even if I could have put the door in my purse and the purse underneath my skin, they would have come. Even if I had been the room myself and had left, they would have come. And even where the apartment no longer was, they would have found everything they wanted to know every day.

On the street, the poem knew that I had to look at every car on the curb, had to memorize its colour, its licence plate, its driver and the time. What for? For nothing other than to talk about it with friends who lived just as hunted. In this way the fear was forced to cling to the facts. It was not allowed to burst in the head.

This poem which includes so many instances of fear – it is about Bettina von Arnim after all – concerned the next two minutes just as much as the next ten years. And many have had their poem. The love of poetry in Eastern Europe is not a beautiful myth. It originated in fear. Utilitarian poetry, in the narrow sense of the word. This is not derogatory because fear is a reliable criterion. Word games don't stand a chance; fear senses precisely the breath every word carries. Authenticity lunges out of what is produced. Many had their poem, recited word for word, stanza by stanza, and with it themselves in the exhilaration. In the case of those devoid of God, this is reminiscent of a prayer.

Fear existed in two languages. In the mother tongue, it was one syllable. In the language of the country, it was two: *frica.*

I knew that according to the orthodox faith, children were stripped naked at baptism and their head was held under water three times. Only twenty years later was I almost frightened by this. For a Securitate officer said: We are going to hold you under water. And: good luck shall strike you dead; thus I understood for the first time where good luck and bad luck meet. Fear drove me in between the foundations of language. This mother tongue and this language of the country, they were two, and completely different. And so foreign to each other. And since the fear which let them loose on each other didn't stop, they didn't stop looking at each other.

German superstition says you should make a wish when you see a shooting star; then it will come true. Romanian superstition says, a falling star means that somebody has just died. Both languages use metaphors to connect the image of the pheasant with man. In German, a pheasant is someone who brags. In Romanian it's a loser. One of the languages uses the outside of the bird as a metaphor, and the other its helplessness *vis-à-vis* the hunter: since the pheasant can't fly, it has to run. The bullet, however, can fly – it hits the pheasant. The German fairy tale begins with the words: Once upon a time. The Romanian fairy tale with the words: Once upon a time that never was.

These opposites existed side by side, became conspicuous every day, prolonged each other. They were two differently formalized possibilities of looking at the world. However, Romanian had the more ruthless images most of the time, that is the daring to be poetic without consolation. The language of the country was never as close to me as the mother tongue, but I preferred its images.

At New Year, I read in the paper that *der gute Rutsch* as New Year's wish originated in Yiddish and that this cannot be found in any German dictionary. And I wondered whether the majority in a country ever thinks about where its language got one word or the other from. Whether it isn't the case that always and everywhere only the minority, out of the corner of its eye, looks at these borrowed words, suspiciously, as if no language got anything for free.

In Romania, any threat was uttered in Romanian. The language of the country in certain moments changed into the language of the state. In this respect, the German language was lucky in Romania. Luckier than in the GDR. Luckier than in the Third Reich. I was forced to realize that the language of the country and my mother tongue make a good language of murderers, even if they look at the world in different ways. And I am forced to observe how all languages in all corners of the world are good for this. And I have seen how fast this happens once it has started.

In Germany you can hear even people who are familiar with each other say when talking about xenophobia: it's also like this in *other* countries. Yes, but we live here in Germany. Never has a German from here said to me: *I* am not like this, and you know a lot of others who are not like this.

It annoys me that *those* who don't have to reproach themselves avoid the question by talking about other countries, that *they* are so quiet and don't talk about themselves as Germans. This also makes me think of the sentence: *And still our heart is frightened.*

Is this possible?

18

Does That Rat Poison Taste Good?*
Herta Müller

'My ladder's gone; it fit so well under the tree; now it is gone. Stolen, where else could it be,' the old woman says, '*they* steal everything; since *they* have been here, you can't own anything any more.' She is talking about asylum seekers.

Complaints like this have become so normal in the village that one doesn't even have to say the word 'asylum seekers' or 'foreigners'. The woman waits for approval.

The sixty-year-old man who accompanies me to the end of the village, to the hills of fruit trees, who lives down in the village like her, nods silently when she looks at him. She knows him and how he feels about this topic from prior conversations. He suffers because he can't say what he thinks now. For I'm right next to him, and he knows I would contradict him angrily. He is silent because he doesn't want a local to know that he has acquaintances who think differently. But also in order to hide the fact that there is someone next to him who is a foreigner.

Weeks ago, he wanted to explain to me that, as a Romanian-German, I was different from the foreigners. Since then, he knows that I don't accept his distinction, his backhanded kindness which is aimed at others.

He bends down for some apples, and the woman leaves dissatisfied. He acts as if the woman had never been there at all.

An hour later, I walk next to him on the way 'home' through the village, which looks like a thousand other villages in West Germany: taken care of with such precision that you can't tell that it was ever exposed to wind, rain, frost or heat which eats the paint. As if time here passed over the houses, only affecting the faces of the people. And even they age later and differently from people in poverty-stricken countries. And I think to myself that those who live in these streets with timber-framed houses,

---

* 'Schmeckt das Rattengift?' from *Hunger und Seide. Essays* (Reinbek: Rowohlt Verlag, 1995), 39–49.

decorative plants and late-September weeds don't want to hear the word poverty. Old people know that they were poor after the war and only half of what they used to be. For they knew that Hitler had started the war.

They lost the war, and they lost house and home; they had even their songs and traditions put into the service of the war. Therefore, they didn't have the right to complain. And they were considered monsters in the outside world, which Hitler had destroyed in their name. And they slaved away so that they wouldn't notice what was left of them.

And the young people know that what they take for granted is wishful thinking for many and a luxury for a very few in poor countries. When the poverty of the poor touches this village, its inhabitants become afraid. Old and young. Their fear is exaggerated because it is imagined; it is fear which turns into hatred. They find poverty degrading, they find foreign poverty especially unacceptable. They feel above such things. And when they think of poverty, they think of the foreigners. They consider looking at foreign poverty to be beneath them. This is the kind of thinking that you find in someone who considers himself a member of the master race. Because they protect their village from poverty, they feel that they are at home.

Those who say the word 'foreigner' in the streets of these villages pair it with hatred. And they've hit upon a topic of conversation which appeals to everybody who passes by. A conversation which is effortless and goes the same way every time. There are enough clichés and prejudices about foreigners to make the conversation last a while, to enable the people involved to rid themselves of private dissatisfactions which have to do with something completely different (which one would never admit to or say out loud).

The regional newspaper had printed a pamphlet about foreigners a few days before. A piece of German 'folklore' harnessed with every prejudice possible, written in the entertaining tone of contempt for humanity. The half-hearted commentary of the editors, which stated that it only reflected the current mood and that the pamphlet was circulating in the area a hundred times over, reflects a hypocritical morality. The editors didn't say anything about its content.

Most of the letters to the editor in the following days were letters of gratitude: finally somebody had said it. Outraged letters were few and far between – the editors probably knew this before they printed it.

The old woman, who talked herself into a rage under the apple tree, didn't talk about *one* asylum seeker; she meant *all* of them. How could she mean just one, she hadn't seen the thief. She knew that an asylum seeker didn't have a house, a roof, a tree. And she knew also that he wouldn't have any use for her old wooden ladder. But this didn't make her question her prejudices.

The local woman accuses indiscriminately, slanders and knows she can get away with it; she will never have to prove what she says. And if it was one of them, she would wish all foreigners to disappear from this village and from all parts of this country. She is one of many; she does what is customary in this area, slanders every day, whenever the opportunity arises. She talks to different people, but the topic is always the same. This is what keeps her and her small village alive.

Keeping this hatred alive becomes normal. The common image of the enemy doesn't have to be corrected because his traits are invented. People who talk to each other affirm one another through a common concept of the enemy without having to accept any responsibility. This is addictive. Xenophobia becomes public opinion. It produces a feeling of belonging, which is so important because envy, intrigue and competition determine relationships in all other realms. Those who stay out of this commonality are suspect and pressured by the community to justify themselves.

Three years ago, I still said: They are 'yesterday's people'. They will talk less and less and be silent more and more because their environment doesn't accept them. They will fall back upon themselves, I still thought three years ago. Three years ago I had no idea how flexible the sentences of hatred can be, how quickly the thinking of the master race can spread again and again, how seamlessly cowardice can be extended into a quality of preparedness for life. And I had even less of an idea of how fast the thinking of the master race can adhere to young people, because it connects self-pity and arrogance in one breath.

I knew that the Wehrsportgruppe Hoffmann and other scattered Nazi groups existed. I also knew that *Republikaner* and DVU were getting more and more votes. I did not believe in the designation 'protest-voters', either in Berlin or in Pforzheim, Stuttgart or anywhere else. And still, I thought that what these rabble-rousers were saying didn't make any sense.

My trust in the consequences of the 1968 generational conflict made me too calm. I thought that there had been a break, once and for all. And that the great majority of those born after 1968 would stand by this break. That sons and daughters back then had looked for and found the perpetrators and silent supporters of Hitler in their parents, that they thought about guilt, especially about personal guilt – I thought this would remain binding in this country.

A pediatrician from Hamburg tells me that young parents in particular who take their children to the hospital tell the doctors: 'I don't want my child to be in a room with foreign children.' These parents often have children who are seriously ill, says the doctor, and amidst all their fears and worries these parents are concerned about this. And they are not afraid to say so.

Those who throw stones and set fires, those who hunt fellow human beings from Hoyerswerda and Rostock are not marginal groups. They move around in the centre. They can rely not only on applause in the streets, but also on the approval of those who don't appear to be skinheads on the outside. Good citizens who do not shave their heads, but, inconspicuously and quietly, create the personal and public opinion which makes manhunts acceptable. For at least two years now, neo-Nazis have been the executioners of public opinion with their clenched fists. That's why they don't try to run away. They act in front of the cameras of reporters and go wild night after night in the same place. There is no reason for them to disguise themselves or to go underground. They present a legal version of organized crime. They feel asked to do so by the community. What their elders no longer tackle because of the physical effort involved, they do for them. They gain respect and turn into heroes.

It won't make a difference if the Chancellor of the Federal Republic prays a thousand more times: 'We are a country that is friendly to foreigners.' Today nobody believes this any more. He is insensitive, blind, a provocation.

The politicians claim to be 'concerned', but not even by accident can they come up with a true sentence which makes people take notice. Not a single thought comes from their lips. Only empty phrases from dead metaphors. They utter these so that they don't have to deal with the facts. They roll off their tongues. Language itself, German language gets goose-pimples when German politicians talk. Their images are metaphors with goose-pimples. The EC (or democracy or the state) has to 'remain capable of defending itself, a strong anchor in a stormy sea' (Minister of Foreign Affairs Kinkel). It's all interchangeable, it says one and the same thing, nothing.

Why don't people who go into politics, for whom public speaking is just as much a part of their job as decision-making behind closed doors, why don't these people at least read enough for them to master the basics of a reasonable language? Why do they use language against neo-Nazis which is hardly any different aesthetically from the linguistic images of the Nazis? All of their linguistic images take the same ugly line:

'Roll up your sleeves', they said after unification; then there was the 'bottom of the valley', which was 'not reached yet'; then it was reached.

Now, 'the boat is full'. On his tenth anniversary as chancellor, the chancellor still maintained: 'Everyone forges his own destiny.' All of the above: linguistic images with goose-pimples.

Where foreigners are set on fire, 'shame' comes more easily to politicians' lips than 'crime'. But 'shame' doesn't mean anything other than concern for damage done outside of Germany. Hunting men is not a 'shame', but a crime.

A week ago, a German was knocked down by skinheads. 'He looked like a foreigner,' the perpetrators said. Therefore a mistake. By setting fire to the accommodation of asylum seekers, the wrong person can't get hit. But, in the street, even a race-conscious expert eye can make a mistake.

When one tries to think this through from the perspective of a neo-Nazi, foreigners ought to make themselves visibly identifiable when they leave their accommodation to avoid this error: they should wear a sign on their clothes.

The few perpetrators in front of a court of law talk about 'boredom'. There is no place for this word in a criminal court of law. Xenophobia cannot be explained by a lack of discothèques and youth projects. Boredom, whatever this means, does not lead to manhunts.

And the lack of 'bloodshed' during a revolution doesn't lead to manhunts either. Those who ride this horse of the philosophy of history turn it into a brown mule. The blood of the dead has never made the living more reasonable. A look at Romania proves this. When Ceauşescu was overthrown, people were killed: there were hidden mass graves filled with people tortured to death. There were people shot to death in the streets. And afterwards?

One year later, church bells ringing, Romanians went to the end of the village and set fire to the houses of gypsies (Roma). Whole streets.

I can't get help thinking that people from the ex-GDR in united Germany are in a similar situation to me: Germans through their language. But not West Germans. Foreigners in all other aspects of biography and socialization. People from the ex-GDR have more in common with Poles, Czechs, Hungarians, Romanians than with West Germans. The dictatorships in Eastern Europe were similar in the appearance of their streets and inner spaces. They created and left similar worlds – and people similarly damaged – sometimes involuntarily through the same planned misery, and sometimes on purpose through the similar structures of their repressive systems.

People from the ex-GDR are not 'second-class citizens' but West Germans on the surface and Eastern Europeans on the inside. This is not to exclude them. This is the truth of the matter. But next to the studied hypocrisy of being the same, it sounds like sacrilege.

Hatred arises because people from Rostock, in so many details, recognize themselves in every asylum seeker, because these fugitives are their immediate past. Unification was supposed to bring about and guarantee a safe distance from the immediate past. It did so, but only on the outside. It can't change years of experience. Unification doesn't extend to the Eastern Europeans, who are now in the same position that people in the GDR were themselves in two years ago. In addition, people expected wealth from unification, wanted to leave the lack (it was not poverty) behind once and for all. And now the poverty of others resides on their doorsteps. The East Germans, released from dictatorship, protect their turf from the poverty of others. Furthermore, it is easier to assert one's own identity *vis-à-vis* the poverty of foreigners than it is to assert it *vis-à-vis* the West Germans.

In the spiteful dealings between the locals from the ex-GDR and foreigners from Eastern Europe, the denial of their Eastern European identity manifests itself. It is similar to that of upstarts, and this behaviour, occurring on a massive scale, is just as repulsive and morally untenable as it is in the case of individual boasters. Only much more dangerous. The new hatred reaches back into history. Antifascism, abused as a pillar of a despised ideology, is stripped away. Now, one feels 'liberated'. The anger, which should be directed towards those who abused antifascism ideologically, instead draws swastikas on Jewish graves and sets fire to the memorial in Sachsenhausen.

Politicians stammer their metaphors with goose-pimples. In order to distance themselves, they suggest new criminal laws. As if the old laws were dead, those against intimidation, blackmail, bodily harm, arson, murder.

Even today, the chancellor cannot pronounce 'right-wing extremism' without its counterpart 'left-wing extremism'. He knows that it is not about the latter this time. And it is precisely from the time of left-wing extremism that there are laws and clauses and an exhaustively trained special police unit. In Brokdorf or Kreuzberg, this unit proved itself to be surprisingly 'capable of action'. Back then, only streets were occupied and supermarkets set on fire. Where are the police when people are set on fire?

Politics doesn't take action any more. Now and then in the daily competition between parties, they are struck by common panic and run about in different directions after what's already happened. Instead of taking action against right-wing extremism, they react to it.

Debates focus on the inherent magic of the changed asylum law. Once this is in effect, everything will be back to the status quo, if an immigration law doesn't come into effect at the same time. It is neither the first nor the last time that everything will stay the same. And yet, politicians make a pact with shortsightedness every day.

The right to political asylum shall continue to exist in its 'essence'. What is this 'essence'? There shall be a list of countries free of political persecution. This also means without persecution of minorities and religious groups. Romania is supposed to be on this list. Even if Romanians return in state-run buses one day, as in Tirgu Mureş, and hunt down Hungarians with sticks, even if there are pogroms against the Roma. Even if the new old secret service appears together with the old Securitate personnel and is long since at home again in factories, post offices and offices. Even if people belonging to opposition parties and publishing houses are spied on and threatened.

That everybody is born and dies an individual – this banality is suitable for a metaphor with goose-pimples. It never occurs to politicians. They think of countries when too many individuals come.

Talking about political persecution is just as hopeless for those who are really persecuted as it is for the refugees from poverty. For now it has been decided that they are not to be believed. Now politicians expect countries to make out written certificates for those they persecute.

The concept 'political asylum' was degraded due to lack of an immigration law. Those who fled poverty were forced to use political asylum as their only excuse, as a compulsory lie. The law makers are to blame for this, not the refugees.

To differentiate between those escaping poverty and those who are politically persecuted is no longer possible once the concept 'political asylum' has been appropriated, had to be appropriated for all kinds of needs. But the motto of politics today is: Close your eyes, and we'll find a way.

Those who still promise the population today that there will be a time with fewer refugees from poverty are consciously deceiving because the reason for the flight, poverty, will not disappear. Poor people will not let rich countries keep them out.

People whose only possessions are miserable junk and temples pounding with weariness and hopelessness are not at home in their countries of origin, either. Their junk doesn't keep them there. And hopelessness and pounding temples drive them out.

The effect of thinking in terms of a master race, through which German mediocrity tries to gain attention, does not stop at the Italians, Greeks, and Turks, who have lived in Germany for twenty years. Outside of Germany, Goethe Institutes have come under pressure to justify their existence; Japanese businessmen cancel investments in East Germany because they are afraid of xenophobia.

At the farmers' market in Hamburg, a young woman begged with a note in her hand. People, both old and young, looked repulsed as she held the note out to them. Some pushed her away. A vendor at one vegetable stand shouted to another who was selling ham: 'Give her something to eat. Why don't you give her a whole ham?' The two men laughed, and the customers in front of both stands laughed along with them.

In front of the Gedächtniskirche in Berlin, a young man pulled at my sleeve and said: 'Does that rat poison taste good?' I was walking along eating a kebab. I said: 'The rat poison isn't in my mouth, it's in your head.' He stuck out his tongue and made a choking sound and contorted his face.

Part V
Guest Workers: Permanent Guests or Temporary Residents?

A workforce diminished by two wars together with the rapid economic development of the 1950s (the so-called *Wirtschaftswunder*) caused the Federal government to recruit workers from several Mediterranean countries.[1] Organized labour migration into the Federal Republic began in the mid-1950s when the Federal government signed contracts with Italy (1955), Spain and Greece (1960), Turkey (1961), Portugal (1964), Tunisia and Morocco (1965) and Yugoslavia (1968). These contracts prescribed that the workers were to leave after a set number of years to be replaced by new recruits; this so-called rotation principle (*Rotationsprinzip*) and the term 'guest worker' were designed to make it obvious from the very beginning that this labour migration was not to be confused with immigration.

Because of an economic recession and the concomitant rise in unemployment, the Federal government banned any further recruitment in 1973 (*Anwerbestop*) and offered incentives to workers already living in Germany to return to their home countries. Between 1955 and 1973, fourteen million workers had come to Germany; by 1973, eleven million had returned. Once workers returned to their native countries, they could only come back if their country was a member of the EC. A great number of workers from non-EC countries such as Turkey and Yugoslavia, however, chose to stay on and, what is more, sent for their families to join them. And this development naturally had enormous consequences for Germany's social infrastructure.

Initially, it had only been men between twenty and forty years of age who came to Germany from these areas; they left their families behind, worked in low-prestige jobs and saved most of their money with the aim of eventually returning home. Starting in the 1970s, however, families followed husbands and fathers, and children were born in the Federal

1. For accounts of the history of migration into Germany from these Mediterranean countries and problems related to migration and integration, see Nora Räthzel, 'Germany: One Race, One Nation?' *Race and Class* 23.3 (1990): 31–48, Eva Kolinsky, 'Non-German Minorities in Contemporary German Society', in *Turkish Culture in German Society Today*, eds David Horricks and Eva Kolinsky (Oxford: Berghahn, 1996), 71–111 and Klaus J. Bade, *Ausländer, Aussiedler, Asyl. Eine Bestandsaufnahme* (Munich: Beck, 1994), 38–52.

Republic. Consequently, although the numbers of foreign workers decreased because those who left were no longer being replaced by new recruits, the number of foreign residents increased. This signalled a change from transitional stay to long-term residence.

Despite this development towards long-term residence, however, the social situation of the 'guest workers' has not improved significantly over the years. They still work in mostly low-prestige, low-income jobs, predominantly in production and service; their children's education is below the level of that of the rest of the population, and their housing is often inadequate. In the 1970s, admittedly, politicians started a campaign to integrate foreign workers and their families during their stay, but the resulting policies do not constitute any real improvement. What is more, most of these foreign residents have to deal with prejudice, discrimination and xenophobia on some level or another at some point in their lives. And unification and the ensuing wave of violence against foreigners in East and West have proven to be further obstacles on the road to a coexistence based on tolerance and respect.

The texts collected in this section reflect the experiences of the first generation of postwar foreign residents in Germany. The authors come from Italy (Biondi and Chiellino), Greece (Torossi), Syria (Schami) and the Lebanon (Naoum). Like their fellow 'guest workers', they worked primarily in restaurants and factories and in construction. However, and here their biographies depart from those of their fellow 'guest workers', almost all of them went back to school and received advanced degrees. Franco Biondi studied psychology at Frankfurt University. Rafik Schami has a PhD in chemistry, and Gino Chiellino studied German literature. He has also worked as a teacher of Italian and is currently employed as a Research Assistant at Augsburg University.

In their writings, these authors depict the life and work experience of the foreign worker in Germany, his problems with housing and the job and above all the prejudices he has to deal with on a daily basis. Through their poems, short stories, fairy tales and fables, they criticize and protest against these inhumane working and living conditions as well as the ever-present prejudices. They try to enlighten their readers about the experiences of this particular minority group and to teach them a lesson in tolerance, respect and mutual understanding.

19

Dead Soul Costs 200 Marks*
Franco Biondi

I have known this country for almost fifteen years. With its apparent coldness, which impressed us so much, its harmony, which doesn't exist, and its love of order and obedience to the law at all costs, which in reality unveils itself as appearance, just like the activity in the centres of many cities. If one of us is thrown into the Federal Republic, he believes he can safely assume that everything he sees is the essence of the German people. But then, when one of us is standing in front of a red light, waiting for it to turn green, he rubs his eyes as soon as he sees that a neatly dressed German crosses the street in spite of the red pedestrian light or that a car – with a sticker on the wind shield saying 'Out of Love for Germany' – dashes through the red light.

I'm not surprised about anything any more; I have learned that my image of the Germans was often wrong; fifteen years as guest worker in this country are not chicken-feed. Not only have I had to fight my image of the natives, but just as much their image of us.

But enough of that. What happens here and there and what this story is about cannot be seen as detached from all of this; it cannot be categorized in a scheme of random probabilities; but it also does not originate in the experience of just any writer. It is a story which happens to many in my situation and, at the same time, it debates many a moralizing writer, who limits himself to showing the failure of German society as so pale and blurred as if being seen from a distance.

It began on a day much like any other day; I didn't even know whether it was the twentieth or the twenty-first of the month. Oronzo, not such an old friend, in whom the sufferings of emigration had left deeper traces than in me, called me and said he had finally found work for me; if I accepted, he could put in a good word for me with his foreman. I had

---

* 'Tote Seele kostet 200 DM', *Die Tarantel. Erzählungen 2* (Fischerhude: Verlag Atelier im Bauernhaus, 1982), 7–22.

already been unemployed for a year, and the unemployment office had simply deleted my name from their lists of unemployment recipients; so I agreed. Oronzo had been without work even longer, at least legal work. How long exactly, I didn't know, in any case, longer than our friendship. But over and over again – I didn't know how he managed it – he was able to find illegal work even though it never lasted long; he had psychological problems which indicated 'guest-worker schizophrenia'.

Well, in any case, two days later Oronzo led me to his foreman, and I got the job. I want to mention explicitly that I would be working without papers, six hours a day for 5.25 marks an hour and without benefits, that is less than half of what one usually makes, and that I would have to work on Saturday and Sunday as well. At the same time it should be mentioned here that it is not necessary to start with the lowest aspects of illegal work in order to get to its essence; 'dead souls', whether they are in trailers or in single rooms, can be found at the intermediate level as well.

The work was easy: packages of magazines had to be stacked on pallets, tied together and then loaded on to trucks and vans. The magazines were popular magazines, the best-selling ones in the Federal Republic, among them also those which often denounce scandalous conditions in peripheral phenomena, and ignore those which are the order of the day at home.

Comme il faut, Oronzo and I could work together: the foreman had a soft spot for a sense of community. In addition to the magazines, we had to load the daily newspaper into the vans, which showed up very early in the morning fresh from the printing-press. There was nothing special about the work; we could do it without thinking and daydream while doing it; there was almost no danger that a work-related accident could happen; otherwise the company would not have used workers without the right papers.

So we loaded one pallet and went on to the next: the whole yard was at our disposal. When it wasn't early morning any more, the normal workers streamed into the main building, and even later the ones with ties on.

On the second morning I worked there, a beige Mercedes appeared in the yard. He must have a special permit, I thought, because at the entrance there was a sign which indicated this, 'Loading only'. He drove in the direction of the main building, passing us. Suddenly Oronzo, who hadn't noticed the car, stepped back a bit and got caught by the car, which passed us at that moment. I'd seen it coming and wanted to hold Oronzo back, but was only able to touch his sleeve. I saw him flying over the hood and hit the ground, where he then lay. The driver, without a tie and a nice suit as I was sure he would be dressed, looked pale and shocked behind his modern wire glasses; he had jumped out of the car and looked at us; I – how could I have done otherwise? – had rushed to Oronzo; the man checked to see whether his car was dented from the crash.

I pulled Oronzo to the pallet, leaned his upper body against the magazines. He was moaning quietly then, his facial expression distorted by pain. Blood was streaming out of his nose, above the corner of his right eye, on his forehead, the skin was grazed a bit, but other than that I could see no injury.

I turned back around, looking for the man with the wire glasses. Where had he gone? Inside his car, he was looking for something in the glove compartment; then he finally came over.

Bad? he asked; and: How could this happen?

He has to be taken to the hospital, I said; and he looked around seeming embarrassed, his face still very pale; then he looked over to the main building. A man with a briefcase was going in just then.

Yes, sure, he said whispering, and again he looked towards the main building. I'll call the ambulance. But where is your foreman?

Quickly, I yelled: Oronzo tried to sit up gasping; the blood had soiled the front of his old sports jacket. I held him underneath and pushed his head back. Finally I found a handkerchief in my pocket and held it under his nose.

The driver of the Mercedes had disappeared already, and after a while he came trotting back with our foreman. The foreman didn't really listen to what I said and immediately felt all over Oronzo's chest, checked the origin of the blood; and, mumbling, he swore.

No need to take him to the hospital, the foreman called conclusively. I'll take him to the doctor. When I asked whether it wouldn't be better to take him to the hospital, the foreman didn't answer. Instead he said to the other man: Are we going to take your car?

The driver of the Mercedes hesitated; and then said: The cover . . . and there's a hot item . . .

Okay, I'll get mine, the foreman called, visibly annoyed, and disappeared. The driver of the Mercedes stayed with us briefly; when he took his eyes off Oronzo, he looked over at the main building, as if we were keeping him from something important.

I thought: get the hell out of here, you son of a bitch.

The foreman came driving in his Ascona; he wasn't wearing his grey coat any more. We put Oronzo in the car, in the back, so that he was lying on his back; and the man with the wire glasses disappeared, got into his car and drove to the main building, where he originally wanted to go.

Don't get blood on the seat, the foreman said to Oronzo in a threatening tone of voice. Or else . . . Whether Oronzo heard that seemed questionable to me. His head was swinging to and fro.

I'm coming with you, I said; the foreman made a face to indicate his disapproval; he got in and started the car. I pulled at the door vehemently, and he opened it. You stay here, he yelled; and I replied: He's my friend. I just got in without looking at the foreman. He stepped on the gas. I noticed that the foreman checked the rear-view mirror nervously and observed me from the side. Oronzo was moaning more heavily now.

Very bad? the foreman said and turned around to him. I think so, I said, better hospital; and I watched the traffic. We drove in the direction of the suburbs; the signs indicated this, too. I remember that the hospital was in the opposite direction.

Where are we going?

The foreman was silent, then he mumbled something incomprehensible, his eyes angry, when I asked again.

We are not going to the hospital, he said suddenly; a private physician is better. When I asked for the reason, he didn't respond.

You'd better sit in the back with him, he said; and he stopped. I got out of the car to get in the back. Hardly had I closed the passenger door than the engine gave a roar. The foreman raced off, leaving me behind at the side of the road.

I swore against God and the foreman, the company and the driver of the Mercedes, but that didn't help. There was no taxi rank nearby; and I wandered around the neighbourhood hoping to see the foreman's car parked somewhere. I also looked for doctors' practices; but all of this was futile.

I turned around and took the tram to the newspaper building. The yard was sparkling clean, no trace of blood or anything suggestive of this morning's incident. Shortly after a man in a grey coat had seen me sitting on a pile, the foreman appeared. He acted very cold; when I asked why he had dropped me off and where Oronzo was now, he said that Oronzo was fine and that I could see him at his place that night.

He asked me into his office. Long-windedly he began to explain that the company had been thinking for a long time of reorganizing the loading process and that there had been a plan for this for more than six months and that this plan had to be executed now. The first measure of this plan concerned me and Oronzo directly: He was sorry to have employed me for such a short time only, but that was it; and the company had to sever its ties with me.

He got an envelope out of a drawer; I think it was a green one. I was surprised, speechless; before I could say anything, he continued his monologue: The company wanted to be generous and wanted to pay you a whole week's wage even though you were only with us for two days. Look at it as a settlement. Then he counted the money out for me, exactly 157.50 marks; and he locked up as he rose and opened the door for me: You will certainly find a new and better job.

Without realizing it I was outside in the yard. The porter nodded in greeting to me as I walked through the gate. I walked the city streets for a while, stopped in front of shop windows, looking, but without registering anything, and I noticed that it was peak shopping time only because people in a hurry bumped into me every once in a while. This morning's images, the foreman's words were buzzing in my head; and Oronzo. What had happened to him, where was he? I simply didn't know what I should have done.

Oronzo's room was locked, and nobody opened. He lived above a former middle-class bar. The landlady, who also owned the bar, said that he most certainly had not come home yet. At night, Oronzo always ate in the bar, and once he got home he always came to the bar first.

I waited at a table in the bar. It was almost completely empty at first, but then it filled up; particularly at the bar, where the men were standing. But I didn't really notice them; for I was consumed by thoughts and restlessness. Nevertheless I felt hungry; I ate, what else? Wiener schnitzel, chips and salad, but drank only moderately; because I wanted to keep a clear head; because the beer didn't taste good that night.

The hours passed by, and no Oronzo in sight. Impatient, I approached the landlady, told her everything, concluding that something very bad had happened to Oronzo, that he might even be dead and that someone had done away with him. The foreman, yes the foreman, was responsible for all of this.

The woman only listened half-heartedly while she was drawing a beer; and the two men at the bar smiled.

I thought only Arabs told tales from 1001 nights, one of them said; and the other one: Something like that couldn't happen here; things here proceed according to regulations.

I thought I must have told everything incoherently and started again; my voice excited, stammering and looking for the appropriate words (this damned German language, which never wants to flow out of my mouth properly!), I presented my story, working without the right papers, illegally that is, the accident, driving with the foreman, his successful drop-off and the settlement in the end.

They smiled again, the two men; one of them even interjected: Just like Delvecchio. And casually he drank from his glass.

No, no, the other one said, more like Kojak, don't you see? copied from Kojak. He said this confidently; and he took a big sip from his glass.

And suddenly I was shocked, not because my tongue was getting sticky in the course of my explanations or because I was sweating terribly; no, not because of this; I was shocked because I realized that they were turning the whole thing into a part of a cheap crime story, like the ones people watch on TV every day; because my experiences were being compared to a TV show, and one I didn't even know, and not the other way round.

The woman rolled her eyes and said: You have no idea what you're talking about. I've known Oronzo for six years. Only he could come up with a story like this. And he knows why. He comes up with crazier and crazier stories, so that he doesn't have to fulfil his duties. Last time he came and babbled about his foreman, who had let him work on the side, on his own house. In the end the foreman only paid him twenty marks. I know the likes of him: he only babbles like that so that he doesn't have to pay. But not with me.

She turned to me: Surely he used you as a front man, right? So that you put up this performance here and pick up his stuff. But not with me.

I denied this vehemently; but she was not willing to discuss this any further and continued: Not with me. First the money, then the belongings: he still owes me this month's and last month's rent and the cost of meals, altogether 680 marks. First the money on the table, then his stuff. She breathed in deeply: 680 marks and not a penny less, you understand?

My shock turned into surprise; depressed I returned to my table after I had asserted the truth of my story again and again. The two men continued to joke about it for a bit. Closing-time was approaching, and Oronzo was still not in sight; the bar was emptying. There was only an old man left at the bar.

I made another advance to the woman, and this time she lent me an open ear. She said afterwards: Okay, I believe you this time. Call the hospitals, there are only three in this city. If something happened, they'll know.

In none of the hospitals had they heard the name Oronzo Mazzotta before. I asked the woman whether it wasn't appropriate to turn to the police. She waved that aside. It doesn't make sense to bother the police with something like this. He'll show up by tomorrow morning.

I remained persistent until the end. The woman came to clear off the table, she swept the floor, washed the glasses; then she opened the door for me and wished me good-night.

I stood outside for an hour smoking one cigarette after the other. The moist, cold air crept into my bones. I set out looking for the closest police station. It took a long time to find it, even though it was only three blocks away. There was light only in one window; the officer, friendly and courteous, listened to the beginning; one could tell from his face that he was surprised; then he interrupted me.

What am I supposed to do with this? he butted in; and I continued as if nothing had happened. Then he remarked: If my wife was missing, my concern would be understandable; but a friend – he gestured dismissively – maybe he was still sitting in some bar or even in a brothel; this was normal for guest workers, he was familiar with these things; and if my friend – this time he emphasized the word – could not be found by early next morning, then I could turn to the police. By the way, the business with working illegally, if this was even possible at such a respected newspaper, was not part of his job, but the next day I could present all this again.

I had to admit to myself that presenting my case any further wasn't going to help at all. I gave up. I was dismayed; my thoughts constantly stumbled against my perceptions. People created order in their world by making it fit a certain framework, I thought; only that which fits it seems true to them; everything else is just fantasy. I think if I'd said that Oronzo had killed the foreman, the landlady and the men in the bar would have acted immediately. That was the point; that was perhaps what made Oronzo a dead soul. I wondered whether his psychological difficulties were a consequence of this.

The window of his room was still dark; and the street was dark as well.

How I slept that night, one can well imagine; and early in the morning, tense, I set off, first to Oronzo – nobody opened up – then to the newspaper building. Two men, who looked like they were from Pakistan, foreigners in any case (I seem to have assimilated to the German way of seeing things), were loading the pallets. They seemed to be worried about my presence there; they looked around nervously.

When I asked whether this was their first day on the job, they didn't answer. Why should they? I wouldn't have behaved any differently in a situation like this.

Searching for the foreman didn't take too long; I found him, or rather we met, at the unloading ramp. He looked at me surprised, his face perhaps twitched nervously, but he collected himself right away. He asked seemingly politely: What do you want?

Of course I asked for Oronzo, about yesterday's events, which he seemed to have forgotten about all of a sudden. He pulled a face as if he couldn't remember any of it; and he shook his head. Oronzo Mazzotta? Never worked here.

I was thinking – as if there was nothing more important to think of – that the German, who is usually quite forgetful when it comes to foreign names, was able to pronounce my friend's name well and clearly the first time. Oh well, I thought, let's seize the bad luck with both hands. I yelled: Let's hear the truth! Where did you bury him?!

I had said this in perfect German; and he looked so surprised that I didn't know whether it was because of this or because of my accusation. For I'd spoken badly pronounced and at times broken German to him since he had employed me. I had been afraid that he wouldn't have employed me, had he known that I knew the language well.

After taking a deep breath, he first looked around. Trembling he said: How dare you say something like that! Then he pulled himself together; he said in a calmer tone of voice that he was sorry but he didn't know anybody of this name and that he'd never seen me before, either.

It goes without saying that this left me speechless; it was important, however, that he kept calm about my threat to bring in the police. That made me feel insecure because I knew that this threat was one of the most powerful German weapons.

That's why – even though I had been determined to do so – I didn't go to the police station. The way the police officer had responded to my report the night before held me back as well. I wandered around the building like a beaten dog; then the Mercedes driver crossed my mind. His car was neither in the yard nor in the car park of the company. Had the Mercedes been dented at all? Too bad that I hadn't even looked; had I done so I might possess some kind of proof now. Thinking about this, I wandered around the company. I observed everybody who drove in and out, even trucks, although I realized that this didn't make sense. I noticed that the two foreign-looking workers weren't working in the yard any longer; in place of them two Germans in company coats were loading the pallets. I sensed vaguely that this change in personnel was probably due to my threats; and I was annoyed at myself for not turning to the police immediately.

He's here, his landlady called, when I opened the door. He's been here for about an hour. He was lying in bed, something seemed to have happened after all, but he wouldn't say anything, was her report.

Oronzo was lying covered up to his chin, his eyes looking at the ceiling. He was completely unapproachable; it wasn't until the evening that one could talk to him; he started to speak in a confused way. He told me then that he had been taken to a house, which was like a toothpick; there a white man with two fireplaces on both cheeks had tried to paint him white, too. This man had been very dangerous; he had wanted to burn Oronzo

– 182 –

with his fireplaces; he had burnt him in two places, on his nose and on his chest. But then he, Oronzo, had escaped; and a woman with eyes like knives had followed him; at the tip of the toothpick he had not been able to go any further, and the woman had been able to catch up with him. The woman's eyes had turned into needles, and he, Oronzo, was stung by them, once in his arm and once in his butt; he had defended himself and tried to break the needles; once he had even bent one of the needles causing its tip to bleed. Afterwards he was overwhelmed by a great darkness, which he was still fighting.

He fell asleep after this story. I decided to stay with him in his room.

He woke several times suddenly and started to cry, to cry for help. Once he went wild; I believe it was at four o'clock in the morning: It's so dark in here, help, I'm in a coffin! I can't breathe in here!

And when I turned on the light and he had regained consciousness to a certain extent, he called out relieved, his face covered with sweat: Thanks, friend, for getting rid of the coffin lid. I was not allowed to turn off the light any more because he was afraid of suffocating.

The following morning he seemed more lively; his gait was unsteady, but he could get up and even go to the bathroom. He didn't seem to have internal injuries or broken bones; but his chest hurt incredibly; in addition, he complained about severe pain in his pelvis. His nose was still red and a bit swollen, and the scratches on his forehead were covered with a shiny layer.

Where he had been taken to, he didn't know; he couldn't remember anything, only that he had felt like he was in a coffin there. Only when he was put in a car and driven home had it felt as if he was returning from heaven to earth.

His condition improved visibly. Slowly he understood what had happened to us. And, as I assumed, he had received an envelope as well. Somebody had put the money in his jacket while he was being treated. In the envelope were his wages and the settlement, exactly 357.50 marks. 200 marks difference from what I had got was probably due to Oronzo's injury. A kind of sickness benefit. Obviously, this was supposed to make good the fact that Oronzo had felt like being in a coffin there. Obviously they assumed that they could buy our silence. Thus nobody was supposed to find out what happened. Like an exchange: Silence in exchange for 200 marks. Mute and motionless like in a coffin; this is what you find money for in your pocket.

The events became clear for Oronzo as well; and he cursed the foreman and the company. He couldn't grasp it. And he talked about suing them. He had tried something like that a year ago with the foreman of the construction firm he was employed at. Oronzo had spent a week of his regular work hours renovating the bathroom in the foreman's home without the company's knowledge. He smashed his thumb on the job; as settlement the foreman gave him 20 marks and reported the accident as a regular work accident; he claimed that Oronzo had only started with the company the previous day. Then he let Oronzo go immediately. In the months that followed, Oronzo went to charitable institutions, the Italian consulate, even to the Union's department of foreign workers. It all came to nothing. Back then I thought: because he wasn't capable of making himself understood, but I sensed now that this wasn't the only or the most important reason.

After I achieved nothing – already when looking for Oronzo – I thought our chances against the newspaper company were very small. We didn't have any evidence other than ourselves. The evidence of two unemployed guest workers, our skin, our eyes, our mouths, that wasn't enough. But we didn't give up yet.

We decided to go to the foreman together. The porter didn't let us in. We don't have any work for you, he said, although we just asked to talk to the foreman; and we stayed in front of the gate. The foreman finally appeared, however; apparently the porter had informed him.

What are you doing, lingering here, he called. No work, get lost or I'll call the police.

Now he had turned the tables, I thought; and in turn we threatened with the police.

Do you have any evidence? he called; and he was laughing slyly.

We will tell everything, one thing after the other; Oronzo pointed to his not so swollen nose.

The foreman was laughing harder. And he yelled: everybody can babble away that this and that happened in the company; why the work papers then?

Regarding the last sentence I said to myself: he's right, and how right he is.

Brief and succinct: as he appeared, so he disappeared; and we wondered for a long time whether we should have gone to the police. We didn't do it in the end: for the police and the judge, if it had even gone that far, it would have been one person's word against another's , and the ruling would have been in favour of those in power. And we knew this much: it wasn't us.

The driver of the Mercedes, Oronzo called then, everything is his fault.

It's funny how we could have forgotten what triggered everything. The reason for that was maybe that he was too high for us, the driver of the

Mercedes, like lightning from a cloudy sky; he came, destroyed and disappeared. Let's look for him, I thought, maybe this will lead to something.

I said nothing; and the next day I started my search. The beige Mercedes was sitting in the car park, no dent or anything, everything perfect. Of course I was disappointed and thought that now we really didn't have anything any more. Through the window I could decipher the name of the Mercedes driver. It was drawn in bold letters on a red strip which was attached to the dashboard: Siegfried Winter.

I rushed home, put on my nicest suit, shaved carefully, and bought a cheap briefcase in the department store. Everything went smoothly in the newspaper building, like clockwork: I simply asked for Siegfried Winter, and they directed me to the editorial floor. His office was empty; I double-checked the name on the door and slipped into the office.

There were several piles of notes on his desk. On a few sheets of paper which he was obviously working on was the microphone of the dictating machine. Other sheets, which were spread out on the table, were printed.

I read a few headlines and thought that I had to work on my German again; if you don't practice constantly, you easily forget this angular language.

Chancellor's Report on the State of the Nation: More Courage to Venture. The German Mark Soon the Most Favoured and Stable Currency of the World. Then an article with the following headline struck me: To Fight Illegal Work: The Order of the Day. Interesting, I thought, they sense the problem; and I read on, a good exercise in the German language. Illegal work did great damage to the economy, especially of the community, it said there. Furthermore it said: Many foreigners are brought to Germany by their fellow-countrymen, where they are sold to dubious companies; the people who help them into Germany collect more than half of the illegal workers' wage. The illegal workers: they live outside the community, often in condemned houses or in trailers on the periphery of the cities. He himself, the writer, had seen them. Every citizen should be asked to do something against these people on German soil since the trade in human beings is degrading and inhumane. This article was signed by Winter.

Suddenly the door opened; there was Winter with a briefcase in his hand. He didn't see me right away; and only when I moved did he look up.

I got the impression that he didn't recognize me immediately; but then horror settled in his eyes. What are you doing here, he screamed, his face all pale, white as a sheet, like after the accident. He pushed his wire glasses up, glanced at the telephone, and looked at me, unsure of himself. You know what this is about.

He dropped the briefcase on the table. I don't know what you're talking about.

All right, I thought, the man claims to have a bad memory; this is why he's a journalist; and I yelled: You knocked Mazzotta over!

Beside himself he started to scream. About intimidation, calling the police.

Do you know that we were working illegally in the company? And that Mazzotta and I lost our job because of the accident?

First an 'And?' slipped out of his mouth, and then he pulled himself together. He said that, although he didn't know what I was talking about, he thought it was sad that I and this other person had lost our jobs. But after all he couldn't help me; he was no unemployment office, and he was swamped with work. Besides that, he had never met me before, he didn't even know me. He glanced at the telephone again; and I was certain, I had this feeling, that he would have called the police, like the foreman, and would have denied ever having knocked Oronzo over. Perhaps this thing would have become complicated for us in the end. The situation being schizophrenic as it was, it could have happened that they would have cut our unemployment benefits because we worked illegally.

I left. But full of anger I added: I won't be idle: I'll tell our story to the newspaper. And it will be published. I had read the first sentence somewhere in the newspaper and kept it in my mind without intending ever to use it.

20

The Flying Tree*
Rafik Schami

In a little field, there once lived an old, gnarled apple tree and a young, tall apricot tree. They had enough space to live and were standing so far apart that neither one of them had to live in the shadow of the other. Year after year, the apricot tree produced more and more blossoms, and the old apple tree became annoyed at this neighbour.

'You are carrying too many blossoms. The bees are running out of time to pollinate mine.'

'I am after all industrious,' the apricot tree answered proudly, 'and so are the bees. You are old and only good for the stove if anything at all.'

This bickering stopped towards the end of spring because the industrious bees had pollinated the blossoms of both trees. So, in the summer, the apple tree was beaming.

'Look at your miserable fruits! There are too many; the slightest breeze will make them fall off. Look at me, every apple is a star. It doesn't surprise me that the farmer only makes jam out of you. What a pathetic dorky jam head you are!' the apple tree said mockingly, looking proudly at his big, rosy-cheeked apples.

'Bonehead! Your apples are only good for tasteless juice. What a lousy juice outfit you are!'

But, when autumn approached, the trees talked less and less to each other; for their fruits were harvested, and they did not know what to argue about any more. They were bored all day long until autumn turned into winter; then they fell into a deep sleep.

One nice day in spring, however, a small tree pushed its way out of the ground and came into the world. The apple tree noticed him first.

'This apricot scoundrel has secretly dropped a stone into the ground, and soon the farmer will fell me and only accommodate apricot trees on

* 'Der fliegende Baum', *Der fliegende Baum* (Kiel: Neuer Malik Verlag, 1991), 170–82.

his land. I am old and bear less and less fruit every year. The farmer doesn't leave a single apple on the ground to rot so that I could take pleasure in an offspring!'

'Good morning!' the small tree said cheerfully and startled the apricot tree, who had been busy courting the bees.

'Good morning! But who are you?' the latter asked back, surprised. He thought to himself that the apple tree, in his old age, was trying to seduce the farmer with an offspring.

'Meee? A tree!'

'Well yes, but what kind of a tree?' the two old ones asked in chorus.

'That I don't know. Isn't it enough to be a tree?'

'No, you have to become something specific! Look, apricots are the most industrious. Don't you like them?' the apricot tree said flattering himself.

'Yes, I do,' the young neighbour answered, and immediately grew two delicate apricot leaves.

'Do not let yourself be seduced by this pathetic jam head. Apples are the most beautiful things in the world!' The apple tree spoke so convincingly that the little tree grew two apple leaves.

'That's not how it works! You have to decide. Apple or apricot?' the other neighbour said furiously.

'I don't know yet! I need time!' the young tree said surprised.

'What a pathetic fool you are!' the two old ones sighed and tended to the bees again. The little tree watched the sun, and he liked it because it was so round and bright. Shortly before it set, he grew a round leaf. It turned dark, but the little tree was so excited that he could not sleep. It was his first night. The stars greeted him, and soon he noticed that no one star was exactly like any other; each one had its own (hi)story. The moon enchanted his listeners with stories until he fell asleep at dawn.

The next morning, the neighbours were surprised about the many new leaves; some of them looked like stars, and from the top of the little tree grew a small stalk with a green half-moon.

'That'll be fun!' the apple tree said mockingly.

'What a useless thing you are! Every tree just carries one kind of leaves and takes care of its fruit,' the apricot tree enlightened him.

'But why? Isn't it wonderful to carry stars and the moon?'

'No, what for?'

'They tell the most beautiful stories!'

'What good is the most beautiful fairy tale to a tree. You are supposed to bear fruit.'

'But I like stories a lot. Can you tell me some?'

'This is getting funnier and funnier! You're asking for stories?'

'Yes! You're old enough, aren't you?' asked the young tree.

'I can't tell you any stories. I can tell you the truth,' the apricot tree moaned.

'And what is the truth?'

'The world is a huge apricot! That's the truth.'

'He's lying,' the apple tree interrupted nastily, 'that's a fairy tale. The truth is, the world is a round apple.'

Because of their argument, the two neighbours forgot the little tree. A swallow was hunting a mosquito in gracious flight. Suddenly, she saw the splendid tree.

'You look strange. What kind of a tree are you?'

'I don't know yet. I am a tree. Isn't that enough?'

'Yes, yes! I think you are great,' the swallow called out.

'Can you tell stories?'

'Well, you are a funny fellow! Hold on, I'll be right back with my friend. She is the best storyteller of us all!' and she flew away.

After a little while she returned accompanied by another swallow, who was giggling at first, when she saw the strange splendour of the leaves; for she had thought that her friend had really exaggerated. She sat down on a branch and searched her memory for the most beautiful stories. Swallows are the greatest storytellers. They travel around the world and nest under roofs of houses and stables. They see and hear a lot and can remember everything. The swallow told the young tree everything about the colourful world, and, when he finally asked admiringly whether the world looked like a swallow, she almost fell off the branch with laughter. At that moment, the young tree ceased to believe that the world looked like an apple or an apricot.

When autumn approached, the swallows said goodbye with a heavy heart, and flew south. The young tree was thinking of his friends all night, and, at dawn, two swallow leaves were unfolding on his branches.

'You should stop growing new leaves; autumn is coming,' the apple tree advised him. But the little tree was only surprised at the paleness which discoloured the leaves of his neighbours.

'Why are you turning so pale?'

'It has to be this way; otherwise we could not survive winter.'

'Why?'

'It has always been this way!' the apricot tree called, and the wind swept away many of his leaves.

'Drop your leaves!' the apple tree shouted in the roaring wind.

'But I love my leaves!' The little one clutched them stubbornly and defended them doggedly against the rage of the storm.

Winter approached and spread icy silence. The little tree felt lonely and deserted. He was trembling more from fear than from the cold. In order to fight his fear, he told himself the swallow's stories. 'Let us sleep!' the apple tree was complaining. 'He doesn't want to bear fruit, but has a big mouth, our young neighbour,' the apricot tree was moaning, and the two enemies agreed for the first time.

It was a cold winter, there was hardly any rain or snow. The colder it got, the more the young tree thought of the swallows and dreamt of their stories.

Exhausted and almost dead from thirst, the trees awoke from their hibernation. They drove their roots deep into the dried-out ground in order to find some moisture. They stretched their branches high into the sky to absorb the sparse dew. Desperately, the little tree tried to quench his thirst also. Searching for water, his fine roots hit again and again against the stronger roots of his neighbours, which were blocking the way; and when he asked them for a bit of space, they shouted:

'Sorry, kid, we have to nourish our fruits.'

Often, the tree dreamed of rain and clouds, and his young leaves were like the images of his dreams.

The swallows listened to the grief of their friend, who no longer wanted to listen to fairy tales. When a tree is thirsty or hungry, it no longer wants to hear stories.

'My neighbours leave hardly any space for me. Can't you help me?'

'But how?' the swallows asked concerned.

'I want to fly south with you because I wouldn't survive another winter here.'

When the swallows gathered in the autumn to fly south, the little tree said goodbye to his neighbours.

'What do you mean by "goodbye"? A tree doesn't travel anywhere!' The apricot tree was incensed.

'But yes! When you don't have anything to eat and to drink any more, then you leave, no matter whether you're a tree or a swallow.'

The young tree used his roots to pack some soil and stretched his branches high into the sky. Hundreds of swallows pulled him out of the dusty, dry ground and flew away with him.

'I have never seen such a crazy tree before!' said the apricot tree and gave a wide yawn, and the apple tree nodded in agreement.

The swallows flew higher and higher. They hurried south without rest. Astonished, the little tree looked down at mountains, valleys and rivers. After several days, they reached their destination together.

'Where are you going?'

'To the rock-face over there,' the swallows answered.

'Can trees live in a rock?'

'No, but you can live in the forest at the bottom of it!'

The little tree was looking at the dense forest. 'No, there's no space. Carry me down to the shimmering river! I can live there.'

The swallows glided down and lowered the little tree gently on to the water.

'We will visit you!' they called and flew to their nests in the rock-face.

The water carried the tree downstream to a calm bend in the river. Glad of the cool water, the tree began to wash the dust off his leaves that had collected on the long journey.

'You're a strange kind of fish!' he finally heard a soft voice say. A small red fish was staring at him in surprise.

'He's just lying on the water and swimming. We on the other hand have to work hard so as not to fall over.'

'Who are you?' a black fish pushed forward.

'I am a tree!'

'A tree fish? I've never heard of such a thing before!'

'Can all tree fish swim so well?' the red fish asked curiously.

'I don't know! I can,' the young tree answered embarrassed.

'Trees must be great fish,' the black fish went into raptures, and the young tree was feeling overjoyed. He told them about his journey, and, after a while, a huge school of fish was listening to him. Many young fish had dreamt of flying one day, but older fish just shook their heads over the talkative little tree. Whether old or young, they listened attentively to his exciting stories and were happy to have him as a new neighbour. Fish usually don't talk much and like to listen. While the young tree washed and told his stories, the water rinsed away the soil from his roots.

'I'm hungry,' he cried.

'And what do tree fish eat?' a small red fish asked him.

'The ground and the sun have given me life, that's why I have to stand upright. Trees like me can only live upright. Please help me to drive my roots into the ground.' A large school of fish grabbed his roots and pulled them deep down. The water helped, and after several tries, the tree was standing upright. He drove his roots deep into the soft ground. Proudly, but somewhat tired, the fish watched the tree and were surprised at the many young leaves, which looked like green fish. On this first day, the tree told fairy tales until late at night.

When he woke up, the sun was already high in the sky. There was not a single fish in sight. He called them, but they did not seem to hear his voice.

'A pelican is lurking nearby,' explained a swallow, which was passing and heard his call. 'That's why all the fish have escaped.'

Suddenly, the young tree was reminded of his loneliness up north. He was furious at the pelican.

'Don't be afraid of the pelican! I'm your friend after all!' the young tree called to the fish. 'As long as I'm nearby, no pelican will dare to do you any harm.'

Only after several calls did a small black fish dare to leave his hiding-place.

'Are you not afraid of the pelican?' he asked the young tree in a soft voice.

'No! And I will prove to him what it means to be a tree!' His branches were whipping the water. He didn't know the pelican, and trees are not afraid of anybody they don't know. But fish do know the pelican. That's why only three small fish dared to leave their hiding-place and kept as close as possible to their friend's trunk.

Suddenly there was a bang. Because it was accompanied by splashing water, the tree could no longer see anything. As if through a veil, he saw the pelican emerge from the whirl of water. The three fish had disappeared. Furiously, the tree stretched out his branches and grabbed the pelican by the neck. The latter wriggled wildly, but couldn't get free. The tree pulled the pelican towards him and hit his head with one of his branches.

'Don't you ever do this again! Return my friends immediately?' he yelled at the frightened bird.

'What's it to you? You're not their father, are you!' the pelican croaked hoarsely, gasping for air because the branches were strangling him.

'I'm not their father, but their friend. Spit them out!' He shook the pelican and hit his head once more.

The pelican was afraid for his life. He opened his enormous beak, and the small fish were able to jump into the water.

'Come here everybody and look at the pelican!' the tree shouted, and more and more fish came out of their hiding-places. For the first time, they were able to laugh at the pelican, who was trapped in the branches, flapping his wings furiously.

'Off with you and never show your face here again!' the tree ordered, slapping him again.

The fish watched cheerfully, as the bird left.

'Friendship between trees and fish is the worst possible bad luck,' the pelican cursed and disappeared.

But his bad luck was greatly enjoyed by the fish. Merrily they danced around their friend's trunk. And if you listened carefully, you could hear them sing for the very first time.

21

The Last Words of the Migrant Rat*
Rafik Shami

It's time to say goodbye. Your presence drives away my fears and fills me with mourning. I know now what I'm about to lose when I leave you.

All my life, I have outwitted death, and, when I come face to face with death now, I do so in order to secure the safety of my community.

There is food everywhere, as ample as never before, and yet it smells suspiciously of jasmine. We are driven to it by hunger, but held back by fear. It is my intention to break through the border between our suspicion and certainty.

I will try this food, and, if I die, please avoid everything that smells of jasmine; multiply and tell your grandchildren tirelessly: Not everything that smells of jasmine is the much sought-after blossom. Death is lurking behind many a pleasant scent.

You might have wondered already why I called you here. At this moment, I am standing face to face with death, and I am not afraid of anything in the world. So urgent was my wish to tell you this before I leave you that I could no longer sleep. It was burning stronger and stronger in my chest. This is my last gift to you; remember it well.

None of you has ever asked me where I come from. Where one is from is not important, only that one is here. This is the most beautiful aspect of our community. But today I want to tell you: My parents lived in Egypt. My father died very early, and my mother had always been very timid. There had been hardly any rain for several years. The drought tormented us as well as all the people there. But we heard of people in the harbour who were hoarding maize and rice. This is customary for human beings. Whenever some go hungry, others hoard food. Like many young rats, I wanted to run to the harbour. My mother cried out of fear. The harbour, she said, swallows young rats, and the demon of the ships

---

* 'Das letzte Wort der Wanderratte', *Der fliegende Baum* (Kiel: Neuer Malik Verlag, 1991), 208–15.

enchants them so that they forget their way home. Nevertheless, I left our little home in the delta of the Nile, and, together with a few friends, I hurried to the harbour. Honestly, I was not afraid. My stomach was growling louder than a cat. Why should I be afraid of demons in that state? Some friends stayed on the bank of the river, others crept with me on board one of the ships. In a huge storage room, where we found enough to eat, I met an incredibly beautiful female, and we spent some hours of tenderness together. My friends and I debated for a long time whether we should stay on the ship or return to the shore. Suddenly, there was a loud noise, and a terrible howling scared me and my friends. Immediately we remembered the demon, and we ran quickly to try to escape to the shore, but the ship was already at sea.

Oh well, I said to myself, I'll be able to live somewhere else as well. As you know, the world is the homeland of us rats; it's only people who are separated and excluded by barbed wire.

For more than five days, I lived in the belly of this ship. There was enough maize, wheat and onions, but everything tasted of salt – I'll never forget this – as if the farmers of Egypt watered their fields with their tears.

Whether in fields or in the basements of houses, I found friends everywhere! How enriching it has been for me to live with you! Our community is rich in experience because of the many different rats who build it. The frugality of the desert rats is paired with the generosity of those who inhabit the pastures. We like to have fun and never go hungry. The experience of our brothers from the north, which enables them to survive any temperature, is coupled with the experiences of our brothers from the south, where the heat is deadly at times. We are equal to any kind of weather. This is our strength. So close to each other and yet so different.

Look at our brothers and sisters, the laboratory rats. Since man began catching them, he has made them as pale as snow and crammed them into cages. Then they stopped talking to each other. There is nothing more to be said because they have turned into pale reflections of themselves. They're not alive. They're waiting for death. They sleep like clockwork, eat and drink like clockwork and get shots like clockwork.

Once I sneaked from the yard into the laboratory through an open window. Almost one hundred brothers and sisters were squeaking in an iron cage. I was furious with rage and forgot my hunger. It took hours of fighting with the latch before I was able to open the door. Sweating, I shouted at them to hurry. But do you think they were happy, happy like one of us who'd been helped out of a trap and forgot the pain of a bleeding leg in the joyful jubilation of our community? They only looked at me with their dull, red eyes. And now? Run away. A beautiful night in the forest is awaiting you. Your way is lit by bright stars. And who will bring us breakfast? some asked. Do you have clocks? others wanted to know. I explained to them that freedom tastes better than all the clocks in the world. But man has poisoned their spirit and planted invisible latches into their hearts, which no rat can destroy any more. They didn't understand my words and scoffed at freedom. Some of them even started to make fun of my dirty coat, explaining to me that they would rather stay in their cage and keep the velvet coats which man had given them. What craziness! It wouldn't occur to any rat, not even in his dreams, to turn arrogant, just because of a reddish or brown coat.

Man is different. When man cannot find anything else to make him feel superior, he looks at his brother disparagingly and calls out arrogantly: We'll show you southerners who is the master of the house. Well, you're giggling and rightly so, because man is stupid. We'll only become smarter if we avoid his stupidity. Man has a bad memory. He doesn't learn from his history. For us rats, the past is the mother of our present. Therefore, I am going to tell a story for the sake of our young friends, a story that proves how short man's memory really is.

Hamlin is a small town in northern Germany. It is situated on the Weser. Once, thousands of people and several hundred rats coexisted there peacefully. One day, a murderer came to Hamlin and told horror stories about us every day. When somebody was sick, he claimed this was due to a rat's bite; when someone's business was bad, he claimed the rats had eaten his stock. The people believed the murderer, and they became intoxicated with the blood of our fathers and mothers. Only a few rats were able to escape from the swords and fire. Afterwards, the murderer kidnapped the town's children. It is said that he abducted one hundred and thirty three children before the people finally drove him out of town. But do not breathe a sigh of relief yet. Man is forgetful. Instead of being ashamed of his dreadful deeds, he forgets them. In Hamlin, there is a memorial named the pied-piper house. Not only are rat murderers forgotten, but murderers of human beings are even admired afterwards.

Man thinks he's the most intelligent being of all. His arrogance is without limits. When someone can add and multiply, but doesn't see that his home is going to ruin, he's a calculating fool. Who has turned rivers into sewers, cities into dumps, and oceans into contaminated death traps? Neither fish nor seagulls. Not us, my dears. Not us! Maybe mother nature thought it wise to equip such a violent being with a bit less sense; for, if man were more intelligent, no rat could survive since man would have uncovered our secret. Whatever malicious poison man may use in his war against us, nothing in the world is going to destroy our will to survive. Do you remember the poison that smelled of apples? It is said that thousands of people were employed to produce it. One house rat from the Ruhr sacrificed himself, and people no longer knew what to do with all the barrels of poison sitting around without a use. Imagine, innumerable huge barrels had all of a sudden disappeared. People were afraid since the poison could be stored in anybody's backyard. The company no longer knew where the barrels were. Just disappeared. But the poison was lurking somewhere among the people. No rat in our community, in contrast, keeps silent when poison is discovered. We know that an individual's life is nothing, while the community will live on eternally. Man is ignorant; that's why he works as if he were going to live eternally and that's why he lives as hurriedly as if he won't survive the night. We have learned from the long life of our community that a rat only has one life to live, work and enjoy.

Now, my dear friends, I will go and try this piece of meat. Watch me carefully, love each other and multiply.

The wise rat walked to the meat. He turned around once more to the congregation and smiled. Many wiped a tear from their eyes and stared sadly at their courageous friend. Only after forty-five days did the rat lose his hair. The rats covered his trembling body with leaves. On the forty-eighth day he died. Hundreds of rats carried him to the river and left his corpse to the mighty waves. They returned, removed the food that smelled of jasmine, loved each other and multiplied.

22

After Yesterday*
Gino Chiellino

– for those friends who would like to give up now, now of all times –

. . . . the sons will
mock and forget
the land of their mothers
the daughters the language of their fathers
                              and even if!
sensitive tellers of untruth
hold our longing
hostage against us
                              and even if!
no peace is promised us
in foreign graveyards
                              and even if!
after yesterday, we will
walk this path of minorities
together, friends,
and if our strength
should fail
our will
will bring us happily
to our goal
                                        for
don't you feel
the tightness of the skin
the sharpness of the wish

* 'Nach dem Gestern', from *Mein fremder Alltag. Gedichte* (Kiel: Neuer Malik Verlag, 1984), 82.

the resoluteness of our thoughts
about what is new?

What is new in us

               we are what is new.

23

Integration, a Thought Consisting of Seven Theses*

Gino Chiellino

Thesis No. 1

For all those who mourn for Italy as I do
– Ballad –

Yes, it's true
in the October wind
– this friend of the rain –
I no longer
feel the music of the chestnuts
the joy
of seeing them falling
before my basket
has gone away

Yes, it's true,
heating doesn't suit me, it can
never
replace the warmth of conversations
the times when
leaning against the wall of the school
beneath the changeable light
of a wintry sun
without beer and wine
with our feet in the snow
words came without effort

---

* 'Integration, ein Gedanke in sieben Thesen', from *Mein fremder Alltag. Gedichte* (Kiel: Neuer Malik Verlag, 1984), 83–91.

Integration, a Thought in Seven Theses

Yes, it's true
Coca-Cola will
never
still
my thirst for water
from our mountains from our sea
The bread is not warm
it doesn't taste of trusted hands
although it is certainly less uncertain
here and now

The conflict remains
          so does the contradiction
the basil
grown
by us in the warmth of a bedroom
changes the colour of the room
it no longer has its green
its smell remains broken

From the incision
that separates me
from a familiar life
I feel the knife
cutting my skin in two
for it is not guided
by me

The retreat to the place of wishes
after yesterday
stills the tears of self-
deception:
arduously to glimpse
the new
is the force that
urges one to live.

Thesis No. 2

On the position of silence
(For G. Fiorenza who wrote:
'I subdivide freedom into three stages:
Easter, August, Christmas,
nine weeks altogether. The rest is
only work.')

As if we had never come to
this country, in which we
have been invisibly silent for 25 years
we have changed life into a train
and forbidden our longing
to leave the tracks

The journey stops
it is April, August, December
a part of it is living
the everyday life of the railway stations
where for a long time no one more is
wanted under the foreign
sky the sharpness of thought is
endangered
it is difficult to refuse
to fight
with thoughts in foreign parts

An arrival was not
planned in the old
new timetable
the country has betrayed
its train stations: the journey comes to a halt.

Thesis No. 3

The enemy of foreigners and his friends

the efforts of everyday life
attack

the limits of contempt
with gawdy head scarves
and jarring demands
the borders
to the outside are broken
the conflict
tracks down those present
in the ghetto
turns them into foreigners
to enemies of foreigners
before the conflict
treasured politicians
turn themselves into
concerned caregivers
planners of the future
external changes
remain unforthcoming
their decision
is still awaited
people are still pressing
for their care
people conform
to their planning
goodness lives on in them
horribly normally
and remains unharmed
for they do not attack
defence is
their art. Today already they rescue
the air and the tongue
from the danger of a possible
future of foreigners
in their country
a decision
against a minority
finds support in the applause
of
their friends.

Thesis No. 4

On the happiness of being full up

your discontent
in front of the Sunday roast
your complete pride
at having already tasted
the honey of life
at fourteen
have a seductive effect
on my children
you still owe
your father
polished by the hunger
of three generations of emigrants
proof
that you are closer to
happiness
until then, I say unto
you
share your happiness
with no one.

Thesis No. 5

Necessary Friends

annoying but tough
in their desire to be sympathetic
strangers interrupt
more often than before
the protective circles
of shadows
around my eyes in foreign parts
no colour
will reach the thoughts
if the eye
nourishes itself on shadows
claim acquaintances

against the backdrop of my black–white–everyday life
with thoughts of affection
belated friends add
colourful lines
to the crevices of my shadows
the eye in foreign parts
should learn to distinguish
shadows crevices
colourful lines
entrust wishes to thoughts
necessary friends maintain
they are right
I still feel the crevices
of rejection
mutual longing is
all the stronger
if there are many friends
if the enemy is nowhere

Thesis No. 6

Longing for a ghetto

. . . . . . with a bus-ticket in my hand
I leave the house
past the garages
I come to the chestnut tree
then to the grounds along the stream
I walk behind myself
check every step
and the glances at me
when I walk past
      the letter
      yesterday's gossip
      the death in the city
at the end of the grounds
I turn back
I will not drive
to the city market
I get into my car

drive to an Italian
shop to
buy groceries there
to break the silence
to be of the same opinion
about the death in the city

3.10.83. 'In an as yet unexplained shooting involving an unmarked police patrol car, 2 step-sons of an Italian died in Augsburg. The father and his 3rd son were seriously wounded.'

Thesis No. 7

The German Passport

It smells of betrayal
of the weaker
amongst us
this deceptive reward
for conformity
hides in vain
from the others
from the conflict
deeply buried in the trouser pocket

    No!
at the end of the Foreigners' Law
and my insecurity
there will
be
no German passport
I myself
falsified
before the future
the tangible future of the children
of my children
and
not by any new border.

−24−

The Café Tales of Abu al Abed*
Jusuf Naoum

At exactly nine o'clock the next day, Abu al Abed entered the café again. He greeted the guests and sat down on his stool. After the circle had formed and there was peace and quiet, Abu al Abed swallowed some tea to moisten his throat and asked as always: 'Where did I leave off last time?'

One of the guests replied: 'You took leave of the wolves at the source of the Nile and then rowed from there to Beirut.'

'Exactly, but that story is already over. Today, dear guests, I will tell you of Sinbad's last journey.

'One day, during the time that I was a vet in West Berlin, my receptionist announced the arrival of Sinbad the Sailor. Oh, I was amazed that this famous man was coming to me personally because I believed like everyone else that he had already died a couple of thousand years ago. We only know him after all from fairy-tale books.

'Anyhow, I thought, what is Sinbad the Sailor doing in West Berlin? Is he looking for new treasures or does he want to experience new adventures? I let my customers and their animals, who were sitting closely packed in the waiting-room, wait and asked my receptionist to show Sinbad in immediately.

'I quickly put on a freshly washed and ironed new white lab coat and put on my glasses. Then I stuffed my pipe with the best English tobacco and sat down in my leather chair behind my big desk. I wanted to make a good impression – after all, I was the most famous vet in West Berlin. That was certainly the reason he had come to me. Moreover, I was looking forward to the visit of an Arabian brother since – as you know, dear guests – Sinbad comes from Baghdad.

'Now, as you know, Sinbad is immensely rich and so the thought entered my head that he was perhaps looking me up so that I could use my connections to help him with the purchase of a few high-rises, plots of

* *Die Kaffeehausgeschichten des Abu al Abed* (Frankfurt-on-Main: Brandes & Apsel Verlag, 1987), 61–76.

land, hotels and restaurants in the city. In West Berlin, you see, every purchase of land or a property is subsidized by the city so that the city doesn't die out. By the way, a high wall runs through the city; the West Berliners built it themselves so that the inhabitants of the other part of the city can't see how rich West Berlin is.

'This is an excellent opportunity for me, too, I thought. Of course, I will let Sinbad benefit from my contacts with the authorities. But I will also charge my brother a handsome commission. You know: if you scratch my back I'll scratch yours and you can't make something out of nothing. After all, we doctors have to live as well.

'Then I heard a timid, quiet knock at my door. I quickly got up to greet my guest. What I saw was a man in his early fifties, perhaps, with broad shoulders and short legs, a fat moustache and black hair. He was wearing a rather old, grey sports jacket and his legs were squeezed into brown tweed trousers that were much too tight. I was very surprised since I had, after all, been expecting an elegant gentleman with diamond rings and a silk caftan.

'The gentleman noticed my surprise and said to me: "You must be disappointed. You almost surely believed I was the rich and famous Sinbad the Sailor from the fairy-tales. I, however, am Sinbad the Aviator. Like my namesake I've travelled around a lot but it didn't make me rich. I lost the only fortune I ever owned – which meant a lot to me – in the Grunewald lake."

'I was completely baffled: "Pardon? Lost in the Grunewald lake? What did you lose then?"

'"That is a long story. But first of all I need a vaccination card for my donkey. Please help me."

'I was once again astonished. I hadn't reckoned on a donkey. In my entire career as a vet I had never had any dealings with a donkey. My customers consisted of dogs, cats, guinea-pigs, rabbits and occasionally also snakes and lizards. Once I even had a baby tiger. But this was the first time I'd ever come face to face with a donkey.

'But I quickly pulled myself together: "Yes, of course, I will always help an Arabian brother. Please, bring me your donkey."

'Sinbad went back out into the waiting-room and led the donkey in. It was a handsome donkey, dear guests, with a shiny, white coat, muscular hindquarters and friendly, gentle eyes. Its hooves were well rounded and freshly shod; on its back it carried a hand-embroidered saddle. Its mouth, which was full of ivory-coloured teeth, looked very healthy. Without my having to say a word, the donkey lay down on my examination bed. Never before had I encountered such a clever animal.

'I asked Sinbad why he needed the vaccination card.

'"For the German authorities."

'"Why?" I enquired. "Do you have a circus? Perhaps elephants, bears and lions as well? Should I vaccinate them too?"

'"No," Sinbad reassured me, "I don't have a circus."

'And then he began to tell me his story.

'Like myself, Sinbad the Aviator had travelled around a lot in the Arabian countries, in Persia, India and Turkey. Travelling was easy for him. He only needed to get aboard his flying carpet and, swish, it would rise into the air. When travelling, he was always accompanied by his donkey. He had taught it how to speak and could therefore communicate quite well with it.

'This time, too, Sinbad had, as always, spread out the map and pointed to a spot with his finger. That was where he wanted to fly to. If he hadn't miscalculated, the journey would take a whole week, even if the winds were favourable.

'He went to the bazaar and bought the necessary provisions: coffee, tee, round flat bread, dried lamb and water melons.

'On the day he flew off it was nice and warm, the air was perfectly clear and the sky was dark blue.

'Towards evening the carpet, along with Sinbad and his donkey, rose up and glided through the air like a sailing-ship. The stars were shining like diamonds and were twinkling down at the earth below. It was the time of the half moon. It looks like a string of jasmines, thought Sinbad happily to himself.

'When the carpet had reached the proper height and was heading north, where Sinbad intended to visit the Eskimos, he closed his eyes contentedly. He was not afraid of oversleeping because his donkey was accustomed to wakening him during journeys.

'No sooner had Sinbad closed his eyes than he began to dream: He was playing with two lionesses at the edge of a river. The predators were as trustworthy as domestic cats. He stroked them without the slightest fear and they suckled him with their milk. Then, in his dream, he caught sight of innumerable fish; small and large fish were swimming peacefully alongside each other in the ocean, and no fish was harming another. He also dreamed of Solomon's treasure. It was lying in a large temple and everyone could take a few pearls and rubies from it because there were enough for everyone.

'Suddenly he saw a huge, black animal which looked like a scorpion. The animal wanted to sting Sinbad in the neck and he became so afraid that he woke up.

'When he opened his eyes it was already broad daylight. He was annoyed at his donkey because it hadn't woken him up. But the donkey was still sleeping itself.

'Sinbad shook it awake and they began to prepare breakfast together. The donkey made coffee and Sinbad cut the bread and meat. They put everything on a sliver platter and began to eat breakfast.

'"Did you have pleasant dreams?" enquired the donkey.

'"I dreamt about lions, fish and a large treasure," replied Sinbad, "It was wonderful! But then a large, black animal came along. It looked like a scorpion and wanted to sting me in the neck. I was terribly frightened and woke up. What could this huge, black animal signify?"

'"We will often meet the huge, black animal. It most surely wants to disturb our journey. You behaved wrongly, Sinbad. You should have defended yourself instead of running away. You have strong hands and a sharp dagger. Why didn't you pierce the heart of the black animal? It would now be dead. But, as it is, it will not leave us in peace, it will continue to follow us."

'"It was much stronger than me. I couldn't do anything on my own," Sinbad countered. Secretly he was thinking that it was only a dream, over and done with, and that he would never again encounter the black beast.

'Sinbad drank another mouthful of coffee, was satisfied that he was full, rinsed out his mouth and wiped off his beard with some water. Then he admired the sky around him.

'Seven days and nights passed. According to Sinbad's calculations they would arrive at their destination on the eighth day.

'He looked down curiously at the ground. There he saw a large forest.

'"What could that be down there?" he asked his donkey.

'"Let's land here," the donkey suggested, "and then we'll find out where we are."

'"We can't land in the woods, we'll have to find flat land," explained Sinbad.

'They searched in all directions. Suddenly the donkey cried out loudly and shook its head with joy: "There, there, look, the big town. We are at our destination!"

'Sinbad took his telescope and looked in the direction the donkey was pointing. In amazement he shouted: "Such an enormous city as that can only be Baghdad! But how? We're seven days journey from Baghdad. Did I perhaps calculate wrongly? That would be most annoying. What am I supposed to do in Baghdad? I know the city like I know my carpet."

'He steered the carpet nearer to the city. Then he realized that it wasn't Baghdad but rather a strange city that lay before him. He had never been here before. There were no mosques here. Instead there were buildings with at least thirty stories. They frightened him, because he was afraid that his carpet would collide with one of these enormous houses.

'He deliberated and looked for a place to land. Then, unfortunately, a bad storm got up. A crosswind caught hold of the flying carpet and forced it to the ground. Sinbad and his donkey fell into a lake and lost the carpet.

'A deep sorrow overcame Sinbad because he felt lost without his carpet.

'The donkey consoled him: "Calm down, it could be a lot worse. We are still alive. Let's gather all our strength and swim to the bank. It'll take half an hour at the most for us to reach land."

'Sinbad hesitated.

'"You're a good swimmer," said the donkey encouragingly. "You told me once you were the crocodile of the Nile. Now you can prove it."

'"But the carpet," objected Sinbad, "where can it be? How can we get home again if we don't like the strange city?"

'They swam for more than half an hour until they reached the bank. They were exhausted and freezing all over. But no matter where they looked they couldn't see any people.

'Sinbad lit a fire and dried his caftan. When it was finally dry he could hardly recognize it. It was completely black and the donkey, too, was very dirty for both had fallen into the filthy sludge of the Grunewald lake. Sinbad brushed his donkey's coat but he couldn't get it clean again.

'Presently, they set off through the Grunewald area. They passed beautiful white houses. Some had marble entrances and a swimming-pool. There were large parks with neatly cut lawns and the flowers were arranged in rows. The place reminded Sinbad of Baghdad but even there he hadn't seen so many palaces. He had never seen anything like it in his life before and he believed that all the people in this city lived in such wonderful villas.

'This thought inspired him with courage and hope because he thought that those who owned such beautiful houses must surely be hospitable. He and his donkey would most certainly receive a warm welcome.

'There was a light on in one of the villas. Sinbad knocked at the door, but no one answered. Then Sinbad knocked harder until a man appeared in a silk dressing-gown, accompanied by an enormous mastiff. When he caught sight of Sinbad and his donkey he began to curse loudly: "What are you guest workers doing here in the Grunewald?"

'Sinbad none the less greeted the man friendly in Arabic: "Peace be with you!" and asked if he could spend the night at his house.

'"Leave my property at once," the man roared back, "or I'll call the police!" And with that he set his dog upon Sinbad who had no choice but to flee.

'They carried on through the Grunewald. Sinbad knocked at another door. An elderly woman looked inquiringly out of the window and was alarmed when she saw Sinbad and his donkey. She thought he was Ali Baba and that the forty robbers were lurking in the background. Her face turned pale and Sinbad could see how hard her heart began to beat beneath the thin gown. She quickly shut the window.

'Disappointed, Sinbad and his donkey continued on their way. On his way through the Grunewald he knocked at more than twenty doors but no one opened up for him. Nobody wanted him as their guest.

'"If only I had my carpet I wouldn't spend a second more here," he moaned.

'The donkey trotted pensively behind him. After a while it said: "Don't be sad. We've always been lucky in the past. People were friendly to us and treated us like guests. Perhaps we'll also find someone here who will take us in. We just have to look around a little more."

'They left the Grunewald and arrived at a very wide street. It was brightly lit and in both directions there were shops, hotels and flats.

'"If it wasn't for these high-rises this street would look like the Baghdad bazaar," said Sinbad to his donkey.

'The pungent smell of half-burned curry sausage emerged from small kiosks at the side of the road. The smell was made worse by the exhausts of cars racing by. The donkey stuck a cork in its nose; it couldn't stand it any more. And Sinbad felt the same way, even though he didn't follow the donkey's example.

'On the other hand, Sinbad liked the splendid shop windows with their pretty mannequins. At first he thought they were real women and so he winked at them and chatted them up; but none of them reacted. He couldn't understand that. He had always been successful with the ladies in Baghdad. He only had to say: "I am Sinbad," and a number of them would follow. Here, however, he was knocking at the windows to attract the girls' attention and still they remained stiff and motionless.

'Sinbad and his donkey carried on. They met a few drunks. One of them cursed at Sinbad and his donkey, another laughed at them both, and a third said sullenly: "Have the guest workers already bought so many Mercedes that they have converted to donkeys?"

'Sinbad spoke to a few passers-by. Most of them dismissed him instantly, others didn't understand him.'

Abu al Abed took a small break, drank a mouthful of tea to moisten his throat and continued with the tale of Sinbad:

'"Allah has abandoned me, doctor. On the Ku'damm, at a bus-stop, I met a Turk called Mustafa Bülbül. He noticed right away that I was desperate and invited me and my donkey to his home. Mustafa lived on the fifth floor of a semi-derelict building in a fourth courtyard of a building in Kreuzberg. There he inhabited a tiny, little, dark room with an outside toilet. His mattress and three cushions lay on one side of the room. In another corner stood an orange box with a hotplate and two pots on top of it. When I saw this tiny room I felt inhibited about staying there. But Mustafa removed this feeling with his hospitality. He prepared a kebab for us to eat and in the evening he fetched two blankets from friends so that my donkey and I could sleep.

'"I slept for seven days and seven nights. Mustafa Bülbül was very worried about me, but my donkey explained to him that I wasn't ill. It told him I usually slept like this after long journeys so that I could gather new strength."

'But now I am also tired,' said Abu al Abed, interrupting his story, 'and I want to go home. Tomorrow, dear guests, I will tell you of Sinbad's other experiences in West Berlin.'

And with that Abu al Abed took his leave from his audience and went home.

The next evening, at exactly nine o'clock, Abu al Abed entered the café again. He greeted his guests and sat down on his stool. After the circle had formed and peace and quiet reigned, he drank a mouthful of tea to moisten his throat. Then he asked as always: 'Where did I leave off last time?'

One of the guests answered: 'At the point where Sinbad had slept seven days and nights in Mustafa Bülbül's room.'

'Oh yes, now I remember. Well – when Sinbad woke up on the eighth day, towards noon, he looked around himself in amazement. He wasn't sure that he wasn't still dreaming and he didn't know where he was until he caught sight of his donkey and Mustafa Bülbül.

'Mustafa offered him Kufta meat with tomato sauce and they drank Ayran along with it.

'Then Mustafa told him what he had been up to in the meantime. He had enquired about a job for Sinbad in the factory where he worked. Unfortunately, however, he had met with no success since the firm wouldn't employ anyone without a work permit. But he told Sinbad that he shouldn't give up hope. It was still possible that he could work for a slave dealer. When Sinbad heard the word "slave", he gave a start: "I was born a free man and I want to die as one, too."

'"Slavery is a little bit different these days," Mustafa tried to explain, "the slave dealer is an employment agent who offers work to foreigners who don't have a work permit. In return he takes half their pay as a commission. The agent sends you to a factory or a large department store and you have to do what is requested. Sometimes you're lucky and you can work there for several days; but most of the time you have to change your workplace on a daily basis."

'Hard though it was, Sinbad had no choice but to go to the job agent for he didn't have any money and so couldn't return to his homeland.

'The slave dealer gave him a job in a lift factory.

'Mustafa Bülbül lent him a shirt, a pair of trousers and a jacket and accompanied him to the factory gate at five o'clock, for Sinbad wouldn't have found it on his own.

'A secretary came up to Sinbad. He showed her the yellow piece of paper that he had got from the slave dealer.

'"Speak German?" she asked while looking at the paper.

'"No understand," said Sinbad, "I Arabian, Turkish, Persian, Indian."

'The secretary called a foreman over. He understood a few words of Turkish and took Sinbad along with him.

'He stopped at a large area covered with many iron bars. He showed Sinbad how to sort out the bars according to length and strength. Then the foreman disappeared.

'Sinbad worked like crazy. He thought he would be able to go home if he finished earlier. But scarcely had he sorted out the last of the bars than new ones were delivered. Ten minutes before finishing time, Sinbad sat down on the floor, completely exhausted. But just at that moment the boss came by. "Get up immediately!" he shouted at Sinbad. "You don't get paid to sit around here! You are in Germany here, not Arabia. We can't use layabouts here!"

'Thereupon Sinbad was sacked.

'Mustafa was not in the least surprised when Sinbad told him what had happened. He knew only too well that a guest worker without a residence and work permit has no rights. He therefore suggested to him that he would go with him to the aliens branch of the police; he hoped that he would maybe get a residence permit. Then the donkey pricked up its ears: "Do I need a residence permit, too?"

'Mustafa explained to him that he would have to go to the vet to get a vaccination card.

'"And now I'm here, doctor," said Sinbad, "to ask you for such a vaccination card for my donkey."

'I, Abu al Abed, first of all carried out a careful general examination of the donkey. I didn't discover any illnesses, all tests were negative. Then I gave him two injections and issued the relevant vaccination card. Finally, I wished Sinbad and his donkey luck.

'That was the first time, dear guests, that I had ever treated an animal free of charge in my West Berlin practice. As you know – Abu al Abed has a soft heart.'

Someone in the audience interrupted Abu al Abed and shouted: 'Did you do anything else to help Sinbad? After all, you had good connections in West Berlin.'

'But, of course,' replied Abu al Abed. 'I sacrificed a whole day and went with him to the police. The room there was full to the ceiling with foreigners. We had to wait for over seven hours for our turn. For the first time ever, even my business card didn't help. Sinbad and I had to wait like everyone else. Then we finally heard Sinbad's name being called. When we went into the room, we were received by a female official with a sullen expression. She constantly asked for information she could have taken from the passport: what was Sinbad's name, where was he born, and if he had come to West Berlin illegally.

'"Yes," I replied, "he came here illegally. But not via Schönefeld or Tegel airports as you perhaps suspect. He landed in the Grunewald."

'The official was very confused: "Since when has there been an airport in the Grunewald?"

'"He crashed there with his flying carpet and his donkey, which accompanies him, in the middle of the Grunewald lake," I informed her.

'The official got very angry, because she thought I was making a fool of her. For fifteen minutes she flicked through Sinbad's passport. Then she explained to us that she would have to turn down the application for a residence permit and that the employment office wouldn't issue a work permit either.

'I, Abu al Abed, got very angry at this point. "Sinbad doesn't want to stay here for long. He just wants to work a bit to save money for his trip home. I will vouch for him!"

'The official, however, did not take this offer up. Sinbad only got a tourist visa that was valid for a month.

'During this time he had no legal right to work. Sinbad was once again forced to work illegally.

'Fortunately, he was able to help out in a Turkish grocery in Kreuzberg and could save a little money for his trip home. And after a month, he broke open his piggy-bank. But, unfortunately, he didn't have enough.

'Then Mustafa Bülbül collected money from his Turkish friends and Sinbad went to the travel agency straight away. He ordered two air tickets to Baghdad, but the employee at the travel agency made it clear that he couldn't take his donkey with him. It could only be transported in a transport plane and that would be very expensive.

'Sinbad left the travel agency in despair. On the street, he cried like a small child who had lost his mother. He ran sobbing through the streets.

'It just so happened to be the day that the bulky refuse was being collected. Some people were throwing old things on to the streets and others were diving on them like vultures: washing machines, televisions, fridges, mattresses, blankets, cushions, armchairs, shelves and many other things, which, in some cases, were like new.

'Sinbad looked closely at the things. He was thinking he could maybe find something for Mustafa's room. And while he was fishing a few blankets out of the mountain of rubbish he suddenly came across a carpet.

'He couldn't believe it: it was the flying carpet he had lost in the Grunewald lake. Overjoyed, he pressed his carpet to his chest and kissed it. He did a song and dance through the streets, until he reached Mustafa's room.

'On this day a big farewell party began at Mustafa's. It lasted seven days and seven nights.

'I, Abu al Abed, was also invited.

'Dear guests, I had never before experienced such a wonderful party. There was grilled lamb, Kubi, tabouli, hummus, stuffed vine leaves and courgettes, zucchini, and the wine flowed like water. Sinbad had bought them with the money he had saved for the two air-tickets and he no longer needed since he had found his flying carpet.

'Up till then, I had attended many parties in West Berlin, in the Hilton, the Bristol, the Kempinski. But I had never felt so much at home as at Mustafa's farewell party for Sinbad.

'On the eighth day of the festivities, shortly before midnight, Sinbad asked all the guests to gather on the roof. Before this, he had returned the jacket, trousers and shirt to Mustafa and had put on his caftan and wrapped his turban around his head. He thanked Mustafa Bülbül and myself, shook hands with his friends, kissed Mustafa and embraced me.

'He mounted his flying carpet and his donkey sat down beside him. Then the carpet rose up and soon the smoke-blackened layer of smog lay beneath Sinbad and his donkey. Above them, they once again saw the bright, clear, shining stars.

'Sinbad steered the carpet in the direction of Baghdad and shut his eyes contentedly.

'When he woke up, he found himself in front of a café in the Baghdad bazaar. He met a crowd of farmers who had left their fields and were waiting to be able to travel to Germany to work in a factory there.

'They were curious when they heard that Sinbad and his donkey had just come from that country and they wanted to hear how guest workers lived there.

'But when they saw Sinbad's empty hands they were very surprised and one of them called out: "Where is the car, Sinbad? Where is the TV, the video, the washing-machine then? Where are the beautiful shirts and suits?"' With these words, Abu al Abed ended the story of Sinbad the Aviator and promised his audience that he would tell them of further adventures the following day.

Without any protest or pressure they allowed Abu al Abed to go home. They were very pensive and quiet that evening.

Margarita's Diary*

Elina Torossi

I love the district I live in. A lot has changed here over the years. I was three years old when my family moved here and the grey façades of the old houses made a dismal impression. The entrances to the houses were dusty, the wooden stairs creaked, and there was a lot of sadness and anxiety lurking in the streets. I was especially afraid of the older German women, who always used to shout at us children when we were playing. And the grown-ups were afraid as well: mum was afraid of the Turkish women in their headscarves, dad was afraid of the German police in their green uniforms, and our neighbour, a slightly built Italian, was afraid of the strong voice of his fat wife. His vegetable shop with its brightly coloured fruit and vegetables was the only swab of colour in our street. Later my uncle opened a snack bar serving Greek food around the corner. People would often gather in front of it and during the day you could hear Greek music when you went past.

Then more and more students and young people moved here because, as my dad said, the rents were cheaper. Shortly, two of them opened a little flower shop with a funny awning over it. With time the brightly coloured awnings grew more common and a few of the grey façades received a fresh coat of paint. Pavements were paved to make footpaths and here and there trees were planted and benches set up. Now the old women often sit in the sun and complain less and less. They remind me of my grandmother and the aunts in our village in Greece. And they are happy when I greet them in Bavarian as I cycle by. 'Grüss Gott, Margarita!' they shout back at me.

* 'Margaritas Tagebuch', *Gute Reise meine Augen: Texte von Griechinnen und Griechen in Deutschland* (Stuttgart: Peter-Grohmann-Verlag, 1992), 68–9.

Part VI
Turks in Germany: From German Turks to Turkish-Germans

Numbering around two million, the Turkish minority is the largest foreign minority resident in Germany today. This group has been the focus of much of the recent right-wing xenophobia. It was Turks who were murdered in arson attacks at Mölln and Solingen. Since unification, moreover, the already prevalent verbal and physical abuse of Turks in *reality* everyday life has vastly increased, while they continue to encounter prejudice when seeking housing or a job.

As a response to this widespread and apparently increasing prejudice and, more particularly, to the wave of xenophobia that has followed German unification, young Turks have begun to form youth gangs to protect themselves. Others, however, have responded differently: Turks (and Germans) have taken to the streets to demonstrate against the violence. Turkish representatives have engaged in discussions with German authorities in search of safety and solutions. And a number of Turkish intellectuals, attributing the intense intolerance and violence against foreigners largely to ignorance, have set out to engage in a dialogue with the German population about the history as well as the current situation of Turks within German society.

The writings collected in this chapter present interesting accounts of the reasons for the migration of Turks to Germany, of the socio-economic and legal position of Turks within German society, of their religious orientation, and, perhaps most importantly, of experiences and aspirations of young Turks who have been shaped by two very different cultures and who are searching for an identity.

These accounts depict a complex picture of Turks in Germany differentiated along generational and gender lines and thus undermining the monochrome image that seems to be prominent in German society. Difference within the Turkish minority in Germany, moreover, also arises from ethnicity. Conflicts between the Turkish majority and the Kurds are not only a problem in Turkey, but have also surfaced in Germany.

The first generation of unskilled Turkish guest workers, who entered German society from the mid-1960s onwards, emerges as a low-paid "underclass," segregated from the German population in cheap housing, which they not only tolerated but often preferred in order to finance summer trips home to their families or to fund the business they dreamed of establishing upon their ultimate return to their homeland.[1]

The experiences and dreams of this generation, as well as the difficulties of living between two cultures and two countries, inform much of the so-called *Gastarbeiterliteratur* of the 1970s and 1980s, as seen in the previous section. In the accounts of the 1990s, however, this group is nearing retirement age and facing the prospect of exchanging their low-paid jobs for even lower pensions, on account of the fact that they entered the German pension schemes late in life. In most cases, furthermore, the dream of returning home has not been realized. In their old age, they feel not only estranged from their homeland, where they are considered to be German Turks, but also from their children, who followed them to Germany in the mid-1970s subsequent to the end of recruitment (*Anwerbestop*) and who have been influenced by German ways.

The second and third generations of Turks in Germany, who came to Germany as children or were born in the country, live, like their parents' generation, between two worlds. While they learn or work in a German environment, they live, for the most part, in a Turkish one. However, although influenced by and attached to both cultures, they are much more fully integrated into German society than the first generation. In most cases, the Turkish homeland is something they know only from brief holiday visits.

Yet, while Germany is the main point of reference for these younger generations, this does not mean that, by and large, they consider themselves German. Rather, the majority view themselves as Turkish-Germans and, insistent upon their dual identity, do not see much point in exchanging their Turkish passports for German ones at the age of eighteen, particularly if that means having to give up Turkish citizenship in the process.

As becomes particularly obvious in Ayse's and Devrim's contributions to this chapter, the young Turks' life and identity between two cultures also lead to conflict with older Turks, in which generational and gender issues are intertwined. Young Turks have begun to question Turkish practices and values, such as the authoritarian and patriarchal family structure prevalent in the Turkish community, kinship networks, the Islamic tradition of arranged marriage and female dress, as well as the influence

---

1. For English-language accounts of the history of Turkish migration into Germany and the problems connected with it, see Elçin Kürasat-Ahlers, 'The Turkish Minority in German Society', in *Turkish Culture in German Society Today*, eds David Horricks and Eva Kolinsky, (Oxford: Berghahn, 1996), 113–35 and Dursun Tan and Hans-Peter Waldhoff, 'Turkish Everyday Culture in Germany and its Prospects', *Turkish Culture in German Society Today*, 137–56.

of Islam and the Turkish government and authorities on the lives of Turks in Germany.

Competent in the German language and politically self-assured, the young generations of Turks have also begun to articulate critical views not only of Turkish but also of German culture in public. Criticizing German xenophobia and racism, Kemal Kurt and Zafer Şenocak and Bülent Tulay in their contributions to this chapter insist on dual citizenship and equal rights rather than complete conformity to German norms. The writer, actress and director Emine Özdamar for her part writes from a position of resistance to dominant German culture, but simultaneously engages with that culture. Her text, 'Karagöz in Alamania/Blackeye in Germany', mixes fragments of German culture and Turkish narratives and at the same time serves as a link to the writings of an earlier generation. The initial culture shock that was experienced and thematized by the first Turkish 'guest workers' to arrive in Germany resurfaces in this text, forming a parallel to the earlier autobiographical accounts on a different level of literary expression. Ismet Elçi, the Kurdish actor, writer and director, is also a master at mixing cultural traditions. The passage presented in this chapter, taken from Elçi's most recent, not yet published novel *Die verwundeten Kinder des Zarathustra* (Zarathustra's Wounded Children), tells the story of a young boy who is smuggled into the 'holy land' (Germany), where he has to struggle with the bureaucracy to gain asylum. The boy, who was sent to this foreign place by his father so that he would escape persecution, does not feel at home in paradise. The text chronicles his search for a home between two cultures, societies and religions. The child experiences these different worlds in fairy-tale manner: he moves between the 'holy land' and the home of the mountain people (the Kurds), between past, present and future in the hope of finding a home(land).

–26–

Karagöz in Alamania/Blackeye in Germany*
Emine Sevgi Özdamar

IT GREW DARK.
IT GREW LIGHT.

Now they stood before the Door to Germany. The path that led to this door was clogged with bundles and suitcases. Two Turkish women: one without a headshawl told another with a headshawl that her husband had moved to another house in Alamania because he had found a German woman, and now she did not know where to find him. The Turkish woman with the headshawl gave her some advice: 'The German police will find him immediately. I know men go to Alamania, grow feathers, strut about like a peacock and think German women are beautiful and smell beautiful.'

The Turkish woman without a headshawl said: 'I have seen their women. They iron and iron their hair. They sew up their bosoms every day or flop, let them hang down. Allah gave each of them an arse, but they only jiggle with it, zirr – zirr – zirr.' The Turkish woman with the headshawl said to the Turkish woman without the headshawl: 'Allah should curse your husband. Inshallah, go then, report him to the police and pull out one of his molars.'

Other Turks were waiting at the Door to Germany: a man with a sheep, a *hodsha* with his minaret.

An illegal worker masqueraded as a soccer player, hoping to get through the border patrol. The farmer and his donkey also waited. They waited and they waited. The Door to Germany opened and closed again. A Turkish dead man arrived, carrying his coffin. The man with the sheep asked his sheep: 'When you are going to a burial, should you go in front of or behind the coffin?'

* From *Mother Tongue* 77–95. © Coach House Press, 1994 and Rotbuch Verlag, 1990. Translation © Estate of Craig Thomas. Reprinted by permission of Coach House Press.

The dead man said: 'It doesn't matter whether you go in front of the coffin or go behind the coffin: it's all the same. Just don't go in the coffin.'

The farmer asked his donkey: 'Why are people coming and going?' The donkey answered: 'I think if they all go in the same direction, the world will get drunk and tip over.'

Then the Door to Germany opened again and a Turk with gold teeth came out. The people waiting at the door asked him: 'What is the weather like in Alamania, Aga?' The man with the gold teeth told them how quickly you can grow rich in Alamania.

The man with the gold teeth:

> You good shit – bowel movement every day.
> Good. You go in, you buy tent, set up in park and
> have a shit in the middle: you understand?
> Then just wait. People come.
> Ask: What's to see?
> You say: Direk, Dreck, dirt.
> Tell truth. Infidels are good men, infidels love truth.
> Infidel ask: 'Direk?'
> You say: 'Yes indeed, Direk.'
> What it cost?
> You say: '99 Pfennig.'
> Infidel pay.
> Infidel go in.
> Infidel go out.
> Much angry.
> Other man comes along.
> Asks: 'What is there to see?'
> The infidel say: 'Many angry. Direk.'
> Many angry people later.
> Another man is asking you: 'Really?'
> You say: 'Of course!'
> 99 Pfennig, 99 Pfennig. Many infidels go in.
> 99 – 99. You make much money.
> But must have permission from the Big police.
> Nix so, nix – no papers.
> Must have really good Direk.
> Bye, bye, friends.

The man with the gold teeth turned on a cassette-radio. A song:

> Alamania, Alamania
> I'm in love with you.
> You'll never see
> One as stupid as me.

Then he went away. The people kept waiting at the Door to Germany. They didn't say a word for a long time.

The illegal worker, dressed as soccer player, began to play with the ball. This upset the man with the sheep. He said to the soccer player: 'Why are you hopping about like that? Send your wife to Alamania. Women get in faster.' Then he said to his sheep: 'He won't send her anywhere. He wants to fuck her himself.'

The Turkish woman without the headshawl said: 'Can't you spend one day without taking your cocks in your mouth?'

The man with the sheep said:

> Woman, do I have to get up from my seat,
> grab you by the collar, by the neck,
> and throw you under my heavy heel?
> Woman, if you don't want to take the man's
>   smelly cock in your mouth,
> then you should have cut off your legs
> and stayed at home.

The Turkish woman with the headshawl answered: 'Your sheep should shit in your mouth, I hope. Inshallah, you should eat some pig meat!'

The farmer began to read aloud from a book so that the fight would end. It was a book that the Turkish employment agency had written for workers going to Alamania. It was called: *A Handbook for Gastarbeiter Who are Going to Work Abroad*. It said: 'Dear Brother Worker! Toilets in Europe are different from here at home: they are like chairs. Do not stand on top of them, you must sit down on them. For cleanliness, do not use water, leaves, earth or stones, but very fine toilet paper.'

The donkey laughed aloud, saying: 'Or else someone will lick your arse.'

The farmer read on: 'When you piss, you absolutely must lift the seat because the next person will sit on the seat.' The donkey laughed again at what was written in the book. 'In the bus and in the streetcar, do not pick your nose, Brother Worker. Do not look left or right and do not get ill,

Brother Worker. Every country slaughters animals in its own fashion. Many countries first stun the animals before slaughtering them. That is allowed by our faith, so feel free to eat everything.'

The donkey said to the man with the sheep: 'The shepherd must be careful that the fools don't slaughter the sheep with the same knife as the pigs, otherwise Brother Mohammed will be angry.'

The man with the sheep said: 'When I sharpen the knife, I don't yet know who I'll lay under it. Perhaps I'll send you to donkey paradise.' Then the man with the sheep ran after the donkey with his knife. The farmer said to the man with the sheep, in order to save his donkey: 'Dear little father, tell me a story.' So the man with the sheep told everyone that was waiting at the Door to Germany stories from the Koran. Everyone sat down around him and listened. He told how the Angel Gabriel had shown himself to Mohammed for the first time, how the first message came out of Mohammed's mouth. He also said that the wine was not forbidden to Moslems at first. Allah had said: 'Believers, we give you dates and grapes, eat and drink your fill.' But once a gentleman named Abdurrahman drank a great deal of wine before praying with the believers, then sang the Koran without a high C. Allah sent another message to Mohammed: 'Believers, if you are drunk, please wait until you can again speak properly.' The man with the sheep told them that a gentleman named Malik gave a feast. They ate and drank and began to compose poetry about their tribes, and a gentleman named Ebu Vakka recited a poem that made Mr Malik very angry, and one of Malik's men picked up a camel bone and bashed in Mr Vakka's head. Then they went to Mohammed and said: 'Yes, Mohammed, finally you must say something about wine.'

Then the Door to Germany opened. Two border officials called the man with the sheep to come into the passport control. He was allowed to enter with his sheep through the Door to Germany. As he was leaving, he finished his story: 'Mohammed said he had received a message from Allah: No wine.'

The man with the sheep went away, the others had to keep on waiting. The farmer read out of the *Handbook for Gastarbeiter*: 'In Europe, no headshawl is worn. If Turkish woman wears headshawl, Europe not like her. *Gastarbeiter* walk without headshawls. If she wants wear headshawl, then make like European women wear headshawl.' He read that on purpose, to the Turkish woman with the headshawl who was waiting there. The woman opened her mouth and said that the headshawl had come into the world because of Mohammed's wedding guests. Because the men, when Mohammed took Zeynep as his fifth wife, had sat too long with him. They sat there, eating, drinking, and Mohammed's wives had to bring dish after dish, and Mohammed was ashamed to say anything, but the men were not ashamed even of the newborn morning dew. Allah didn't stand for this and sent His first message about the headshawl. 'Women should not show strangers their hair, breasts or stomach. Because that is their beauty.'

Then the border officials called the woman with the headshawl to come into the passport inspection office. The donkey said to her: 'A Moslem woman should walk, but her foot should not strike the earth so hard that her beauty jiggles, making men feel lustful.'

The farmer said to her: 'Sister, you may still show your beauty: to your husband, your father, the father of your husband, your sons, the sons of your husband, your brothers – he pointed to himself – your nephews, men who are not men, children who know nothing of women.'

The woman with the headshawl said on leaving: 'Do I understand beauty and headshawls? Not understand! But I love my headshawl. I not understand, what does a Turkish employment agency's *Handbook for Gastarbeiter* want with my headshawl?' The border policeman said to her: 'Your residence permit has expired. Understand? You back home. All clear?' The woman said: 'I back? I stay home? Not clear. My husband fuck Alamania woman, I say.' She had to turn back from the Door to Germany.

The donkey read on further: 'Civilized people refrain from fighting. Europe does not like knives and pistols. Please, dear Workers, do not buy any knives or pistols. You can always buy potatoes, rice and frozen chicken and eat. For example: Mr Mahmut Tarak drank a glass of beer with his German girlfriend. At the end, he and his knife received six-and-one-half years of prison.'

The passport official asked the illegal worker, who had dressed as a soccer player: 'Your papers, please. Turkish?'

Soccer player: '*Türküz.*'

The passport official said: 'Going into the Federal Republic, into the *Bundesrepublik*?'

Soccer player: '*Bunepislik.*'

'What is the purpose of your visit?' The soccer player said the name of a famous soccer club: Futbol – futbol: *Fenerbahce.*'

The passport official said: 'A guest game?'

'Not guest, not work, *Fenerbahce.*'

He started to play soccer. The passport official said: 'No discussion, sir, you may not enter.'

The soccer player wanted to go through the Door to Germany, behind his ball, but a whistle threw him out of the Door to Germany.

IT GREW DARK.
IT GREW LIGHT.

A few months passed. The farmer stepped out of the Alamania Door. He had on a street-sweeper's uniform. Suddenly he felt great longing for his wife whom he had left behind in the village. He took off his street-sweeper's uniform and said to the donkey that he had to get away. The donkey held fast to his jacket and said: 'I'm coming with you, I want to see my wife, too.' The farmer said: 'Have you gone mad, you son of a donkey! Now pay attention. If tomorrow the boss comes into the hostel and asks where the sick man is, then you tremble under my bed clothes and call out: "I'm sweating, I'm sweating." Now I must go away, my Sugar, my Rose.' The farmer went off in the direction of Turkey, a shopping bag with him. The donkey composed a few lines for his farewell:

> A man sick with love
> doesn't need a doctor's prescription,
> nor does the hopelessly ill need
> to be a physician's victim.
> Remember me to the hens at the farm
> and let them all hang from the very first branch.

Then he sat down and began to philosophize because he had read a great deal while being an unemployed donkey.

'Our hens lay eggs whenever they want and whenever it . . . how should I say . . . rains, yes – some other thing? Snow! When it snows, not at all. There goes a chicken off to the executioner, one that does not lay six eggs a day. Light on, light off, light on . . . Here the people are smart and the animals stupid: at home animals are smart and humans are stupid.'

The donkey smoked a cigarette, a Camel.

'Money is smart here, too. It knows where to go: into the wallet. The people hang on to their wallets like on to Holy Scripture. Money is sought after like the Virgin Mary. Our people have their money in their trouser pocket. If you want to pay, you reach into your trouser pocket and sometimes you can even play with your own balls while you're looking. At home, money is tattered, it stinks like a junk dealer, like his long bedsocks, someone may have written a love poem or a telephone number on it.'

> Why then doesn't a donkey go faster?
> Should you beat him to go faster?

Or: The people in my homeland have earned
recognition and respect through their work abroad.
At home, that's true of every donkey.
Let's take a look.

The donkey drinks red wine.

'My farmer climbs into the bus between the hostel and the factory, and notes where he must get off every day, and nevertheless he always gets off at the wrong place. Why? Because he has written down *Stop*. Sweet thing.'

'Do we have to admit that we understand immediately what we perceive through our eyes or ears? Even foreigners, whose language we haven't yet learned? Should we deny that we hear them when they are speaking in their language? Or should we say that we don't just hear them, but that we all understand what they are saying? Just the same, if we don't know our letters yet, but direct our eyes at them, should we maintain that we don't see them or that we even understand them when we nevertheless see them?'

Then a *Gastarbeiter* came along wearing sunglasses and he asked the donkey:

Excellent Rabbi, Socrates.
You tell me: where is
whorehouse?

By then the donkey was drunk and said:
'Go to City Hall.'
The *Gastarbeiter* said:
'Nix City Hall, whorehouse.'
The donkey said:
'Yes, go to City Hall; behind the City Hall is whorehouse.

Then the farmer came back from Turkey. He was carrying his wife on his shoulders. The farmer saw his drunken donkey and asked him, 'How are you, how are things, Maestro, what's wrong with you?'

The donkey said: 'Nothing. I am in the Left Movement now.'

The donkey asked the farmer's wife where her child was. She said she had left her in her mother's village. She got a stamp in her passport at the Alamania Door: Tourist, three-month permit to stay. The Alamania Door closed, then opened immediately. The farmer's wife came out. She was pregnant, she went off in the direction of Turkey and said: 'I can't stand

Germany.' Then she came back again from Turkey towards the Alamania Door. Now she was very pregnant and carried her first baby in her arms and said: 'I can't stand Turkey.' She stood at the Door to Germany and called out loud to her husband. Germany was noisy. Her husband was working as a miner. She called out: 'Come here, I have something to say to you.' The farmer called back: 'I can't, you come here.' She screamed: 'No.' The farmer threw a pair of new shoes and a headshawl out of Germany and said to his donkey: 'Speak to her, I must go on working.' The donkey showed her a key at the Door to Germany. He said: 'Come, there is an apartment.' This was important because until then the farmer didn't have a residence. When his wife was last in Germany, they always spent the night in the home of generous Turks or Germans. The farmer's wife put on her shoes and her headshawl and went, very pregnant, with her baby into Germany. She told her husband that his uncle had done something to her back in the village. The farmer asked her: 'What did he do?'

'He did *Pssst* to me.'

'Again: what did he do?'

She told him. One day she had been working with the uncle and his wife in the village in the apple orchard. The farmer had sent his uncle Deutschmarks from Germany for the apple orchard. That day, she had worked much more than the uncle's wife. The uncle's wife had quarrelled with her. Then the farmer's uncle came and struck his wife.

'Five days later – while I was eating cherries – your uncle came and began to eat cherries right from the cherry tree. He told me that he'd had to strike his wife for my sake, she no longer allowed him into the bed with her. Now whenever he needed a woman, he would go into the city, once a month. "You must pay the bus and the cost of women for me," he said.' Then the wife said to her husband, the farmer: 'My poor head can't make out what your uncle wants.'

The farmer was so disturbed that his nose began to bleed, but he answered his wife: 'My uncle is a bit of a chatterbox, he didn't mean anything.'

The donkey tried to save the situation and said: 'One word sets up another word, and that word puts your arse out in the cold. We must go to bed.'

Then the Door to Germany opened. The farmer's wife came out with two babies and pregnant again. She had a black eye. She set off in the direction of Turkey, shushed her babies and said: 'He doesn't love me any more. Did you know my husband? I don't see him now, he goes around walking with ghosts, like this, hand in hand. He fetched me back. It was, I think, winter. It wasn't summer. It was raining. Yes, no daylight. No sun. Went by taxi. People said: "Here is a room." We went into it, then we stood there, and my insides went *tzzz*. "How could they live like that here?" I thought. But I didn't say that to him. Then evening came. Went to sleep. Next day he went off to work and left us alone in the room . . . My daughter cried. I said: "Aische, I'll cut my head off for you. Don't cry." He took us out for a walk, once, twice. We saw cars. He said: "I building cars, I building cars." I said: "I think you hit by car." I'll tell you why. When he did sins[1] for his cars, he'd come into the room and forget that I too am born of a mother. He'd hit us, always, again and again. For Allah, he's a good man: he doesn't smoke, he doesn't drink, but why does he send money to his uncle? Once I went away. A neighbour said, at the train station there is big department stores. I had the girl with me, then it became dark so fast. She cried . . . Then Allah showed me the church. It went: *Bim Bam, Can Can*. I knew it: the broken church. Walked to church, and from church I found the room again. From morning dew until stars came out, I turned about in the room like a blind mill-horse. I often thought, Allah has buried us, we must have many sins, but what have I done? Have I smoked? What is a human being? A human being is a plate full of wet earth. Wherever they throw us, we stick. But I can't. I don't know. So small was I, with my grandmother, sky-blue-eyed Aische, we looked between the pages of the Koran for Mohammed's eyelashes. Grandmother said: "Mohammed wept so much for humanity, that's why his eyelashes rained down." It is true. I shivered. What is wrong with my husband? I look to the left, I look to the right. My mind has diarrhoea from talking to myself. The donkey, for example, is smart. He doesn't stay in the room like a stuffed red pepper in a headshawl. He has his air. Oh, what do I know! My grandmother used to say: "Humans are like birds. Open eyes and you are here. Close eyes and you are there." Good-bye, Alamania!'

When she left, the farmer looked in her direction through the Door to Germany. He couldn't get away because he was working in the street with a compressed-air hammer. He spoke in her direction: 'Go, go. I thought I was the front wheel, wherever the front wheel goes, shouldn't the back wheel go also? I say yes, but this woman drives about on her own. And as she drives, she can make a man go mad if he doesn't have a tongue in his mouth. Leave me alone, donkey!'

The donkey said: 'I'm only gong to wipe off your sweat. You are so wet.'

---

1. The German text has *Übersünden*, a pun with the words *Überstunden*, overtime, and *Sünden*, sins.

The farmer said:

'Let me sweat until there is nothing left of me.'

'Keep working!'

'I must go back to the village. Why did she eat cherries with my uncle from the same tree? I have to know, I want revenge.'

The donkey said:

'Oh, my son, what revenge? You don't have any time off work, wait until Christmas.'

'I am going now.'

'Drink some *raki*, it puts an end to worry.'

'I find no more rest.'

'Then leave it alone.'

'What?'

'Looking for rest.'

'Come, Christmas, come, I've got to, got to know.'

'What?'

'Was my uncle already under the cherry tree when my wife went to him, or was she under the cherry tree first and my uncle went to her. Let's say, there is the cherry tree, there she is, there is . . .'

'Christmas is here,' said the donkey.

The German foreman came and said: 'Merry Christmas, this bottle of champagne is a present to you from the company. And a goose, too.' The farmer asked: 'Why are you crying, boss?' The foreman said: 'All one hundred men, we have been let go. You go on the dole, I go on the dole . . . See you, friends.'

27

Terrible Times under Dursun*
Ayse

Like the other kids I always wanted to play outside after school. I wasn't allowed to go out. My father didn't allow me to do this until I told him that my little sister ought to be able to go out and play. From that day forth I was able to go outside but had to take my little sister Sergül along with me. I wasn't allowed to go to the playground, which was 100 metres away. We weren't able to play in the yard either because the caretaker, a Turk, was very bad and gave us what for whenever he saw us there. What is more, my parents wanted to be able to see me whenever they looked out the window. My elder brothers didn't have to be visible.

I was told precisely how far I could go. I could go left as far as the corner, which was about 50 metres away, and I could go right as far as the cobbler's, which was another 50 metres away.

These boundaries did not bother me until I was in fourth grade. At that time a community centre opened up nearby and my brothers were allowed to go but I wasn't. My brothers were instructed to give me a whack if they saw me overstep the boundaries. My elder brother took this matter very seriously.

I suffered a great deal under my elder brother Dursun. My parents raised him as a genuine Turkish son. Of course he didn't put up any resistance because he reaped a lot of benefits from it. In Turkey he had been top of his class and my parents were very proud of him. The rest of us were treated as inferiors because my parents believed that Dursun was the cleverest and the best of all of us. Even later, when I had better marks than Dursun and even after he only made it into the secondary modern, I was still considered to be inferior.

At the outset here in Berlin, I suffered terribly under Dursun. Sometimes I was even more afraid of him than of my father or my mother. I always

---

* From: Ayse und Devrim: *Wo gehören wir hin? Zwei türkische Mädchen erzählen* (Ayse and Devrim: *Where do we belong? Two Turkish Girls tell their story*), eds Michael Kuhlmann and Alwin Meyer (Bornheim: Lamuv Verlag, 1983), 20–5.

had to go to bed when he ordered me to. I couldn't watch any music programmes or any other entertainment on TV until I was in the sixth grade. As the eldest he was able to choose the channel and determine who could watch. The worst times were when my parents weren't there and a kids' programme was on TV. He would then lock the door and watch by himself. Then I would often take the fuse out and he would thump me. If I wasn't tired and wanted to watch a programme along with him that began around 7 p.m. there would always be a row. Dursun wouldn't allow it and would send me to bed. Our parents would take his side and go on at me too. Sometimes I would then purposely cut my finger in the kitchen so that I could at least see a few minutes of the show. For the bandages were in the living-room. But that never lasted more than ten minutes and Dursun made sure that I didn't get to stay around longer than that.

He hit me whenever he got a chance. One day he came in and gave me his jacket to hang up. I hung the jacket behind the bedroom door. But when someone opened the door the jacket fell down. Dursun then thought that I had deliberately dropped his jacket and hammered me. I will never forget that. He took my head and banged it on the wall. Afterwards I wanted to die and I took some tablets. But they just gave me a headache.

Altogether I tried three times to commit suicide by taking an overdose of pills. Each time was after a terrible beating, twice from Dursun and once from my father. It never worked. I simply lay in bed for two days with a headache and completely listless. No one realized that I had taken pills. They thought I had flu or something.

For Dursun I was a slave. I always shook when he came home. I was at my happiest when he was away on a school trip. When I was in the eighth grade and wanted to go on the class trip he was against it. For that reason my father also opposed the idea. I couldn't go along.

Whenever Dursun brought his friends home with him I had to serve them. He acted as if I was his servant and he the lord of the manor. I always tried as hard as I could to please him so that he wouldn't beat me but he always found some fault.

My parents always agreed with Dursun. Whenever I told them that he had hit me unjustly they would just say that he would never hit me if I hadn't done something wrong. Sometimes I even got another blow from my father if I complained.

One day when I was going somewhere with one of my cousins, Dursun came towards us. My cousin had just told me something funny and we began to laugh. When Dursun reached us he struck me a sudden blow. He thought we had been laughing because we wanted to attract the attention of the boys on the other side of the street. When I told my father what had happened he was outraged that Dursun had only whacked me one time.

No matter what I did Dursun always believed he had good reason for hitting me, which he then eagerly did. And then, as always, I would hear: you only get hit if you've done something wrong.

It wasn't until I was twelve that Dursun stopped hitting me like he used to. I only got a slap now and then, when, according to him, I had been too cheeky.

Sometimes I felt very sorry about the fact that I didn't have a very good relationship with Dursun. I would have liked to be able to have a conversation with him. He never talked to us. He always thought he was too clever and we were too stupid to understand him. But I only believed that until I was thirteen.

At the age of thirteen I entered the upper school. That was the start of the worst phase. I knew that through Dursun I could persuade my parents to let me out. But Dursun, of course, never spoke to me. And certainly not about things like that. As far as he was concerned there was nothing to discuss: I was a girl and therefore had to sit at home. Instead of the expected help I would have got a couple of slaps at best.

I always had to make sure that three people didn't learn what they weren't supposed to. Firstly my father, secondly my mother and lastly Dursun. I could expect worse punishment from Dursun than from my parents. That didn't change until some time between my sixteenth and seventeenth birthday, when he had a German girlfriend he used to bring home.

One day when she was there, he asked me if I would like to join them. That wasn't so unusual. He had often called me when he had visitors but mostly to serve them. This time I sat down with them and we began to talk. In time the conversation was so relaxed that I plucked up the courage to ask Dursun why he treated me like a slave and like a piece of dirt. I also listed a couple of occasions on which he had, in my opinion, behaved like a father even though he was my brother and ought to have helped me. He agreed with a lot of what I said, or at least he claimed to. And somehow I could also understand him. My parents were forcing him into the role of commander-in-chief just as they were forcing me into the role of future housewife.

Turkish sons are raised from day one as radical dictators. It is dinned into them that their sister represents the family honour, which must be protected at all costs. The question of honour is actually a whole other chapter. Because honour is so prominent and one hears from an early age that it is the most important thing to protect, one cannot, especially as a son, avoid taking it very seriously. And since we Turks are an extended family the honour of the individual daughters is the honour of the whole family. That is why the guardians of honour are not only to be found in one's immediate family but are scattered throughout the entire extended family.

I'm not sure if my second-oldest brother Kamil took the business of honour so seriously. In any case I didn't suffer so much under him. I could even talk to him about things that Turkish girls don't usually discuss with their brothers. He never interfered in any decision regarding me. But my parents didn't treat him as seriously as they did Dursun either.

I liked my younger siblings most – not, of course, when I was still young myself and wanted to play but couldn't because I had to look after them. But in time they became more independent and I could leave them unattended. The little ones always came to me when they had worries or questions. I almost felt like their mother. They had no relationship with our parents, which was a great pity, I think, because I couldn't be like a real mother to them.

I always tried to see that my sister Sergül had it better than me. I didn't want her to be as fenced in as I was. I managed to arrange for her to go to class parties on her own. When my class had a party I usually couldn't go, or if I did someone had to come along to look after me. She is now thirteen years old and has more freedom than I had at thirteen, or even seventeen. I had no one to cover up for me. All I had was someone trying to pull me down.

After the conversations with Dursun, the situation had changed so much that he got off my back and I had enough confidence to tell him to his face what I thought. I was now able to smoke in his presence, something he would never have allowed before, and I was able to express outrage about the way Turkish children were raised without risking a slap from him. I still don't know what brought about the change in him. I only know that it had something to do with his German girlfriend. But I cannot say whether she alone was responsible for it.

Dursun's metamorphosis showed me that it really wasn't his fault that he was the way he was and treated us the way he did. It was the fault of his upbringing, which he couldn't do anything about. What Turks understand by upbringing is still a mystery to me. From the outset children are raised to believe that the stronger, the physically stronger, will win. I always felt sick when I saw my uncle make his sons fight with each other to determine which of them was the strongest.

28

My Two Faces*
Ayse

In the morning I got up a Turk and got ready for school. On the way to school I was neutral and considered what was good and bad about the one and compared it with the other. At school I was German. After school I had to go straight home because, for one thing, there would be trouble if I came home late and, for another, I wasn't allowed to go anywhere else. On the way back I was once again neutral, although I must say that I felt better on the way to school than on the way home. As soon as I was home I had to put my Turkish face on again, or else I didn't get along with people.

My true self was more in the German face because I was more honest with that one than with the Turkish one. The Turkish face was full of lies or rather discretion. At home, after all, I couldn't say everything I thought and wanted to say. They even forced me to lie to them.

I didn't find it particularly funny having two faces. It bothered me a lot that I had to change constantly. I couldn't arrive home with my German face because I then felt worse and there were arguments because my parents didn't understand me any more, or didn't want to. I loved school and hated my home because I couldn't reveal myself there as I really was, which I could do in school. The people at school accepted me as I was and never looked outraged if I had a different opinion from them. Among my parents and other Turks I was allowed to have my own opinion but if it deviated from the usual, typically Turkish view then it was better for me to keep it to myself or perhaps even to conform if I didn't want my life to be hell.

In conversation with my parents and others I was only considered an equal until I began to get worked up about some aspects of Turkish beliefs

* From: Ayse und Devrim: *Wo gehören wir hin? Zwei türkische Mädchen erzählen* (Ayse and Devrim: *Where do we belong? Two Turkish Girls tell their story*), eds Michael Kuhlmann and Alwin Meyer (Bornheim: Lamuv Verlag, 1983), 35–7.

and behaviour. When I expressed the view that I felt as if I were in a golden cage they just said that I had all the freedoms imaginable. And then when I asked them why I couldn't go out, why my brothers never once helped in the household, why I was guarded like a prisoner, why I couldn't have a boyfriend, then I was advised that if I really thought I wanted these things I should quickly think again. Otherwise we might bang heads. Then I was reminded that I am a Turkish female and that such things couldn't even be discussed.

I often tried to reach some kind of agreement in conversations with my parents, but unfortunately without any success. By unsuccessful I mean that they did listen to me and even agreed with me but couldn't change their ways and always made it clear to me in the end that my wishes were Utopian and that I would have to accept things as they were.

The greatest fear of my parents and most Turks is that people could speak badly of their daughters. They are very dependent on the opinion of those around them. Their surroundings consist of the extended family to which we belong and on which every member of the extended family makes himself dependent. Before important decisions are made the opinions of the oldest and most respected family members are heard. The result of the decision does not depend on the person who is actually directly affected by it but on almost the whole extended family. That is the case, for example, in matters of marriage. If the family does not consent to the chosen partner then it is very rare that the person concerned gets his or her way and marries the partner. If he does, it can very easily happen that he is not fully accepted or that he even becomes an outcast.

My father often told me that he would let me go out if he weren't so afraid of talk. The good will he possessed didn't help me very much though. I went to school in the mornings, came back in the afternoon and didn't leave the flat until the next morning. The weekends were the worst. I hated them. I came home to the flat on Friday afternoon and left it again on Monday morning. The holidays that we didn't spend in Turkey were just as bad for me. I never got out and, if I did, it was only to relatives and family friends, and with my parents, of course. There wasn't a lot of variety there. Sometimes I didn't even go along, but stayed home alone or with my sister. But now and then I had to go with them because they were afraid to leave me alone. If I didn't see why I should come with them, they would say that a stranger could come and rape me.

If my parents happened to stay at home on the weekend, which hardly ever happened, we were very rarely alone. Promptly, without prior warning – as is customary for Turks – visitors appeared at the door. I always hated it when we had visitors because I had to wait on them like crazy. After I had poured tea I always had to situate myself so that I could see when people had emptied their cups and then had to fill them up.

At weekends a lot of things coincided that made me mad. I had to clean the whole flat, iron all the shirts – around fifteen on average – repair zips, alter trousers, serve food, etc., etc. And then there were the special requests of my brothers, among whom Dursun was outstanding. He couldn't even fetch his own socks, even if he happened to be standing right next to the cupboard they were in. If I sat down to rest for a little while I would immediately hear that I was lazy, that I did nothing and left all the work to my poor, sick mother (who always had some complaint or other).

29

Women are Property and Honour*
Ayse

Whenever I spoke with acquaintances or relatives it didn't take me long to bring the conversation around to my biggest problem. I began to get upset about how we girls are treated. People tried to convince me that I should give up my daydreaming and behave at long last like a real Turkish woman, which I did in fact always try to do when I was at home, without always being very successful.

One evening, during such a conversation, a distant relative told me I was as valuable as gold in his eyes and then he asked me a question that I didn't quite understand: whether I knew when gold had its true value. I asked him to explain what he meant but he just responded with the stupid comment that I was otherwise so smart and such a know-all. After that I was pretty mad and didn't want to talk to him any more but then he told me what he had meant, namely: 'Gold only holds its true value when it is lying in the window and out of reach.' For me that meant I should sit at home and not let anyone near me.

When I then tried to explain to him that I did not value being as valuable as gold he responded that I had no option as a Turkish girl because I was the honour and had to be safeguarded and protected. Unfortunately he was right. I had to be guarded and protected and I couldn't do anything about it.

This man also told me that he would kill me if he saw me on the street with another man. And if he weren't able to kill me himself he said he would find someone to do it for him. My parents were sitting there and heard their daughter being threatened. They said nothing. Any relative or acquaintance could have beaten me and my father would simply have believed that I deserved it.

---

* From: Ayse und Devrim: *Wo gehören wir hin? Zwei türkische Mädchen erzählen* (Ayse and Devrim: *Where do we belong? Two Turkish Girls tell their story*), eds Michael Kuhlmann and Alwin Meyer (Bornheim: Lamuv Verlag, 1983), 44–6.

I hated the fact that any idiot could interfere whenever I did something that Turkish girls don't usually do. An uncle of mine implored my parents not to allow me so many liberties. (I would have loved to find out what he found libertarian about my life.) They shouldn't allow me to visit my friends, he said. What is more, he warned my parents that I might take off with a German some time if I didn't change my views about the unjust conditions among Turks. My leash was instantly shortened.

Of course, there were relatives and acquaintances that I got along with. Whenever I was in trouble with my parents I could go to them and talk to them about it. An aunt of mine, for example, was always especially nice, to my brothers and sisters too. For that reason my father often forbade us to go to her house. One reason for this was that she was my mother's sister and he didn't much care for my mother's family. (This wasn't only his fault.) Another reason was that he thought that my aunt was trying to take us away from our own parents. (No one needed to encourage us to do this. My parents' behaviour towards us was encouragement enough.)

A distant relative who had a young daughter of her own was also close at hand if I was having a difficult time with my parents. She would often tell me of her own youth. Her father would even beat her in the morning if it seemed to him that she had combed her hair too conspicuously. In the end, she married to get out of her parents' home. I often asked her why she didn't treat her own daughter better. When she came to Germany with her husband he took off with another woman and left her with their daughter and son. She had to bring up the kids on her own. I thought therefore that she could allow her daughter more liberties and that it was a sign of mistrust when she wouldn't let her daughter out on her own. She countered that by saying she would like to do so but was – as usual – afraid of gossip. We used to talk about this for hours but the outcome of the conversation was always the same: 'We are Turks. What would people say?' No one saw a way out. No one could imagine how things could be done differently. Everything that wasn't Turkish was rejected outright as bad. To live like Germans was out of the question because the German girls, in their opinion, were whores who would give themselves to anyone. Perhaps I would also have regarded the Turkish way as perfect if I hadn't learned in school that things could be different.

30

Putting Obstructions in Young Turks' Way*

Ayse

I can partly understand many Turkish girls who form groups and don't want to mix with Germans. It is logical that people prefer to be with those who accept them. On the other hand, I also think it's a shame because it deprives them of the chance to get along with Germans.

There are Germans who reject us Turks from the outset. It is very difficult to get close to them. From the stories of Turkish girls and from my own experience I realize that it is impossible for some to establish contact with Germans. For that reason you shouldn't think badly of these people if they become resigned and only hang out with their own people.

The German state doesn't exactly help to remove people's fears of one another. If they set up classes composed of only Turks in which Turks are not exactly taught that there are also Germans that they could get along with, it is hardly surprising that Turkish youths simply hang out together. There's a lot of talk about integration but Turks are none the less increasingly cut off from Germans when they are stuck in Turkish classes with the excuse that they can't speak very good German. If you then observe how lessons are conducted in such classes, you can understand that it will take a while for them to learn German. Some Turks who have mastered German are also stuck in these classes. And if the teachers of such classes are Turks themselves, then you can work the rest out for yourself.

No one should be surprised if radical groups form because not all Turkish teachers want the youths to be integrated. If kids and youths – animated by a Turkish teacher – are forced by their parents to attend Koran school and mosques, where they are not exactly taught how to get along

---

* From: Ayse und Devrim: *Wo gehören wir hin? Zwei türkische Mädchen erzählen* (Ayse and Devrim: *Where do we belong? Two Turkish Girls tell their story*), eds Michael Kuhlmann and Alwin Meyer (Bornheim: Lamuv Verlag, 1983) 58–60.

with others, then there is no reason to hope that these people will one day get along with Germans.

All the people I know who attend purely Turkish classes are opposed to Germans because they have never had a chance to interact with Germans and hear only from their teachers, Hocas and parents that Germans are bad because they have a different faith and a different culture. Everything German is rejected outright.

It is my opinion, that if they are only separated on account of language difficulties, these people should receive one or two years of intensive German instruction and should then be fully integrated into German classes. You can master the language in one or two years if you don't have to do any difficult subjects alongside German and if you aren't being taught by Turkish teachers.

There are Turkish girls and boys who attend Turkish classes for more than four years and who still don't learn German well enough. This is certainly not due to the fact that they are too stupid to learn this language or to succeed at school. There are so many Turks who don't even manage to complete the secondary modern and end up in the factory like their parents, even though they would like to learn a trade. But that is made impossible for them from the start because they are stuck in Turkish classes in which they sometimes learn nothing. I call that putting an obstruction in the way of young Turks so that they don't attain much more than their parents, because we were only brought here to do factory work.

If I had stayed in the Turkish class I would have achieved little more than the majority of Turkish girls. I used to run into many of the girls among my former classmates when I was in the tenth grade. They were either already married or about to be married, or else they were working in the factory and wanted to go back to Turkey soon because they didn't want to turn out like their parents, even though, like myself, they only knew the country from holiday visits. Before you form a negative opinion of these girls for marrying so young you should ask yourself why they do it. They have no qualifications and no profession. Even though they don't want to spend the rest of their lives in chastity and in prison, moving out of their parents' home to live on their own is out of the question, even if it were financially possible. And it is not so easy just to leave. To do that you need a lot of strength and good friends, or you have to be very independent, which isn't something you learn to be in a Turkish family.

31

You Will Never Be Able to Learn This Language*

Devrim

Now we were in West Berlin. At first my parents were very nice to us. But this changed over time. My mother got annoyed at the fact that my father always went out on his own at the weekend. We were also annoyed at the fact that we had to stay at home. My mother could speak hardly any German, and neither could we, of course. Maybe that's why we had to stay at home.

After three months I had to go to school. At first I didn't want to go, and neither did my sister. We had no idea how we were supposed to make ourselves understood at school when we didn't know any German. Since I had language problems and there was no Turkish sixth grade at my school I had repeat the fifth form. I was happy that there was at least a fifth-grade Turkish class.

Our class teacher was a German but we also had classes with Turkish teachers. I tried hard to learn German as quickly as possible. It was very hard. It is hard to imagine how you are supposed to manage to learn German through German lessons five times a week. I used to say to myself again and again: 'You will never be able to speak this language.'

No one could help me learn it at home. But I wanted to be able to speak German because I had seen foreigners who spoke German poorly trying to make themselves understood: with their hands. And the majority of people they were trying to communicate with acted as if they couldn't understand them and just ignored them. That was malicious and awful, but what could you do about it if you couldn't speak German? Such foreigners have no other way of making themselves understood, and the Germans consider them ridiculous and superfluous. When you ask them

* From: Ayse und Devrim: *Wo gehören wir hin? Zwei türkische Mädchen erzählen* (Ayse and Devrim: *Where do we belong? Two Turkish Girls tell their story*), eds Michael Kuhlmann and Alwin Meyer (Bornheim: Lamuv Verlag, 1983), 114–18.

why most of them hold this opinion they say: 'Why are you still here then? Go back home if you don't like it here! We've got enough of you lot. And if you don't want to go back then you should learn the language.'

The Turkish pupils had a lot of difficulties at school. They were always oppressed by the Germans and forced to do things for them. If, for example, it emerged that something had been stolen, the foreigners got the blame even though they hadn't done it. And they didn't know how to defend themselves: they were a minority in the class and often their German wasn't good enough.

At home there is no one to help the foreign pupil. Even if a child's parents know more German than they do, they don't have time for the child. They always have more important things to take care of.

The foreign youth must adapt to German ways of doing things. But at the same time he cannot forget his own culture and religion. He must conform therefore without offending his parents' views. And that is particularly difficult for young foreigners who have grown up in a country which is quite different from Germany. If they cannot conform, then they are not respected at all by the Germans. Yes, the life of a foreigner is really awful.

–32–

I thought I Was in Hell*
Devrim

At primary school we mostly spoke Turkish in class. The class, after all, was composed entirely of Turkish kids. But when I switched over to seventh grade in the comprehensive I suddenly had to communicate with everyone in German. I thought I was in hell. It was as if someone was trying to punish me. Sometimes I didn't understand the subjects being discussed in class. But I was the only one who cared if I was following or not. Everything was frightening for me. I was afraid of everyone in this school, even of myself, my voice. The fear drove me mad. I couldn't defend myself physically if someone wanted to hit me and I couldn't defend myself verbally either.

I had found no one who wanted to offer me their hand and say: 'I would like to help you.' I am still aware today of how much I cried. I only understood about a quarter of what the teachers said. But some of them did show some understanding.

Every day brought different problems. I was cursed by everyone in my class. Many of the boys liked to annoy me. No one took my side. And problems were piling up at home. I didn't know what to do. Nevertheless I managed to achieve a B C average on my half-term report.

For my parents I was a nothing. They treated me like a maid who had to do everything. When I asked them what they had to say about my report card, my mother answered: 'We fully expect you to do well at school because you're no use anywhere else.' I was really hurt. I can't describe how my heart bled.

I never dared tell my parents of my experiences at school. That I was always alone, for example. I knew that they would not understand me. They would have said: 'You are stupid and that's why you don't have any friends. No one can understand you anyway.'

* From: Ayse und Devrim: *Wo gehören wir hin? Zwei türkische Mädchen erzählen* (Ayse and Devrim: *Where do we belong? Two Turkish Girls tell their story*), eds Michael Kuhlmann and Alwin Meyer (Bornheim: Lamuv Verlag, 1983) 116–18.

I had never experienced anything like it. It was strange and awful. I could hardly bear it. I had always got on all right before in any situation. Now I couldn't express myself properly when we were discussing something at school. Instead of helping me they laughed at every word I pronounced wrongly. Since I had often experienced this I felt it was better to say nothing. But who was supposed to express my opinion? Since I said nothing it seemed that I agreed with everything.

I couldn't understand my classmates because I considered them childish. They all wanted to do as little as possible in class, or in any case they didn't want to make a constructive contribution. They just wanted to make fun of classmates who couldn't defend themselves. They did the same with teachers. I used to ask myself: 'What are they after here?' I came up with the following answer: 'They don't actually want to come here. They come because they have to.'

I never knew such a thing in Turkey. Teachers there were very strict, and so were the pupils' parents. Discipline was greatly respected. The parents said to the teachers: 'You can abuse my child's skin as much as you want, but leave the bones for us.' The teacher could do whatever he wanted to turn the child into a sensible person. For example, he could give out lines and beat them. After that kids wouldn't even dream of being cheeky. But that didn't mean that we couldn't have any fun. There was a great deal of friendship and solidarity among the pupils.

When I compare the friends I went to primary school with in Turkey with my classmates here I find that the ones in Turkey were much more mature. Perhaps that's because they had to learn at a younger age there how to get along in life. They had to eat the same meal four days in a row. They couldn't spend their time playing. They had to speak to and behave in front of their parents as if they were standing before state authorities on which they were dependent.

Nothing of that is evident among Germans of my age. On the contrary: in this German class they all seemed to me like stones that had just come out of the fridge.

–33–

I Played a Role*
Devrim

After a half-year at the new school I still hadn't made any friends. But in time I managed to recognize the weaknesses and the good sides of my classmates. Slowly I began to understand what I had to do to get close to them. I acted a role, so to speak. I had to do it, even though I hated to and still do.

Since most of them were beginning to smoke and always showed off about it, I finally thought I had found a way. Every week I bought myself cigarettes with my ten marks pocket money. In the first months I bought a packet every week so that I could get by financially to some extent.

From then on I behaved quite differently from before. I started to be as rude to everyone as possible. I became a 'big mouth'. And I swore all the time so that the others would notice my 'mouth'. Whenever anyone asked me for a cigarette I would give them one.

After a while I bought two packets a week. And soon that wasn't enough. Somehow I became addicted. My pocket money began to appear meagre. I didn't eat breakfast in the morning but I hardly had any money to get myself something to eat in the school café. I brought food from home, otherwise I would have starved.

My relationship with my classmates had improved considerably, although it still wasn't rosy. I didn't get along at all with some of the boys.

My parents found out that I had been smoking for some time. My sister had found a packet of ashes and cigarettes under my bed and had nothing better to do than to run to my parents to tell them. Once again it was my mother who got upset the most. But I wasn't punished or beaten. I was happy about that. Girls in my class had told me how their parents

---

* From: Ayse und Devrim: *Wo gehören wir hin? Zwei türkische Mädchen erzählen* (Ayse and Devrim: *Where do we belong? Two Turkish Girls tell their story*), eds Michael Kuhlmann and Alwin Meyer (Bornheim: Lamuv Verlag, 1983), 130–3.

had reacted. In the majority of cases, all hell had broken loose. Only a few of them, who were already eighteen or older, hadn't had any difficulties.

After a while I also wanted to wear make-up. I knew that my mother was against it, but I did it anyway. The influence of my classmates was simply too great. I kept it a secret for a while. I wore make-up at school and when it was over I washed my face in the toilets and then went home.

After a while I didn't want to make myself up in secret. The first time my mother saw me she criticized me right away. But in the end she realized that she couldn't do anything about it. She knew very well that if she forbade me to do it I would just do it in secret.

My father and my brother Resul were also very angry with me and threatened to beat me if I didn't stop. But they also realized that they couldn't do anything about it. From now on no one said anything about my make-up. But the usual rows continued.

I often toyed with the idea of committing suicide. What did I have to live for? Just so that I could cry every day? Why could I never laugh with all my heart? Didn't I have the same right to do so as the others? My mother only had one answer to such questions, which I didn't want to understand: 'Since you are a girl and will later be a woman you must learn all these things now.' Sometimes I wondered if she was my mother after all.

My mother never did anything for her own pleasure. She at least liked cleaning, but we were bored to death. Sometimes we went to the cinema, but only with my father. My brothers were never interested in taking us to the cinema or anywhere else, even though my parents approved of that. They said: 'If we take her with us she'll just be chatted up by boys. That's not on. That will offend our honour.' I almost felt like giving up talking to them. But then I would only have lost out, would have perished even more.

I said to my mother: 'I want out! I am fed up with this house. I'm sick of the air in here, do you hear me, I'm sick of it! I am sick and tired of just looking at the walls!'

She shouted at me as if I were a dog that didn't want to obey: 'Where do you want to go? On to the streets? Go on then, you know yourself what the others will say about you. A decent girl must stay at home until she is married. Then you can live your life.'

'Well, why are you sending me to school then? Instead of going to school I could go to bed with a boy if I felt like it. Please tell me honestly if that's what you're afraid of. If you are then you don't know me very well.'

'Yes, that's it. We would be notified if you played truant. You can see for yourself what becomes of girls when their mothers give them more leeway.'

I screamed: 'Oh, why am I talking to you about this? I say the same thing every day and you make the same stupid remarks every time we talk. But I am not as stupid as you think. You must know that I feel sorry for the girls who don't know what to do with their freedom. They have boys on the brain. I wouldn't waste my time on boys if all they're concerned about is flirting with me. I want to use my time to do sports, dance, sing and learn. But you just don't want to understand me. And as far as marriage is concerned, I've told you a thousand times before that I will never marry, do you understand, because I know that married people are often unhappy.'

'Can you not hold your tongue? You are annoying me. Stop it! You'll not be able to live with these ideas for long anyway.'

'Oh, leave that to me!'

'For God's sake, shut your mouth!' In the end, she threw her slipper at me. 'My God, you don't have a big mouth. We Muslims don't live so that we can do what pleases or what occurs to us. We live for the life beyond. We obey Allah so that we can enter heaven after death. It is my fault for bringing you to Germany. You no longer believe in God here. You've become proper communists!'

'Oh stop it! You don't even know what it means to be a communist. You use that word as an insult for people who don't believe in God. Everything you find bad you attribute to communism.'

Yes, I hate our religion. I am not devout in that sense. I don't want to console myself with hopes of an afterworld. I would like to live my life. I came into this world to live here.

On the other hand, I've never forgotten my culture. I love Turkish folk-songs and folk-dances more than anything else.

34

Mother Tongue*

Emine Sevgi Özdamar

In my language, 'tongue' means 'language'.

A tongue has no bones: twist it in any direction and it will turn that way.

I sat with my twisted tongue in this city, Berlin. A café for foreigners, with Arabs for customers, the stools too high, feet dangling. An old croissant sits wearily on the plate. I give *bakshish* right away, otherwise the waiter might feel ashamed. If only I knew when I lost my mother tongue. My mother and I sometimes spoke in our mother tongue. My mother said to me, 'You know what? You just keep on talking, you think you're saying everything, but suddenly you jump over unspoken words, and you just keep talking. And I, I jump with you and breathe easily.' Then she said: 'You left half your hair back in Alamania.'

I can remember sentences now, sentences she said in her mother tongue, except that when I imagine her voice, the sentences themselves sound in my ears like a foreign language I know well. When I asked her once why Istanbul had become so dark, she said, 'Istanbul has always been this dark, it's your eyes that have grown used to Alamanian lights.'

I can still remember another Turkish mother and the words which she said in our mother tongue. She was the mother of a boy in prison who could not sleep at night because he was waiting to be taken away and hanged. The mother said, 'I came out of the hospital eleven years ago. I saw the garden full of policemen, my mind swam, I asked neighbours. They're probably here to get our son, they said. I entered the garden and went up to the first policeman I saw. Why have you come into my garden? I asked. Your son has been seized, he said. Why would you seize my son, do you have a search warrant at least, I said, I can't read. He said yes. Then go into the house and look around, I said. Soon the house too was full of policemen, and I squatted on the ground and stayed there. When I asked, What is wrong with my son? they said, Your son is an anarchist.'

The mother didn't know how many times she'd wept in the past eleven years. Once when she saw her son for the first time in prison and was unable to recognize him. The second time when he had to stand and hear the word 'hanging'.

'I never went to court, the final trial. The judges will speak, they said. His father went there, came back; when he came through the door, I saw it in his face. The neighbours all came in with him, and we wept together, our *hodsha* from the local mosque stood with us like a half-man on his knees and wept. The ashtray as thick as two fingers broke that day right down the middle, in two pieces. I heard a *shash* and suddenly the ashtray was lying there in front of me.'

These sentences, said by the mother of a hanged man, I can only remember them as if she had said the words in German.

The written language also looked foreign to me, though like that of a language I had learned well. An extract from the newspaper: 'Workers shed their own blood.' Strikes were prohibited, workers cut their own fingers, held their shirts under the drops of blood, then wrapped their loaves of dry bread in their bloody shirts and sent them to the Turkish army. I can remember that too, just as though this piece of news were printed in several newspapers, in front of a tavern; you could see the writing as you walked by, photograph it, then forget it.

If I only knew when exactly I lost my mother tongue. Once I walked past the prison in Stuttgart, where there was a lawn in front and only a bird flying by the cells. A prisoner in a blue exercise suit hung on to the bars of the window; he had a very soft voice, he spoke my same mother tongue, saying aloud to someone, 'Brother Yashar, did you see that?' The other man, whom I could not see, said, 'Yes, I saw.'

To see: *Görmek.*

I stood on the lawn and smiled. We were so far apart from each other. They saw me like a big needle in the grass. I did not know what they meant by 'see'. Did they mean me or a bird? From a prison you can only see, touch, feel, catch. There can be no plucking.

Görmek: to see.

I remember another word in my mother tongue. It was in a dream. I'm in Istanbul in a wooden house, and there I see a friend, a Communist, he doesn't laugh. I tell him about someone who tells stories out of the corner of his mouth, only half-believing them. My Communist friend says,

'Everyone talks like that.' I say, 'What does one have to do in order to talk about deep, meaningful things?' He says, '*Kaza gecirmek.*' 'Experience accidents of life.'

Görmek and *Kaza gecirmek.*

Another word in my mother tongue once came to me in a dream. A train travels along, stops, outside they're making arrests, dogs bark, three ticket collectors come, I consider whether I should say, 'I am Italian.' I want to hide my passport, which lists my profession as *ISCI* (worker). I think, if I can say that I am a student or an artist, I'll get through the inspection. There's a photocopier there as big as a room, it prints a very large self-portrait of me as an *ISCI*.

Görmek, Kaza gecirmek, ISCI.

Once I sat in the Intercity train restaurant, at a table where a man was already seated, happily reading a book. I thought, what is he reading? It was only the menu. Perhaps I lost my mother tongue in the IC-restaurant.

At first, I could not look at Cologne cathedral. Whenever the train arrived in Cologne, I always shut my eyes. Once, however, I opened an eye, and then I saw it: the cathedral was watching me. At that moment a razor-blade entered my body, ran through me, and there was no more pain. I opened my other eye. Perhaps I lost my mother tongue there, then, that time.

Stand up, go to the other Berlin. Brecht was the reason why I originally came here. Perhaps there I'll be able to remember when it was that I lost my mother tongue. In the corridor between the two Berlins is a photomat.

I am at the Berliner Ensemble, at the canteen.

My boots make cracking sounds like a cowboy in a commercial. The canteen workers are smoking, talking about pots and dishes; outside there are beer barrels, gas bottles waiting, everyone talking about work.

Get up. Walk on your fingers tips back to Turkey, sit on a sofa with Grandmother beside me. Sit in Istanbul in the Turkish Bath. The gypsy women working there will wash me. It was a bath for hookers. A gypsy woman washed me once, she asked me, 'What whorehouse are you working in, Beauty?'

I was working at the Communist Commune. One day the police arrived. I was the only girl. The commissar asked me, 'These guys here, are they all over you?' I said, 'Yes, they're all over me, but they watch out.'

The Commissar said: 'Have you no heart for your father? I also have a daughter your age. Allah should curse you all. *Inshallah.*'

They also brought Mahir's brother into the police station – Mahir was known in the newspapers as a local thief. Back then, they killed Mahir with bullets. Mahir's brother sat there as though he had something bitter in his mouth and was unable to spit it out. He was wearing a very thin shirt. I had on a black sweater with a high collar.

'Brother, put this on.' Mahir's brother looked at me, as though I were speaking a foreign tongue. Why am I standing in one half of Berlin? Should I go and look for him? That was seventeen years ago, by now they've puked through their noses all the milk they drank from their mothers.

I'm going to go back to the other Berlin. I am going to learn Arabic, which was once our system of writing. After our war of liberation, 1927, Atatürk outlawed the Arabic script and brought in the Latin letters. My grandfather only knew Arabic script, I only know the Latin alphabet, which means that, if my grandfather and I had been unable to speak and could only tell each other things in writing, we'd have unable to tell each other stories. Perhaps only by going back to Grandfather will I be able to find my way back to my mother, back to my mother tongue.

Inshallah.

In West Berlin, they say there is a great master of Arabic writing.

Ibni Abdullah.

35

Germany – a *Heimat* for Turks?*

Zafer Şenocak and *Bülent Tulay*

A Plea for Overcoming the Crisis between the Orient and the Occident

The discussion of the new Foreigners' Law (*Ausländergesetz*) in the Federal Republic, in so far as it took place at all in the shadow of events in the GDR and Eastern Europe, for the most part left us, the second generation of Turkish immigrants, out of consideration. This law continues to ignore our situation. Having been born and raised here we can scarcely identify with the term 'foreign citizen' that is the operative phrase in the law in question. We can no longer imagine a future in this country without recognition as German citizens. Up till now, however, those responsible have consistently evaded this crucial issue.

The majority of Turks, especially those of the first generation, also seem to have more important concerns than a secure and equal future in Germany.

The media and public opinion of Turks in Germany are extensions of the Turkish media, Turkish public opinion, Turkish consciousness and have hitherto been devoid of all autonomy, their own vision.

Perhaps there would be nothing to complain about here if we weren't already in the thirtieth year of immigration and if we weren't long overdue thinking about the guarantee of citizens' rights for Turks in Germany.

As a result of the inflow of workers, which led to the phenomenon of guest workers, the Federal Republic has become de facto a country of immigration for the majority of the foreign workers and their families. A second generation of foreigners has grown up here and a third is already being born. But the legislation and even the choice of words in the public discussion lag far behind the existing situation. For years, the vast majority

---

* 'Deutschland – Heimat für Türken?', from *Atlas des tropischen Deutschland* (Berlin: Babel Verlag, 1992), 9–20.

of the population has been talking of 'integrating foreign citizens' and the Left has been speaking about a 'multicultural society'. Unfortunately, however, this discussion has not progressed beyond these slogans! Nowhere is it made clear what deep-rooted change of consciousness must take place in all concerned in order for native and future German citizens to live together truly and successfully.

Unlimited Citizens' Rights

'We already have a multicultural society', say some. By this they mean the contactless juxtaposition of cultures and philosophies of life. Everyone should find happiness in his own way, look only at his own plate and settle down in a ghetto.

'Integration', say the others and by that they mean nothing other than complete assimilation, the disappearance of Anatolian faces behind German masks.

But can Germans of Turkish origin, who have decided on a life in Germany, achieve integration without a guarantee of unlimited citizens' rights?

Citizens without citizens' rights – in our opinion no democratic state can withstand such a condition in the long term without social conflicts and tensions. One cannot overlook the fact that forces exist even within the governing parties who regard 'foreigners' who have lived here for decades as a foreign threat and who would prefer to get rid of them again if this were economically viable and could be done legally. These forces, who are not afraid of exploiting moods, are assisted by a widespread, undifferentiated way of looking at foreigners. At most differentiation occurs according to the motto: 'the more foreign they are, the more dangerous'.

Ironically enough, the view of the Left resembles a mirror image of this. Those who make decisions at party conferences on a general right to remain for all foreigners who come here do not appear to be blessed with much ability to differentiate or much of a sense of reality.

Condemnation and glorification of foreigners are pretty much the same thing; both are defence mechanisms which are not based on partnership but rather on power relations.

The Second Generation

When we speak of a universal change of consciousness we mean the start of a long overdue discussion of repressed identity problems and fear of contact with foreigners. The Turks must finally begin to speak in order to locate themselves anew, to orientate and define themselves. This applies especially to the so-called second generation and generations to come. They are the real foreigners because they are barred from looking in the rear-view mirror and live with neither citizens' rights nor a *Heimat*. Moreover, they are often not even perceived as foreigners because their language, their appearance and their consumer behaviour scarcely differentiate them from Germans of the same age.

Is Turkey Still their *Heimat* and Can It Be the *Heimat* of their Children?

We have the sadly often unrecognized fortune of living in a time in which terms such as fatherland, homeland and nation can be seen from various perspectives and are not simply keywords which only fit a particular lock.

Among young Turks there still reigns that spirit which merely laments split identity, i.e. speechlessness. They are writing an endless book of memories, using the shreds of childhood, in lost or not yet found languages, and the pages remain empty. They have not yet found a language to translate this book in order to communicate it to others. For their fathers and mothers they are the lost generation. Will they be the speechless generation for their children? Is there a way out of passivity, of niches, ghettos and half-truths?

The birth of German citizens of Turkish and Islamic origin also poses a test for Germans. For some, the ability of the German people to integrate others into their society appears to be exhausted before integration has even taken place. The Turks are stigmatized as eternal foreigners.

But those at the opposite end of the spectrum, who regard all foreigners as intrinsically better people and believe that they must accept every archaic habit, every strange custom, only help bring about conflict. For, after all, in the final analysis, this position considers it possible to get by without a change in consciousness and without the other. Change and contact, however, are keywords in a multicultural view of society. It is necessary therefore to explore ways to overcome latent and obvious fears of contact, to track down prejudices, to break through the ghetto and create an atmosphere in which foreignness and familiarity are in constant contact, so that something new can grow. This is a process which can be enjoyable but is just as painful as rubbing wounds. In many ways, it resembles artistic work.

Crisis between the Orient and the Occident

The younger generation of the Turks of Germany has a historic opportunity to overcome the crisis between the Orient and Occident in which Turkish identity has been stuck for over a century. In so doing, they must not let themselves be led by the psychologisms of contemporary Turkish society.

It is already clear that the next generation will no longer be neutral but will be right in the middle in a European context. Place and change of perspective condition each other. A change of place, without a simultaneous change of perspective, leads to emptiness. The break with the original *Heimat* took place long ago. But this break and all its consequences must be understood so that the resultant emptiness can be filled.

All too often the interests of Turks in Germany do not coincide with those of Turkey. The incapacitation of Turks in Germany is not only manifest in the Germans' refusal to grant citizens' rights but in Turkey's claim to sole representation. In order to achieve the ability to formulate and perceive their own interests, in order to speak their own language, Germany's Turkish youth must also get rid of their parents' authoritarian thinking and abandon a one-sided orientation towards Turkey.

The Turkish youth cannot cling to the phantasmagoria of the lost *Heimat*.

Multicultural – But How?

Almost all of the organizations that Turks have founded in Germany have their roots in Turkey. That is not unusual if one considers the interests of the first generation. But will it suffice for the future? The German citizen of Turkish origin needs his own face, one that must tolerate differences. Because even conforming cannot prevent him from remaining different, from remaining the other. This otherness constitutes the base of his new, perhaps double identity, or more accurately, of his identities!

It is necessary therefore to abandon the unbroken concept of identity which is still customary everywhere. Identity meant and still means drawing up a border, a piece of defence and, all too often, the destruction of someone else. It is no coincidence that Hans Mayer, in his book 'The Outsider' (*Der Außenseiter*), locates the failure of the Enlightenment in exclusion and methods of segregation of bourgeois society which the others and outsiders experience.

A new concept of identity, which enables coexistence without the sacrifice of personality and difference at the altar of identity, contains gaps through which the other, the foreigner, can enter and exit. Identity would no longer be able to manifest itself as hegemony over others. Whether this remains just a pipedream or can one day become reality also depends on whether we learn to accept differences and use them productively, on whether we learn to have contact with one another.

What is needed is a complete change of consciousness, a reorientation which makes Turks feel connected to Germany's problems and perspectives, which enriches Germans with the cultural baggage of the Turks and finally provides the second generation with the leeway that will enable it to find its own way.

It is precisely the areas of conflict and contradictions of two cultures, the conflict between modernity and tradition, that will make it possible for the Turks of Germany to summon up the creativity that will give birth to a specific culture. In the process they will marvel at their own roots as something foreign and foreignness will be perceived as their own. This will not constitute a mummification of traditional identities but virtuoso dealings with points of view and perspectives.

But this will also require a change of society here, of cultural life, of lesson plans and educational content in German schools. The multiculturalism of a society must reach beyond the satisfaction of desires for exoticism and folklore. It must lead to a serious examination of the culture, language, history, literature and religion of the other. This is particularly relevant with regard to education. But attempts at this are scarcely being taken into consideration in the current discussion on the future of the multicultural society.

Is History Catching Up with Us?

The consciousness of individuals and the collective unconscious always have more staying power than administrative measures and legislative periods. For, in contrast to these short-term phenomena, they are channelled by symbols and metaphors that are thousands of years old. That is why it will be necessary in the future to investigate where, how and why the coexistence of different cultures, the complicated interweaving of interrelationships between the native and the foreign has repeatedly failed in the history of civilization. The bitter experiences of the twentieth century still lie undigested within us!

But who among us, the second generation of Turks in Germany, has really considered the past and the future of Germany in any depth?

Does Emigrating to Germany not also Mean Emigrating into the Recent German Past?

The history of Jews in Germany, as the largest minority of a different faith, and the impulses emitted by them, but also the effect of the Enlightenment on Jewry with all its consequences, which reached as far as emancipation and assimilation, offer us an experiential background that has not yet been analysed. The bitter experiences that led to the destruction of the Jewish minority in Europe must also have some bearing on the conception of a multicultural Europe.

But does the threat not exist that the anti-Semitism of European history will be extended to an anti-Islamism, dug out of the Middle Ages and made topical? The era of depoliticization, of fast-moving concepts, of post-modern arbitrariness is being succeeded today by a neoconservative thrust, which is once again rendering nationalism and xenophobia socially acceptable.

German Question – German Identity

There is no doubt that the majority of Germans was successfully drawn into the European process after 1945. However, the so-called German Question remains a trouble area. This does not so much mean the question of borders but of the German national sentiment, of German identity.

The Germans, especially those in the West, have suppressed all memory of national feeling. This was also part of a strategy of 'overcoming the past' (*Vergangenheitsbewältigung*) that could be described more accurately as a project of forgetting. The ritual of overcoming involves not only expiatory phrases and anniversary celebrations but the suppression of moods, the sublimation of emotions, embedded in a general programme of reconstruction, which didn't exactly follow the most difficult path.

As the French philosopher Alain Finkielkraut explained impressively in his book 'Futile Remembrance' (*Vergebliche Erinnerung*), this ritual of overcoming really prevents making memory contemporary and calls forth a mechanism of impertinent forgetting.

The presence of a minority which can be distinguished from the majority on account of its culture, history and religion could turn out to be an important corrective in the rediscovery of a German national sentiment. Obviously, however, this fact also embodies an enormous potential for conflict. And since conflicts build up and are aggravated by the subconscious something ought to be done quickly.

No Integration without Citizens' Rights

In the thirtieth year of immigration, Germany should no longer remain the rear-light in Europe with regard to foreigners' rights and life prospects. Yet, despite German announcements to the contrary, a serious will for integration is not evident as long as the debureaucratization and liberalization of German naturalization laws and its practice are left out of the discussion.

The offer, 'Foreigners could become naturalized if they really wanted to', remains a mockery in face of the German concept of citizenship, which is orientated towards the hereditary origins of the subject. According to this conception, ethnic Germans from Eastern Europe, whose ancestors have lived outside Germany's borders for 500 years and who can only speak broken German, or none at all, are regarded as Germans. But a second- or third-generation Turk, who was born or grew up in Germany, who can't speak Turkish, but who for that very reason is all the better at expressing himself in German: he is and remains a foreigner. The fact that this can continue to play a central role in a country in which racial concepts led to incomprehensible crimes seems, to put it mildly, alienating.

Islam as a European Factor

The fact that German citizens of Turkish origin are also German citizens of the Islamic faith appears increasingly to arouse fears of contact.

Islam has long been a European factor. Almost two million Muslims, for example, live in Germany. In contrast to many EU states, Islam is not recognized in this country as a state-supported religious community.

The future will show whether extreme positions on all sides will give way to a dialogue or if they will continue to blacken people's consciousness. After anti-Semitism, Islam shouldn't serve as a new enemy image for the self-conception of Europe. The Muslims must also work to ensure this. They must finally begin to examine their tradition critically, to not only tolerate freedom of expression, but to promote it.

Islam does not force itself on anyone. This religion is essentially more tolerant than seems plausible after so much recent violence and arbitrariness done in its name.

The roots for the tolerance of Islam lie in its history, not in a utopically transfigured history, but in the practical, lived history of Moorish Spain, a [*seldschukischen*][1] Anatolia. It is high time that we took this up again and developed that critical, enlightened spirit which determined Western thought from the ninth to the thirteenth century, allowed a high civilization to flourish and decisively influenced the European Middle Ages on its way to the modern era.

Humanistic ideals and the spirit of the Enlightenment were not home-grown in Europe. Rather, they are west-eastern hybrids, crossbreeds. Their practice and cultivation would not represent a process of alienation for Muslims but, on the contrary, would constitute the discovery of their own lost tradition.

This rediscovery and redevelopment of one's own tradition in the critical counter-light of a pluralistic society will only be possible for those who have learned to change viewpoints, to see something of themselves in what is foreign and to look at themselves from a distance. This alone might enable future generations to handle prejudices and enemy images differently in order to one day erase them perhaps from the language of humanity.

January 1990

1. Ethnic Turkish.

36

Not an Oriental (Fairy) Tale*
Kemal Kurt

My family and I lived in the house that burnt down. As children and later in elementary school, Christian and I were friends. He was a quiet boy. I can't believe that Christian turned into a Nazi. He had meals with us and at times slept over. How could he set fire to the house which he had been to so many times; how could he be to blame for the death of people whose hospitality he and his parents enjoyed many times?

> Erkan Temiz (15 years) to journalists in Turkey about Christian R., the presumed arsonist of Solingen.

Ants everywhere.

They crawl under my shirt, in my mouth, through my nostrils right up into my brain.

Condemned to inactivity, when there is so much to do. Permanent vacation as punishment for a workaholic.

Something is crawling and tingling everywhere. Too much peace and quiet makes me restless. Again the windows of the other houses shimmer like gold in the distance. I long for my home. Softly, I pronounce its name: Berlin.

Once upon a time, never upon a time. A long time ago there was a city. It had a beautiful wall.

This wall was the post that the world was fixed to. Since it has been pulled out, the world is shaking. In its very foundations, the parts rub together, it is crumbling.

Neighbours turn into murderers.

Streets turn into trenches.

Houses turn into gas chambers.

---

* 'Kein orientalisches Märchen', from *Was ist die Mehrzahl von Heimat? Bilder eines türkisch-deutschen Doppellebens* (Reinbek: Rowohlt Taschenbuch Verlag, 1995), 150–8.

I have been pronouncing the name of the city softly since then.

My longing has been travelling without a ticket since then.

'How could he set fire to the house which he had been to so many times?' Erkan Temiz asked.

'Why do they do this?' the inhabitants of Aytepe ask and expect me to provide them with an answer.

'Why?' this is the question asked most often here. Why?

As if there was an explanation.

As if the consequences became more bearable because of an explanation.

A three-year-old Turkish boy and his sister want to cross the street. The boy is hit by a car; badly hurt, he is lying in the street. A young woman, who sees the accident from her window, calls the police and, together with her neighbour, goes to the scene of the accident. About thirty curious onlookers have gathered. They pity – no, not the badly hurt boy, but the driver of the car, who for his part is grieving over the damage to the paint. It gets worse when the boy's mother arrives at the scene of the accident, wailing loudly. Then the passers-by start to carry on about the Turks in general and the mother in particular. She is hysterical, they say, and they wonder whether she is going to attack the driver with a knife. Some think out loud about the Turks: They come into the country in masses, they take advantage of the welfare state, and in addition, they bring children into the world. They agree to a great extent: 'Thank God, one less Turk!' When two women try to exert a moderating influence on these people, they are scolded. Nobody does anything about it, not even the policemen who are present.

Those who have experienced something like this don't wonder how Hoyerswerda, Rostock, Mölln, Solingen, Lübeck or Magdeburg were possible. It happened exactly like this, but not in the wild East and not in the past few years when, being confronted with the attacks on foreigners, one could talk about pogrom mood without being contradicted. It happened on 12 July 1983, in broad daylight, in a well-off part of Berlin, Wilmersdorf, in Johann-Georg-Straße. Still affected by what she had experienced, that young woman at the window told me about it a few days afterwards.

'Death is a master from Germany,' Paul Celan wrote. The master has worked overtime in the past few years: In Eberswalde, a man from Angola is beaten to death by skinheads. In a Mecklenburg hall, youths kill the eighteen-year-old Romanian Dragomir Christenel. The Vietnamese Nguyen Van Tu is stabbed to death by right-wing extremists in Berlin-Mahrzan. In Ostfildern-Kemnat, masked men beat the Yugoslavian Sadri

Berisha to death. In Stotternheim, the Polish seasonal worker Ireneusz Szydersi is killed by a right-wing extremist bouncer of a discothèque. The list is long: Saarlouis, Dresden, Friedrichshafen, Buxtehude, Flensburg, Hörstel, Mölln, Köln, Berlin-Mitte, Freiburg, Staßfurt, Schlotheim, Hangelsberg, names one had never heard before – Adenstedt, Lübz, Preetz, Langenau, Vreden. Names one would otherwise have been spared – Mühlheim, Schwerin, Coburg, Solingen, Lübeck, Magdeburg. To be continued.

'Something is not right in Germany,' wrote Elie Wiesel, a writer and Nobel Peace Prize winner and a survivor of the concentration camps Auschwitz and Buchenwald, who usually makes an effort at reconciliation. 'There was a time when I was convinced that Germany would never let itself be seduced again by the violence and ugliness of anti-Semitism. I told myself it would be one of the few countries in the world in which hatred did not have a right to existence any more . . . I was wrong. I say this filled with grief . . .'

I'm filled with grief, too. I also thought that what happened would never be repeated. Unfortunately, however, at present, something stinks to high heaven in Germany. Those who have followed the developments in policy-making concerning foreigners in the past fifteen years know where the stench originates.

Berlin sociologist Helmut Essinger outlines three steps in the escalation of racism in Germany.

In the early 1980s, a change in policy regarding foreigners took place. 'After the abstinence of the postwar era . . . one could again express nationalist, biologist and racist views in public.' A group of Heidelberg professors provided the theoretical superstructure in the 'Heidelberg Manifesto'. 'Integration of foreigners is genocide' was the title of a brochure of someone by the name of Wolfgang Seeger; in the Hanover area, it was put into letter-boxes and sent to offices and day-care centres. In it, there is talk about a 'homogenized mixture of people' and 'state destruction' because of integration. Furthermore: 'Because of natural laws, integration of foreigners into the body of the German people is not possible . . . mixing creates schizophrenic or multiple personalities . . . half-breeds often show criminal character traits . . . Those who do not wish their descendants to be destroyed in a Eurasian-negroid mixture of peoples will support corresponding education.'

In 1981/2, the political atmosphere was shaped by the Berlin Foreigner Decree. According to it, foreign young people should not have the right to a residence permit after they have turned eighteen. Thousands of young people were threatened with expulsion. Since then, compared with other

European countries, Germany has had the most restrictive laws concerning the reunification of families.

During this time, the first Turk jokes appeared. The grounds for racist attacks were prepared verbally. Many politicians liked to lend a hand in this.

'The Federal Republic is not a country of immigration,' it resounded again and again in loud baritone. Even in the most distant corner of the Republic one heard it and pricked up one's ears: there were people who stayed in this country and had no right to do so!

'The boat is full,' it was then said, and people became afraid of drowning. Everybody tried to drown out everyone else. In the cacophony one could hear bits and pieces like 'domination by foreign influence', 'tide', 'flood'. What kind of primary fears were roused when a former governor (*Ministerpräsident*) of Hessen regretted loudly that Prinz Eugen's victory over the Turks – him again? – had been futile since today they were streaming into the country unimpeded! But most eager of all was a small man with great ambitions – the former Berlin Minister for Internal Affairs Heinrich Lummer: 'if politics is not able to master policy concerning foreigners, to find a reasonable solution, then this problem will turn into a security problem one day', he knew already in 1982. 'Of course, tension arises when a German starts to feel: "I'm not at home any more; they stole it from me in a certain way." His whole environment has become foreign to him. It starts with how it smells . . . He doesn't feel comfortable anymore. Then aggression starts to grow. This is natural.' And the minister indicated that: 'when the foreigner problem is solved, the problem of unemployment is solved as well'.

I am the 'problem'. Today, the ghosts that were called up by such irresponsible politicians work on 'solving' the problem.

The second phase of racism in Germany, according to Essinger, began in the late 1980s, when right-wing radical and extremist groups with xenophobic slogans became popular. Its peak was reached with the *Republikaner* TV commercial for the election of the Berlin representatives in 1989; its message cannot be surpassed in insensitivity: Play Me the Song of Death.[1] And already then one could see a reaction one would also witness in the racist attacks of 1992: large parts of the population watched and listened unmoved.

Mainstream politicians drew the wrong conclusions from this and used the same vocabulary in order to avoid losing votes. Foreigners were turned

---

1. The German text is *Spiel mir das Lied vom Tod*, which is the German title of the film *Once Upon a Time in the West*.

into an election campaign issue; people talked about them as if they were simply a problem that had to be solved, a temporary illness that had to be cured. The border between the centre and the right-wing extremist camp disappeared, the politics of exclusion was stabilized.

The third phase, an inevitable consequence of what went before, are the open and brutal acts of violence today. Extremism feeds on the centre, where politicians have stirred up fears. In contrast to the latter, sociologists don't talk of 'marginal groups' but of a 'popular extremism of the centre'. Mölln, Solingen, Hoyerswerda, Rostock . . . a map goes up in flames in more spots than a society has margins. Like Auschwitz and Dachau, such places now carry a stigma – wrongly so since so far the centre has not been lost. But unfortunately the fact remains that not even a dozen wise men can get a stone out of a well which was thrown in by a fool. The causes of neofascism today are the same as those of the crusades then: poverty, unemployment and lack of a vision for the future, accompanied by an effective propaganda machinery. And the crusaders, too – just like the skinheads today – got drunk before they pillaged and threatened to burn. German courts are understanding and accept the influence of alcohol as diminishing guilt.

This is a licence to continue.

Verbal violence has changed into brute force. What can be done?

There are calls for drastic steps by the police and measures for self-protection. Certainly, these desperate calls are justified. For a long time, the police searched half-heartedly and proved to be unmotivated in combating nightly orgies of violence. 'No indications of xenophobia as a motive for the crime,' it was often said after arson attacks. Even though he who confessed to the attack in Mölln used 'Heil Hitler!' as his goodbye, the police assumed personal motives within a criminal milieu. But the problems created by politics can be solved neither by the police nor by counter-violence. Only a fundamental rethinking and a change in attitudes concerning the foreign population – even though they don't have any votes to cast – can avoid the worst. Time is running out; prudent, responsible and quick actions are essential to save the endangered democracy. Lasting and conspicuous examples have to be set, examples which defy the violence, put it in its place instead of being intimidated by it:

1. The politics of exclusion have to be left behind once and for all; the Foreigners Law has to be changed accordingly. Immigration laws have to be instituted, laws which do more justice to political reality than laws regulating temporary stays.

2. It must be made possible for foreigners to participate in political decision making through the right to vote in local and general elections. This demand, which has been raised for fifteen years, has been rejected with reference to the Federal Republic's Basic Law. It is an argument among jurists. The Basic Law can be changed, as we have seen recently with regard to Article 16.
3. An anti-discrimination law like that in Great Britain and the USA has to be introduced. In those countries, the strong words of irresponsible politicians don't fall into the category of free speech; they can be prosecuted as incitement of the people. In the USA, Draconian penalties, prison sentences and fines are imposed for 'hate crimes' – a concept that the German legal system does not know – as in the case of Tom and John Metzgers of the 'White Aryan Resistance', for instance.
4. The 1913 law that still regulates who belongs to the German nation and who doesn't (*Reichsstaatsangehörigengesetz*) must be changed, and the *jus sanguinis*, the principle of origin, must be replaced by the *jus soli*, the principle of place of birth. Dual citizenship must be made possible.

These certainly unpopular measures would send clear signals in a time when they are urgently needed. Unfortunately it still doesn't look as if this will happen. With some relief one estimates that the number of attacks has diminished somewhat. But, today, foreigners are still being hunted down in the streets; today fires are still being set here and there. The arsonists are arming themselves with the most recent telecommunications technology and computers for the next attack; death lists are being compiled. But, as long as there is no scent of corpses in the air, nobody pays any attention. Attacks without deadly consequences have become a normal aspect of reality; they don't count.

The former Berlin Minister of Internal Affairs, famous for his biting slogans and notorious because of his contacts with the NPD and the right-wing radical 'voters' action group of the *Volk* party', was elected as the CDU chairman in the *Bundestag* committee for – they never cease to amaze one – human rights.

'We are a country which is friendly to foreigners,' the Chancellor insisted with childish defiance, while the dormitories were still in flames. Five days after Mölln, the Social Democratic opposition leader said that incidents like this also occurred in other countries, but that it counted for double when it came to Germany. The politicians seem to be so stuck in their positions that they are no longer aware that their well-meaning statements are playing down the events. The pitiable Germans are punished doubly for something that everybody else does as well. But something like a clapping, cheering, jubilant mass of people in face of the attempted murder of brown-eyed children does not exist in other countries. In no other countries do hooligans hunt down Africans in pedestrian zones of big cities in broad daylight – and the police have difficulty distinguishing between perpetrators and victims.

Apart from human rights violations in Iran and China, the 1994 human rights report of the US Minister of Foreign Affairs dealt extensively with violence against foreigners in Germany. Violence was continuing, it said, but the German police were more in control, and German judges have moved to impose tougher sentences after being criticized for their lenient verdicts. Exactly how much the police were in control of the situation we were able to see in Magdeburg, and many verdicts lead us to question the rule of law. The Paderborn district court found in February 1994 that the expression 'Turks out' falls under the right to free speech, and that it neither expresses contempt for humanity nor incites the people. It acquitted the three accused skinheads. At about the same time, the leader of a group of skinheads in California was sentenced to eight years in prison because of a similar accusation; the court found it proven that he wanted to provoke a race war with his statement.

Amnesty International also reproached the Federal Republic of Germany for abuse of foreign citizens. In the case of Abdülkerim B., for instance, who was beaten up in Berlin-Charlottenburg on 16 October 1993 by several policemen, first in the street and then in a police car. Or in the case of Garip M., who was sentenced to one year of prison without parole by the Berlin district court because he had distributed leaflets which talked about Germany as a country of murderers. Cases are known in which foreigners died or were fatally injured in a stranglehold by the police. In September 1994 Nigeria demanded explanations from the Federal Government about the death of twenty-four Nigerian citizens, who died between 1991 and 1994 in Germany while being detained prior to deportation.

Unfortunately the events of the past few years do not seem to have promoted a change of course in policy regarding foreigners as might have been expected. It is only because the Minister of Foreign Affairs has bemoaned feeling 'pressured for explanations' on his visits outside Germany, because protests from abroad have increased, and because the fear has been growing that foreign investors will flee with their wallets that the Federal Government finds itself forced to act. I would prefer it if they acted out of conviction. I would prefer it if they acted because the lives of innocent women and children are significant to them, and not because the reputation of Germans abroad has been dented.

The three-year-old boy who was hurt in the accident in Berlin-Wilmersdorf died in hospital. The woman at the window and her neighbour initiated a campaign for donations to be used for the transfer and funeral of the child. Many helped, and, as chance would have it, they collected 1001 marks, rounded up by 20 pfennigs – unfortunately however, this is not an oriental fairy tale. The mother, who was five months pregnant at the time of the accident, gave birth to a disabled child. The parents were accused of violating their legal parental responsibility to keep their children under proper supervision. The case was dropped later on.

Nobody from the ranks of the smirking onlookers was sued. Even though Article 130 of the criminal code says: 'Those who disturb the peace in a way which attacks the dignity of others by inciting hatred of segments of the population, by abusing them, by maliciously disparaging and slandering them, will be sentenced to at least three months in prison.'

How many politicians would go to jail if this article were applied consistently?

37

Zarathustra's Wounded Children*
Ismet Elçi

Thus I flew on and, with a bad conscience, left my guardian angel behind, who himself needed protection. I passed a wonderful forest, across which a rope was stretched. I dived down and held on to the rope. It started to sing. I understood a few words of this humming song. I recognized that it was the same rope that my poor tortured brother had pulled out of his head in order to forget his thoughts. Then the rope sang about paradise; it advised me to follow it. I made my way hand over hand along the rope so that the invisible spring could not pull me up into the sky again. As I dragged myself along between the trees, suddenly the invisible force which pulled me upward let up.

I fell to the ground, which was covered with moss. The sun was shining through the dark-green trees, insects were humming, birds chirping. In a clearing, I watched a lion playing with a rabbit. I got up and followed a sandy path. Along its edge, huge mushrooms were growing. After I had walked for a while, I heard sighing and wailing. I followed the noise and found my angel in uniform sitting on a big tree stump. When he recognized me, his face lit up, and we continued on the path together until we reached a little river. In its clear water, we could see plenty of fish. My friend was very thirsty and scooped up some water in his hands in order to drink it. Then he asked me whether this was the path that I had been led along back then. When I confirmed this he took exact sketches and notes, got out a small camera and took pictures of our surroundings. Then he wanted to know whether the smugglers[1] were hiding in this forest. I said that this was probably so, but then he added that he didn't have anything to do with this; this was the business of a different organization.

Afterwards he asked me whether I could teach him to fly and if he could fly with me then. I thought for a moment; then I agreed on the

---

* (Excerpt from an unpublished manuscript)
1. The German *Schlepper* refers to men helping people cross a border illegally.

condition that I would have to walk when he flew, since the energy needed for flying was only sufficient for one. He agreed without further ado. Looking into his eyes intensely, I transferred the necessary power to him. Then he flew and I walked; with nimble steps, I walked through the forest. Now and then, I saw the angel fly through the treetops; after a while, however, I lost touch with him; in a clearing, I searched the sky for him. I found him on the horizon and realized that he had gone off in the wrong direction. I yelled after him that it was the wrong way. He turned around and said that he wasn't wrong, that the sun was moving north to south. I had to believe him, he said. I found out that he was in fact right. The sun moved from north to south. I realized immediately that the saintly man, who was writing a new book in which a revolution was taking place, must be behind this change. No wars were ever going to take place again, and all languages were going to be liberated. My angel, the one in uniform, was enthusiastic about this idea, too. We set off in the right direction. After a while, I couldn't walk any more and called him down to me. I climbed on his back and held on to his ears so tightly that he pulled a face. For several hours, we flew in one direction. We landed without any help. After we had rested for a bit, we looked around. We were in an area in which nature had been left to its own devices. Here, torturing men, animals, plants, rivers, oceans and air seemed to be forbidden. Unfortunately, this hadn't got around to the rest of the world – or it simply wasn't followed. We went through forests and meadows, covered with delicate flowers. We drank from brooks, and around us the air was as soft as velvet. From far away, I saw a man who, upon our approach, was hiding in a hole in the ground. We looked into the hole, and I recognized my father. Before he greeted me, he asked right away who the 'unbeliever' at my side was; from this I gathered that he didn't know anything about the book. I turned around to my companion, who had pulled out his camera and was eagerly taking pictures of my father, the surroundings and everything that moved. I answered my father's question with the comment that believers and unbelievers had the same god. For safety's sake, I stepped back from the edge of the hole because I feared my father's unpredictable reactions. His face darkened and he growled something incomprehensible. Then he added more loudly that unbelievers belonged in hell. I shook my head. I answered that I could not understand why God had not created all men equal. I saw the veins on his forehead swell up and his eyes turn red; then he grunted angrily: 'Because the believers believe, and the unbelievers don't believe.'

He crawled out of his hole and approached me. I ran away as fast as I could so that he couldn't hit me. But he could run well, my old man. I could hear him panting behind me. We came to a wide road, which was lined with people on both sides. The onlookers began to applaud and whispered to each other. They assumed that I was the first in an athletic competition. Suddenly, I discovered a shadow followed by a second one. I looked up and saw two helicopters, which were hovering above me. I started to run even faster, and my breath became so loud that this was the only thing I could still hear.

By this time, I had reached a town on this road; behind the people, I saw one house next to the other. As I passed, I could hear the echo of my gasping breath, which was refracted from the walls of the houses. The sound grew louder and louder, and suddenly the windows of the houses burst from the sound, and one wall collapsed. I pushed myself past the people, who were startled, and went into the room through the hole in the wall, where five people were sitting in front of a TV; they had followed my running on TV; it had been filmed from one of the helicopters. There were four men and one woman; she told me that the race had been full of suspense until the collapse of the wall. The TV had been hit by a rock and had imploded. Because of the shock, the men were kneeling on the floor praying; the woman said that they did this because the book written by the saintly man instructed them to do so. Hence I was happy about the book's effect, and I was happy for my saintly friend and about the fact that there would never be another war. The woman lamented that she was happy to have four men at the same time, but that she was also very unhappy since the men never had any time for her.

In the meantime, my father had passed by outside, and I dared to leave the house without responding to the woman's complaints. Among the many people, I noticed a uniform, and I recognized my angel, the policeman. He was running about in a great panic and was taking pictures of everything that seemed interesting to him. In between, he took lots of notes. Every now and then, he pulled a book from his uniform jacket and leafed through it. Some of the people recognized me as the runner and started to applaud again. Because of this, my angel became aware of me and fought his way through to me. We walked together along part of the street and came to a monument made of stone. It represented a man who was almost as tall as my brother back there at home. My companion asked me who it was. He didn't know the name. I answered that he was the father of millions of people and I couldn't understand that he, an educated man, didn't know him. He was very surprised and couldn't grasp that one man could father so many children. I decided not to explain this any further. We turned into a side street, where we saw many children, all about my age. Then he enquired curiously whether all of them wanted to go to the holy land.

'No,' I said, 'the children just want to go to school!'

'But why are they accompanied by so many soldiers?' he asked further.

'So that they can learn faster!' I explained to him.

He muttered appreciatively, 'Wonderful, wonderful!'

Then he produced his camera and quickly took pictures of the studying children with their helpers. Afterwards he wanted to walk on, but I couldn't walk any more. So he allowed me to climb on his back, and I held on to both of his ears, which by now had become as long as rabbit ears. I rode on him through the crowd; when we passed a group of tourists, we were photographed several times. Some of them even wanted to climb on his back along with me; one wanted to pay money to do so. I declined and said that this transportation was private and that my porter was not for rent. My angel didn't mind playing his ferrying role; he had a powerful build, and I was still small. He was only interested in whether, from my elevated position, I had already discovered one of the smugglers anywhere. I said no. He asked me to let him know if I did, because he wanted to speak with one of them urgently. I pointed out to him that this could be dangerous for me. As a corpse, I would not be very useful to him. He thought about it and turned around to me; then he smiled at me, and I smiled back. Then he put me down, and I had to walk again.

After a while, we passed a kiosk, which sold all kinds of drinks. He bought something for us to drink. Then we set out again. Unfortunately, the drinks were so warm from the heat that I suddenly felt sick after only a few steps. I fell down and closed my eyes. The long walk, the heat and the bad air had made me very tired. My angel tried to get me to continue, but I refused. I could still see the clouds, which were passing above me; then it slowly grew dark around me. Suddenly, it was bright again, and I was in a room; next to me was an officer. He said words to me in a language which I was supposed to have learned at some earlier time. Since the bright light dazzled me I wanted to turn my head, but I couldn't move. As if paralysed, I was lying underneath a dripping stone, which was hanging directly above me. Water was dripping on to my head constantly, one drop after the other, with cruel regularity. I counted the drops while the officer next to me was talking to me insistently in the foreign language. He tried to make it clear to me that time had slowed down – one second was as long as a minute now, and a minute as long as an hour; the hour was a day, the day a week, the week a month, and the month lasted a year.

And indeed, from the corner of my eye, I could observe a ray of sun, which remained an eternity in the same spot on the wall. The sun seemed to move only very slowly and thus confirmed the officer's words. I don't know how long I had been lying like this. The drops pierced like needles into my brain, and I lost the consciousness that I hadn't had. When I thought I had regained consciousness, I was able to move again. I sat up and looked around the room in which I found myself. It was huge and seemed to be a real paradise. I recognized my angel and saw that he was surrounded by beautiful, young women. He seemed to be very happy and had apparently completely forgotten about me. I counted the women; there were exactly seventy-five, exactly as many as described by the new holy book. Besides that, all the other prophecies of the book had come true as well, except for the pronouncement of eternal life. For when I looked at him, I noticed that my angel in uniform was visibly getting older; his hair was turning grey and his face wrinkly. The drops from the ceiling had become a thick stream of water; the ray of sun on the wall hurried from left to right, disappeared and appeared again on the left. I was glad to have escaped the stream of water; I no longer knew how long I had been lying underneath the dripping stone. I only felt the roaring of the drops in my head, which had shaken my soul.

Suddenly my angel removed himself from the circle of his women and joined me. He looked at me and was shocked; at first, he didn't know what to say. I must have looked terrible. But he had aged decades as well and looked like his own father. But then he composed himself, smiled at me, and I tried to smile back. Afterwards, he sat down on a chair, which was not far away in a corner. I looked at him, but he didn't say anything. Suddenly, all four walls moved outward; he was sliding away on his chair, too, until he was very small and far away. The only thing I could still see was his face, which was lit by a light from below. Everything else was in the dark. Then a very small girl came out of the shadow; her face was eerily illuminated, too. The child was still very small, but could already speak and walk; and she came running directly towards me. She grinned at me angrily and showed me sharp teeth, with which she wanted to bite me. I was afraid the girl might eat me. In a deep and hoarse voice, she yelled out asking me why I was silent. A man appeared out of the darkness; I could only see his face also. He apologized for the girl's behaviour, introduced himself – he said he was an engineer – then he led the child to my friend, the angel in uniform, who was still sitting far away on his chair. My angel seemed to have fallen asleep. The man with the child approached him, purloined a bottle from him and emptied it. Then he returned it to my angel's pocket and sat down next to him on a chair. He pulled the nasty child on to his lap. Angrily, the girl resisted, her eyes sparked and she gnashed her pointed teeth.

Gradually, more and more people entered the hall. A man in a black coat stepped into the centre of the room, bowed and introduced himself as the founder of the law, while pointing to a thick book which he was carrying with him. Then he went to a corner of the room and sat down. Some men followed him; one of them explained in a few words that they were the helpers of the administration. Then they sat down right and left of the man in the coat. The hall filled up. The faces were bright. The more people that came, the brighter the hall became. The brighter it became, the less threatening the faces seemed. A man entered the room; he wanted to say something, but he couldn't. Only moaning came out of his mouth. He pointed to his mouth – somebody had cut out his tongue. He shrugged his shoulders and sat down on a bench in the front. Four men carried a huge portrait into the room; it was several metres high and wide; they hung it up on the wall. I had seen the face several times before and recognized the 'father of millions'. Someone had explained to me back then that this person was so important that he was not allowed to be harmed even in a revolution, even if this meant sacrificing many people's lives. The murmuring in the room ceased. The helpers rose and with dignity went to the man who had lost his tongue. The engineer, who was by now holding my companion's empty bottle in his hand, joined them. He took up a position and claimed the shape of a bottle was completely impractical. People's inventive genius was underdeveloped in some areas; as designer, he would have given bottles a different shape.

With these words, he knocked off the bottle's neck on a chair and looked at the jagged edge with pleasure. A man in a white coat rose and went to the man without a tongue and asked him to undress. When he didn't do it, the lawmaker excitedly leafed through his book and then gave the helpers a sign. These nodded in agreement and undressed the tongueless man with obvious pleasure. The man started to cry out loud; he seemed to call out a few words in the language of the mountain people, which is after all forbidden. But nobody could understand him because without a tongue he could only mumble. This was lucky for him because otherwise he would have been punished additionally because of his language. He tried to fend off the helpers. He looked up and stammered a word which sounded like the name of the creator. One of the helpers remarked he wasn't home, he was on vacation.

Then the hall became unbearably bright; dazzled, everybody held their hands protectively in front of their eyes. The voice of the Prophet roared from all corners of the room as if through huge loudspeakers. He preached that he was still there, even if one did not follow the holy book, he still existed. Everybody present was very frightened; only the keeper of the law leafed through his book again. Then he said calmly that only his law was valid here and he had to act according to his law. The nasty little girl had been watching everything from the corner. In her deep voice, she screamed at me asking what I was waiting for. I was feeling insecure because I didn't know what this little beast wanted from me. My angel-like friend smiled at me, and I returned a forced smile. Then he took notes again and photographed those present. In the meantime, the tongueless man had been undressed. Naked, he lay on his stomach in the middle of the room. The helpers held his arms and legs. The engineer with the bottle looked at the trembling man; then he inserted the broken bottle into the defenceless man's rectum. Gurgling came out of his throat, a stream of blood poured on to the floor. Those present rose from their seats so that they could see better. The president of the court announced that the sentence had been carried out. He added that the law was going to be applied in full force to anybody who refused to accept that he was born a slave. But the man on the ground didn't die. He changed in some strange way.

Selected Bibliography

Primary Sources

Ackermann, Irmgard, ed. *Als Fremder in Deutschland*. Munich: dtv, 1982.
———. *In zwei Sprachen leben*. Munich: dtv, 1983.
———. *Türken deutscher Sprache*. Munich: dtv, 1984.
Ackermann, Irmgard and Harald Weinrich, eds. *Eine nicht nur deutsche Literatur: Zur Standortbestimmung der 'Ausländerliteratur'*. Munich: Piper, 1986.
Biondi, Franco. *Passavantis Rückkehr. Erzählungen 1*. Fischerhude: Verlag Atelier im Bauernhaus, 1982.
———. *Die Tarantel. Erzählungen 2*. Fischerhude: Verlag Atelier im Bauernhaus, 1982.
———. *Die Unversöhnlichen oder im Labyrinth der Herkunft*. Tübingen: Heliopolis, 1991.
Biondi, Franco, ed. *Im neuen Land*. Bremen: Edition CON, 1980.
———. *Zwischen Fabrik und Bahnhof*. Bremen: Edition CON, 1981
———. *Annäherungen. Prosa, Lyriken und Fotografiken aus dem Gastarbeiteralltag*. Bremen: Edition CON, 1982.
———. *Zwischen zwei Giganten: Prosa, Lyrik und Grafiken aus dem Gastarbeiteralltag*. Bremen: Edition CON, 1983.
Biller, Maxim. *Die Tempojahre*. Munich: dtv, 1991.
Broder, Henryk. *Erbarmen mit den Deutschen*. Hamburg: Hoffmann und Campe, 1994.
———. *Schöne Bescherung! Unterwegs im neuen Deutschland*. Augsburg: Ölbaum Verlag, 1994.
———. *Volk und Wahn*. Hamburg: Spiegel-Buch Verlag, 1996.
Chiellino, Gino. *Mein fremder Alltag. Gedichte*. Kiel: Neuer Malik Verlag, 1984.
———. *Sehnsucht nach Sprache. Gedichte*. Kiel: Neuer Malik Verlag, 1987.
———. *Literatur und Identität in der Fremde. Zur Literatur italienischer Autoren in der Bundesrepublik*. Kiel: Neuer Malik Verlag, 1989.
———. *Fremde: Discourse of the Foreign*. Toronto: Guernica, 1995.

Dikmen, Sinasi. *Wir werden das Knoblauchkind schon schaukeln: Satiren.* Berlin: EXpress Edition, 1983.

——. *Hurra, ich lebe in Deutschland: Satiren.* Munich: Piper, 1995.

Eicheneier, Niki, ed. *Dimitrakis '86. Um eine Heimat bittend.* Cologne: Romiosini, 1985.

Elçi, Ismet. *Cemile oder das Märchen von der Hoffnung.* Berlin: Verlag Clemens Zerling, 1991.

Esselborn, Karl, ed. *über Grenzen: Berichte, Erzählungen und Gedichte von Ausländern.* Munich: dtv, 1987.

Fleischmann, Lea. *Ich bin Israelin: Erfahrungen in einem orientalischen Land.* Hamburg: Hoffmann & Campe, 1982.

——. *Dies ist nicht mein Land – Eine Jüdin verläßt die Bundesrepublik.* Hamburg: Wilhelm Heine Verlag, 1992.

Fraundorfer, Helmuth. *Landschaft der Maulwürfe. Gedichte.* Frankfurt-on-Main: dipa Verlag, 1990.

Friedrich, Heinz. *Chamissos Enkel.* Munich: dtv, 1986.

Gündisch, Karin. *Im Land der Schokolade und Bananen. Kurzgeschichten.* Weinheim: Beltz & Gelberg, 1987.

——. *Weit, weit hinter den Wäldern.* Weinheim: Beltz & Gelberg, 1988.

——. *Liebe. Tage, die kommen.* Freiburg: Kore, 1994.

Gute Reise meine Augen: Texte von Griechinnen und Griechen in Deutschland. Stuttgart: Peter- Grohmann-Verlag, 1992.

Hamm, Horst, Wolfgang Jung and Heidi Knott, eds. *Flucht nach Deutschland: Lebensberichte.* Freiburg: Dreisam, 1988.

Hensel, Klaus. *Oktober Lichtspiel. Gedichte.* Frankfurt-on-Main: Frankfurter Verlagsanstalt, 1988.

——. *Stradivaris Geigenstein. Gedichte.* Dreieich: Schierlingspresse, 1989.

Holzl, Luisa and Eleni Torossi, eds. *Freihändig auf dem Tandem: Dreißig Frauen aus elf Ländern.* Kiel: Neuer Malik Verlag, 1985.

Honigmann, Barbara. *Roman von einem Kinde: Sechs Erzählungen.* Hamburg: Luchterhand, 1989.

——. *Eine Liebe aus nichts.* Reinbek: Rowohlt, 1991.

——. *Soharas Reise.* Reinbek: Rowohlt, 1996.

Kurt, Kemal. *Bilder einer Kindheit. Erzählung.* Berlin: EXpress Edition, 1986.

——. *Was ist die Mehrzahl von Heimat? Bilder eines türkisch-deutschen Doppellebens.* Reinbek: Rowohlt, 1995.

——. *The Five Fingers of the Moon.* New York: North–South Books, 1997.

Klüger, Ruth. *Weiter leben – Eine Jugend.* Göttingen: Wallstein, 1992.

Knott, Heidi, ed. *Heimat Deutschland? Lebensberichte von Aus- und Übersiedlern.* Pfaffenweiler: Centaurus Verlagsgesellschaft, 1991.

Kuhlmann, Michael and Alwin Meyer, eds. *Ayse und Devrim: Wo gehören wir hin?* Bornheim: Lamuv, 1983.

Lappin, Elena, ed. *Jewish Voices, German Words – Growing Up Jewish in Postwar Germany and Austria.* Trans. Krishna Winston. North Haven, CT: Catbird. 1994.

Moníková, Libuše. *Pavane für eine verstorbene Infantin.* München: Hanser, 1983.

——. *Die Fassade: M.N.O.P.Q.* München: Hanser, 1987.

——. *Treibeis.* München: Hanser, 1992.

——. *Prager Fenster. Essays.* München: Hanser, 1994.

——. *Verklärte Nacht.* München: Hanser, 1996.

Müller, Herta. *Niederungen.* Berlin: Rotbuch, 1984.

——. *Barfüßiger Februar.* Berlin: Rotbuch, 1987.

——. *Reisende auf einem Bein.* Berlin: Rotbuch, 1989.

——. *The Passport.* London: Serpent's Tail, 1989.

——. *Der Teufel sitzt im Spiegel. Wie Wahrnehmung sich erfindet.* Berlin: Rotbuch, 1991.

——. *Hunger und Seide. Essays.* Reinbeck: Rowohlt, 1995.

——. *The Land of Green Plums: A Novel.* New York: Metropolitan Books, 1996.

Naoum, Jusuf. *Der rote Hahn: Erzählungen des Fischers Sidaoui.* Darmstadt: Luchterhand, 1974.

——. *Karakus und andere orientalische Märchen.* Frankfurt-on-Main: Brandes & Apsel, 1986.

——. *Die Kaffeehausgeschichten des Abu al Abed.* Frankfurt-on-Main: Brandes & Apsel, 1987.

Oji, Chima. *Unter die Deutschen gefallen.* Wuppertal: Peter Hammer, 1992.

Ören, Aras. *Die Fremde ist auch ein Haus.* Berlin: Rotbuch, 1980.

——. *Bitte nix Polizei.* Düsseldorf: Fischer, 1981.

——. *Manege.* Frankfurt-on-Main: Fischer, 1984.

Özakin, Aysel. *Die Preisvergabe.* Trans. Heike Offen. Frankfurt-on-Main: Luchterhand, 1982.

——. *Der fliegende Teppich – Auf der Spur meines Vaters.* Trans. Cornelius Bischoff. Reinbek: Rowohlt, 1987.

——. *Die blaue Maske.* Trans. Carl Koß. Hamburg and Zurich: Luchterhand, 1991.

——. *Die Vögel auf der Stirn.* Trans. Carl Koß. Hamburg and Zurich: Luchterhand, 1991.

——. *Glaube, Liebe, Aircondition – Eine türkische Kindheit*. Trans. Cornelia Holfelder-von der Tann. Hamburg and Zurich: Luchterhand, 1991.

——. *Deine Stimmer gehört dir. Erzählungen*. Trans. Hanne Egghardt and H.A. Schmiede. Hamburg and Zurich: Luchterhand, 1992.

——. *Die Leidenschaft der Anderen*. Trans. Hanne Egghardt. Hamburg and Zurich: Luchterhand, 1992.

Özdamar, Emine Sevgi. *Mutterzunge*. Berlin: Rotbuch, 1991.

——. *Das Leben ist eine Karawanserei – hat zwei Türen – aus einer kam ich rein – aus der anderen ging ich raus*. Cologne: Kiepenheuer und Witsch, 1992.

——. *Mother Tongue*. Trans. Craig Thomas. Toronto: Coach House Press, 1994.

Özkan, Hülya and Andrea Wörle, eds. *Eine Fremde wie ich*. Munich: dtv, 1985.

Pazarkaya, Yüksel. *Rosen im Frost: Einblicke in die türkische Kultur*. Zurich: Unionsverlag, 1980.

——. 'Stimmen des Zorns und der Einsamkeit in Bitterland.' *Zeitschrift für Kulturaustausch* 35 (1985): 16–27.

Schaffernicht, Christian, ed. *Zu Hause in der Fremde*. Fischerhude: Atelier im Bauernhaus, 1981.

Schami, Rafik. *Die Sehnsucht fährt schwarz*. Munich: dtv, 1988.

——. *A Handful of Stars*. London: Penguin, 1990.

——. *Der fliegende Baum*. Kiel: Neuer Malik Verlag, 1991.

——. *Der ehrliche Lügner*. Weinheim: Beltz & Gelberg, 1992.

——. *Damascus Nights*. Trans. Philip Boehm. New York: Farrar, Straus and Giroux, 1993.

——. *Der Fliegenmelker und andere Erzählungen*. Kiel: Neuer Malik Verlag, 1993.

——. *Fatima and the Dream Thief*. New York: North–South Books, 1996.

——. *The Crow Who Stood on His Beak*. New York: North–South Books, 1996.

Scheinhardt, Saliha. *Drei Zypressen. Erzählungen über türkische Frauen in Deutschland*. Freiburg im Breisgau: Verlag Herder, 1992.

Schindel, Robert. *Im Herzen die Krätze. Gedichte*. Frankfurt-on-Main: Suhrkamp, 1988.

——. *Gebürtig*. Frankfurt-on-Main: Suhrkamp, 1992.

Schlesak, Dieter. *Vaterlandstage. Und die Kunst des Verschwindens. Roman*. Zurich: Benziger, 1986.

——. *Aufbäumen. Gedichte und ein Essay*. Reinbek: Rowohlt, 1990.

——. *Wenn die Dinge aus dem Namen fallen. Essay.* Reinbek: Rowohlt, 1991.

——. *Stehendes Ich in laufender Zeit.* Leipzig: Reclam, 1994.

Seligmann, Rafael. *Rubinsteins Versteigerung.* Frankfurt-on-Main: Eichborn Verlag, 1989.

——. *Mit beschränkter Hoffnung: Juden, Deutsche, Israelis.* Hamburg: Hoffmann & Campe, 1991.

Şenocak, Zafer. *Flammentropfen: Gedichte.* Frankfurt-on-Main: Dagyeli, 1985.

——. *Ritual der Jugend: Gedichte.* Frankfurt-on-Main: Dagyeli, 1987.

——. *Fernwehanstalten: Gedichte.* Berlin: Babel Verlag, 1994.

——. 'War and Peace in Modernity: Reflections on the German-Turkish Future (1994).' *Cultural Studies* 10:2 (1996): 255–69.

—— and Bülent Tulay. *Atlas des tropischen Deutschland.* Berlin: Babel Verlag, 1992.

Sichrovsky, Peter. *Strangers in Their Own Land: Young Jews in Germany and Austria Today.* London: I.B. Tauris, 1986.

Sucharewicz, Leo. *Israelische Geschichten aus Deutschland. Kurzgeschichten zwischen Krieg und Frieden.* Munich: Roman Kovar Verlag, 1989.

Tekinay, Alev. *Über alle Grenzen: Erzählungen.* Hamburg: Buntbuch, 1986.

——. *Die Deutschprüfung: Erzählungen.* Frankfurt-on-Main: Brandes & Apsel, 1989.

——. *Nur ein Hauch von Paradies.* Frankfurt-on-Main: Brandes & Apsel, 1993.

Torossi, Elina. *Tanz der Tintenfische.* Kiel: Neuer Malik Verlag, 1986.

——. *Paganinis Traum.* Kiel: Neuer Malik Verlag, 1988.

——. *Die Papierschiffe.* Pongratz: Bibliophilen Verlag Edition, 1991.

Totok, William. *Die Zwänge der Erinnerung. Aufzeichnungen aus Rumänien.* Hamburg: Junius, 1988.

von Wroblewsky, Vincent. *Zwischen Thora und Trabant: Juden in der DDR.* Berlin: Aufbau, 1993.

Wagner, Richard. *Ausreiseantrag. Begrüßungsgeld. Erzählungen.* Frankfurt-on-Main: Luchterhand, 1988.

——. *Exit: A Romanian Story.* London, New York: Verso, 1990.

——. *Mythendämmerung.* Berlin: Rotbuch, 1993.

Wichner, Ernest, ed. *Das Wohnen ist kein Ort. Texte und Zeichen aus Siebenbürgen, dem Banat und den Gegenden versuchter Ankunft. die horen* 147 (1988).

Selected Bibliography

Background, History, Literary Criticism

Adelson, Leslie. 'Migrants' Literature or German Literature? TORKAN's *Tufan: Brief an einen islamischen Bruder.*' *German Quarterly* 63.3/4 (1990): 382–9.

Amnesty International. *Federal Republic of Germany: The Alleged Ill-Treatment of Foreigners: A Summary of Recent Concerns.* London: Amnesty International, International Secretariat, 1993.

Bade, Klaus J. *Ausländer, Aussiedler, Asyl. Eine Bestandsaufnahme.* Munich: Beck, 1994.

Balke, Friedrich, Rebekka Habermas, Patrizia Nanz, and Peter Sillem, eds. *Schwierige Fremdheit. Über Integration und Ausgrenzung in Einwanderungsländern.* Frankfurt-on-Main: Fischer, 1993.

Basgöz, Ilhan and Norman Furniss, eds. *Turkish Workers in Europe.* Bloomington: Indiana University Turkish Studies, 1985.

Berman, Russell A., Azade Seyhan and Arlene Akiko Teraoka, eds. *Special Issue on Minorities in German Culture.* New German Critique 46 (Winter 1989).

Booth, Heather, Stephen Castles and Tina Wallace. *Here for Good: Western Europe's New Ethnic Minorities.* London: Pluto, 1984.

Brubaker, William Rogers, ed. *Immigration and the Politics of Citizenship in Europe and North America.* Lanham, New York, London: University Press of America, 1989.

Cartner, Holly. *'Foreigners Out': Xenophobia and Right-Wing Violence in Germany.* New York: Helsinki Watch, 1992.

Castles, Stephen and Godula Kosack. *Immigrant Workers and Class Structure in Western Europe.* London: Oxford University Press, 1985.

Chiellino, Carmine. *Am Ufer der Fremde: Literatur und Arbeitsmigration, 1870–1991.* Stuttgart: Metzler, 1995.

Cohn, Michael. *The Jews in Germany, 1945–1993: The Building of a Minority.* Westport, CT, and London: Praeger, 1994.

Cohn-Bendit, Daniel and Thomas Schmid. *Heimat Babylon. Das Wagnis der multikulturellen Demokratie.* Hamburg: Hoffmann & Campe, 1992.

Faruk, Sen and Andreas Goldberg. *Türken in Deutschland: Leben zwischen zwei Kulturen.* Munich: Beck, 1994.

Foreigners in Our Midst: Aspects of Cultural Diversity in Germany, Portrayals, and Background Reports. Bonn: Inter Nationes, 1996.

Frederking, Monika. *Schreiben gegen Voruteile. Literatur türkischer Migranten in der Bundesrepublik Deutschland.* Berlin: EXpress Edition, 1985.

Gilman, Sander L. and Karen Remmler, eds. *Reemerging Jewish Culture in Germany: Life and Literature Since 1989*. New York and London: New York University Press, 1994.

Gorschenek, Günter and Stephan Reimers, eds. *Offene Wunden – brennende Fragen: Juden in Deutschland von 1938 bis heute*. Frankfurt-on-Main: Josef Knecht, 1989.

Grimm, Reinhold and Jost Hermand, eds. *Blacks and German Culture. Essays*. Madison: University of Wisconsin Press, 1986.

Hamm, Horst. *Fremdgegangen freigeschrieben. Einführung in die deutschsprachige Gastarbeiterliteratur*. Würzburg: Königshausen & Neumann, 1988.

Heinze, Hartmut. *Migrantenliteratur in der Bundesrepublik Deutschland*. Berlin: EXpress Edition, 1986.

Horricks, David and Eva Kolinsky, eds. *Turkish Culture in German Society Today*. Oxford: Berghahn, 1996.

Hostility towards Foreigners in Germany: New Facts, Analyses, Arguments. Bonn: Press and Information Office of the Federal Government, Foreign Affairs Division, 1993.

Hügel, Ika, Chris Lange, May Ayim, Ilona Bubeck, Gülsen Aktas and Dagmar Schultz, eds. *Entfernte Verbindungen: Rassismus, Antisemitismus, Klassenunterdrückung*. Berlin: Orlanda Frauenverlag, 1993.

IDEEN-Redaktion. *Einwanderungsland Deutschland*. Göttingen: Lamuv, 1993.

Informationen zur politischen Bildung: Aussiedler. Bonn: Bundeszentrale für politische Bildung, June 1989.

Informationen zur politischen Bildung: Ausländer. Bonn: Bundeszentrale für politische Bildung, October 1992.

Joppke, Christian. *Multiculturalism and Immigration: A Comparison of the United States, Germany, and Britain*. Florence: European University Institute, 1995.

Kegelmann, Rene. *An den Grenzen des Nichts, dieser Sprache – Zur Situation rumäniendeutscher Literatur der achtziger Jahre in der Bundesrepublik Deutschland*. Bielefeld: Aisthesis, 1995.

Korte, Hermann. *Migration und ihre sozialen Folgen*. Göttingen: Vandenhoeck und Ruprecht, 1983.

Kreuzer, Helmut, ed. *Gastarbeiterliteratur. LiLi (Zeitschrift für Literaturwissenschaft und Linguistik)* 56 (1984).

Kreuzer, Helmut. 'Gastarbeiter-Literatur, Ausländer-Literatur, Migranten-Literatur? Zur Einführung.' *LiLi* 56 (1984): 7–11.

Leggewie, Claus and Zaferşenocak, eds. *Deutsche Türken: Das Ende der Geduld/Türk Almanlar: Sabrin sonu*. Reinbek: Rowohlt, 1993.

Leitner, Helga. *Regulating Migrants' Lives: The Dialectic of Migrant Labor and the Contradictions of Regulatory and Integration Policies in the FRG.* Minneapolis: Institute of International Studies, University of Minnesota, 1986.

Lorenz, W. and Yüksel Pazarkaya, eds. . . . *Aber die Fremde ist in mir. Migrationserfahrungen und Deutschlandbild in der türkischen Literatur der Gegenwart. Zeitschrift für Kulturaustausch* 35.1 (1985).

Malchow, Barbara, Keyumars Tayebi and Ulrike Brand. *Aussiedler in der Bundesrepublik. Die fremdem Deutschen.* Reinbek: Rowohlt, 1990.

Meier-Braun, Heinz and Yüksel Pazarkaya, eds. *Berichte und Informationen zum besseren Verständnis der Türken in Deutschland.* Frankfurt-on-Main: Ullstein, 1983.

Meinhardt, Rolf, ed. *Türken raus? oder verteidigt den sozialen Frieden.* Reinbek: Rowohlt, 1984.

Midgley, Elizabeth. *Immigration and Asylum in Germany and the United States: Challenges and Choices.* Washington, DC: American Institute for Contemporary German Studies, 1995.

Munz, Rainer and Myron Weiner, eds. *Migrants, Refugees, and Foreign Policy: U.S. and German Policies toward Countries of Origin.* Providence, R.I.: Berghahn, 1997.

Nirumand, Bahman, ed. *Angst vor den Deutschen. Terror gegen Ausländer und der Zerfall des Rechtsstaates.* Reinbek: Rowohlt, 1992.

Opitz, May, Katharina Oguntoye and Dagmar Schultz, eds. *Showing Our Colors – Afro-German Women Speak Out.* Trans. Anne V. Adams. Foreword by Audre Lorde. Amherst: University of Massachusetts Press, 1992.

Rabinach, Anson and Jack Zipes. *Germans and Jews since the Holocaust. The Changing Situation in West Germany.* New York and London: Holmes and Meier, 1986.

Räthzel, Nora. 'Germany: one race, one nation?' *Race and Class* 23.3 (1990): 31–48.

Reeg, Ulrike. *Schreiben in der Fremde. Literatur nationaler Minderheiten in der Bundesrepublik Deutschland.* Essen: Klartext, 1988.

Rogers, Rosemarie, ed. *Guests Come to Stay: The Effects of European Labor Migration on Sending and Receiving Countries.* Boulder and London: Westview, 1985.

Schmalz-Jacobsen, Cornelia and Georg Hansen, eds. *Kleines Lexikon der ethnischen Minderheiten in Deutschland.* Munich: Beck, 1997.

Schütt, Peter. *Der Mohr hat seine Schuldigkeit getan. Gibt es Rassismus in der Bundesrepublik?* Dortmund: Weltkreis Verlag, 1981.

Seligmann, Rafael. 'Wie in der Judenschul.' *Der Spiegel* 10 (1995): 62–6.

Şölçün, Sargut. *Sein und Nichtsein. Zur Literatur in der multikulturellen Gesellschaft*. Bielefeld: Aisthesis, 1992.

Solms, Wilhem, ed. *Nachruf auf die rumäniendeutsche Literatur*. Marburg: Hitzeroth, 1990.

Suhr, Heidrun. 'Ausländerliteratur: Minority Literature in the Federal Republic of Germany.' *New German Critique* 46 (Winter 1989): 71–103.

Teraoka, Arlene. '*Gastarbeiterliteratur*: The Other Speaks Back.' *Cultural Critque* 7 (Autumn 1987): 77–101.

Tumat, Alfred J. *Migration und Integration. Ein Reader*. Baltmannsweiler: Pädagogischer Verlag Burgbücherei Schneider, 1986.

Veteto-Conrad, Marilya. *Doppelte Nationalitätsmoral: Social and Self-Perceptions and Authorial Intent of Two German-Language Turkish Women Writers*. Edmonton: University of Alberta, 1996.

Wolffsohn, Michael. *Eternal Guilt? Forty Years of German–Jewish–Israeli Relations*. Trans. Douglas Bokovoy. New York: Columbia University Press, 1993.